The M.E. Sharpe Library of
Franklin D. Roosevelt Studies

Volume Five

The M.E. Sharpe Library of
Franklin D. Roosevelt Studies

Franklin D. Roosevelt and Abraham Lincoln

Competing Perspectives on Two Great Presidencies

William D. Pederson
Frank J. Williams
Editors

Routledge
Taylor & Francis Group

LONDON AND NEW YORK

First published 2003 by M.E. Sharpe

Published 2015 by Routledge
2 Park Square, Milton Park, Abingdon, Oxon OX14 4RN
711 Third Avenue, New York, NY 10017, USA

Routledge is an imprint of the Taylor & Francis Group, an informa business

Copyright © 2003 Taylor & Francis. All rights reserved.

No part of this book may be reprinted or reproduced or utilised in any form or by any electronic, mechanical, or other means, now known or hereafter invented, including photocopying and recording, or in any information storage or retrieval system, without permission in writing from the publishers.

Notices
No responsibility is assumed by the publisher for any injury and/or damage to persons or property as a matter of products liability, negligence or otherwise, or from any use of operation of any methods, products, instructions or ideas contained in the material herein.

Practitioners and researchers must always rely on their own experience and knowledge in evaluating and using any information, methods, compounds, or experiments described herein. In using such information or methods they should be mindful of their own safety and the safety of others, including parties for whom they have a professional responsibility.

Product or corporate names may be trademarks or registered trademarks, and are used only for identification and explanation without intent to infringe.

Library of Congress Cataloging-in-Publication Data

Franklin D. Roosevelt and Abraham Lincoln : competing perspectives on two great presidencies / William D. Pederson and Frank J. Williams, editors.
    p. cm.
Includes bibliographical references and index.
ISBN 0-7656-1034-5 (alk. paper) — ISBN 0-7656-1035-3 (pbk.: alk. paper)
    1. Presidents—United States—History—Case studies. 2. Lincoln, Abraham, 1809–1865. 3. Roosevelt, Franklin D. (Franklin Delano), 1882–1945. 4. United States—Politics and government—1861–1865. 5. United States—Politics and government—1993–1945. I. Pederson, William D., 1946– II. Williams, Frank J.

E176.1 .F7895 2002
973.7′02—dc21

2002022197

ISBN 13: 9780765610355 (pbk)
ISBN 13: 9780765610348 (hbk)

TABLE OF CONTENTS

Introduction 3
William D. Pederson and Frank J. Williams

Part I: Dual Greatness in the White House
    1. Franklin D. Roosevelt's Abraham Lincoln 10
       Ronald D. Rietveld
    2. Two Wartime Elections: The Presidential Elections
       of 1864 and 1944 61
       David E. Long
    3. Abraham and Mary, Franklin and Eleanor: Their Growth
       From Private to Public Comprehension 75
       James Chowning Davies
    4. FDR and Lincoln in Stone (and Bronze) 128
       C. Todd Stephenson

Part II: Comparative Political Leadership
    5. Warrior, Communitarian, and Echo: The Leadership of
       Abraham Lincoln, Winston Churchill and Franklin
       Roosevelt 154
       Frank J. Williams
    6. An Evaluation of Franklin Delano Roosevelt 171
       Glen Jeansonne
    7. Franklin D. Roosevelt, Huey P. Long, and Political
       Leadership: Room for Just One at the Top 181
       Glen Jeansonne
    8. Jesus, Lincoln, and Beethoven: Three Notes on the Same
       Grand Chord 185
       James Chowning Davies

Part III: Teaching a Legacy
    9. The Depression, Eleanor and World War II: What Do
       Elementary School Social Studies Tell Us About Franklin
       Roosevelt? 214
       Sherry L. Field
    10. FDR and American Life: Portrayals and Interpretations in
       Secondary School American History Textbooks 227
       O. L. Davis, Jr. and Matthew D. Davis
    11. Teaching FDR to the Next Generation 236
       Matthew Ware Coulter

Chronology 247

Biographical Digest 258

Selected Bibliography 271

List of Contributors 280

Index 281

The M.E. Sharpe Library of
Franklin D. Roosevelt Studies

Volume Five

Introduction

William D. Pederson and Frank J. Williams

Rankings of American presidents by scholars consistently affirm Abraham Lincoln as the greatest president of the nineteenth century and Franklin D. Roosevelt as his twentieth century counterpart.[1] Both were presidents during national crises who guided a country torn by war, one internal, the other external. Commander-in-Chief Abraham Lincoln preserved the Union and Chief Executive Lincoln put a fragile Union back together and ended slavery. Chief Executive Franklin Roosevelt's New Deal offered hope during the Great Depression and Commander-in-Chief Roosevelt's forces won the Second World War, again preserving America's historic experiment in democratic self-government. The contribution of their leadership style to these victories and how successor generations preserve and teach their legacies is the subject of this volume. By examining and comparing personalities, leadership style, and the times in which the sixteenth and thirty-second presidents held office, the ten contributors to this volume help us to better understand why scholars and the public value the enduring contributions of Abraham Lincoln and Franklin Roosevelt to the American heritage.

Styles and Relationships

In more innocent times, everyone had a hero. Today, we tend to be limited to "significant others." The opening four chapters of this volume suggest the role of both heroes and significant others in the lives of these presidents as well as how the legacy of the greatest presidents is publicly perpetuated through monuments in Washington, D.C. The relationships that presidents have with those around them and their connections with historical figures would almost define them and provide important aids in defining their political styles.

Historian Ronald D. Rietveld presents an in-depth examination of the influence Abraham Lincoln exerted on Franklin Roosevelt. Both occupied the White House during the major wars of their respective century. Both exercised maximum extra-constitutional authority to govern in times of greatest threat to the nation. Both made mistakes, but neither questioned that the president must operate within a system of checks and balances with the other two branches of government or that the public retained the final responsibility to pass judgment on them through the election process. Roosevelt understood Lincoln's Machiavellian dimensions in political leadership, and both understood the ultimate nature of America's great experiment in self-government.

The 1864 and 1944 presidential elections were referenda on the wartime leadership of Lincoln and Roosevelt. Historian David E. Long considers the 1864 election among the most important elections in American history. The public ratified the sixteenth president's policies designed to both preserve the Union and end slavery. Despite the often vitriolic and profuse criticism Lincoln endured as president, his actions led finally to decisive battlefield results, confirming his success as a political leader. Similarly, Franklin Roosevelt led an international coalition in defeating the Axis powers' threat to democratic government, prompting the public to allow him to break the two-term tradition for presidents. Both were able to pursue their visions to successful conclusions by using the skills they had developed as flexible and active politicians.

Political scientist James C. Davies traces the roots of both presidents to the standards they practiced with their associates and spouses. It is significant that both married women were far ahead of their times. In fact, Mary Todd Lincoln in many ways set the political standard for First Ladies of the nineteenth century, building upon the legacy of Dolley Madison. Mary Todd Lincoln in her pre-White House years had assumed a role as a political equal to her husband, literally grooming the socially unpolished Lincoln for the presidency. Relying on the controversial insights of Mariah Vance,[2] Davies portrays a vexed but affectionate partnership between the Lincolns, at least until they lost their second son while in the White House. In their last moments together at Ford's Theater, Mary and Abe were holding hands, enjoying themselves. Each had learned to deal with the other's limitations while remaining cognizant of that partner's potential. Despite recurrent efforts by some to downplay the significance of the marriage, Davies recognizes its durability.

A similar durability bound the relationship between Eleanor and Franklin Roosevelt. Although physical intimacy ended early in their marriage, their mutual appreciation of each other's talents created an unbreakable bond of political partnership. It was Eleanor who refused to let Franklin quit politics. From him, she learned the jungle side of politics. From her, he learned about the needs of a public that did not share his life of privilege.

Historian C. Todd Stephenson deals with the public's desire to leave a permanent and public tribute to its greatest leaders. It takes the public a half-century before it can finally judge its leaders, he argues. With passage of time, at some level of consciousness, the public finally comes to terms with political greatness of individual leaders and pays tribute through an artistic rendering. The Lincoln Memorial and the new Franklin D. Roosevelt Memorial in Washington, D.C. are public confirmation of the judgment of scholars that these two leaders, along with George Washington, represent the touchstone of democratic leadership.

The interest in Lincoln for one editor of this volume was first sparked by a portrait of the sixteenth president conspicuously hanging on his elementary schoolhouse wall. That visual contact in childhood sparked a lifelong interest in Abraham Lincoln, an illustration on a small scale of the broader role that public monuments may have by appealing to the right, nondiscursive, side of the brain of the millions who view them. In an age of activism, it is regrettable that emerging groups may advance their immediate agenda at the expense of not understanding the role of the monuments in preserving America's experiment in self-government. In a sense, their narrow concerns driven by immediacy are reminders of the regional factions of the 1850s that became blinded to the universal goals of the American republic.

The second part of this volume extends the analysis from comparative leadership in the White House to encompass a transnational perspective as well as a comparative look at world religious and musical leadership. The four chapters confirm that democratic leadership derives from its celebration of individual dignity and recognition of equality among individuals and nations.

Frank J. Williams in chapter 5 contrasts the dual greatness of Lincoln and Roosevelt with Winston Churchill. While recognizing Churchill's role in the twentieth century, Williams ultimately argues that the dual greatness of the sixteenth and thirty-second presidents was more enduring because their leadership transcended the warrior leader model of Churchill with a recognition that people desire fulfillment of needs beyond bodily security. Williams suggests that Churchill's more limited leadership, compared with the American duo, may be linked to the childhood trauma he suffered from parental rejection. And while Lincoln and Churchill both may have suffered from mental bipolarity, Lincoln showed greater flexibility in adapting to it. Franklin Roosevelt's inherent optimism, even when faced with the devastation of paralysis as an adult, certainly emerged from a psychological background far healthier than that of Lincoln or Churchill.

In chapters 6 and 7, historian Glen Jeansonne compares and contrasts

Franklin D. Roosevelt and Huey P. Long. Roosevelt understood that both General Douglas MacArthur and Senator Huey P. Long posed the greatest threats to his leadership. In contrast to Roosevelt's democratic leadership style, the two were powerful right-wing and left-wing authoritarian models of leadership. If Franklin Roosevelt made an occasional political mistake and had manipulative tendencies, Huey P. Long almost always was a demagogic autocrat riding a populist crest of popularity. Long was trapped by both a state without a strong democratic heritage and personal demons he could not control. He destroyed lawful government in Louisiana, replacing it with despotic rule through the power he craved. In sharp contrast, Roosevelt's upbringing and personality imposed restraints on his behavior. A measure of contrast is that—unlike Mary Todd Lincoln and Eleanor Roosevelt—Rose Long simply abandoned her spouse to bring up their children while Long grew increasingly isolated and paranoid.

In a provocative conclusion to the second part of this volume, James C. Davies boldly offers insights into the careers of Jesus, Lincoln, and Beethoven. Surprisingly, these three seemingly disparate individuals from different centuries and cultures are viewed as pioneers who pushed back the threatening forest of fear that ordinary people were demons. Each stressed a common theme of dignity and equality of human beings. Jesus both preached and practiced these values among those less well off, while Lincoln was able to draw upon his understanding of the democratic experiment in self-government by aligning the values of the Declaration of Independence with the United States Constitution. Relying on Suzanne Langer's insights, Davies suggests how Beethoven used music to celebrate universal impulses in the human psyche. The visions and the practices of these three great figures are democratic.

The third and final part of this volume assesses the teaching of Franklin Roosevelt's legacy in America's schools today. Just as great presidents are influenced by their greatest predecessors—George Washington served as Lincoln's model and Lincoln, in turn, was Franklin Roosevelt's model—today's youth need to be educated about American political leaders. Not all leaders are equal, despite the come-lately creation of a generic President's Day that undermines the legacy of George Washington and Abraham Lincoln. The balkanization of learning about the American political tradition is very much alive among folks who mean well but have difficulty separating the trees from the forest.

Chapters 9 and 10 survey the state of teaching of the Roosevelt legacy in elementary and secondary schools. Sherry L. Field presents a depressing portrait of the message being delivered in social studies textbooks used in Atlanta's public schools, just as she has previously documented in the textbook discussion of Abraham Lincoln.[3] The Davises' findings are just slightly more optimistic in their survey of secondary social studies textbooks.

In contrast, Matthew Ware Coulter reports on some innovative approaches to teaching about the Roosevelt era, and potentially the Lincoln era. He has introduced both into his U.S. history course at the community college level. He proposes a model for integrating primary source materials and short in-class writing assignments to supplement traditional lecture formats. As he states, "watching, writing and discussing" are used to supplement traditional "lecturing, reading and quizzing."

Conclusion

The contributions in this volume enhance our understanding of the elements of greatness in terms of presidential leadership in the world's premiere experiment in self-government. The dual greatness of Abraham Lincoln and Franklin Roosevelt stems from their willingness to use America's most original political office as a creative tool to address slavery, secession, the Great Depression, and World War II, potentially insurmountable challenges to the stability of the nation and its democratic foundation. Each clearly understood and heeded Alexander Hamilton's admonition for an activist presidency, as he described in *Federalist Paper 70:* "Energy in the executive is a leading character of good government." Abraham Lincoln followed George Washington's example in dealing with the Whiskey Rebellion—energy and magnanimity. Franklin Roosevelt followed Lincoln's presidential model. Both were willing to experiment to accomplish their visions for preserving America's great experiment.

Apart from their energetic use of presidential powers, both chief executives also demonstrated their democratic inclinations in their personal lives with spouses and associates. Married to progressive, intelligent, strong women, they supported if not encouraged their wives' interests in public affairs. Despite Mary Todd Lincoln's instability after losing two of their four sons prematurely, Abraham learned to deal with his wife's emotional fragility. Eleanor was Franklin's stalwart following his polio. Eleanor was capable of growing into the role that Mary Todd may have created for herself—and future First Ladies—if she had not suffered from the loss of her sons. While Roosevelt may have been more manipulative than Lincoln, like Lincoln he recognized the essential dignity of human beings and their desire to be equally respected. The personal practices and public policies of both, no matter how imperfectly implemented, were ahead of their times and advanced realization of these transcendent values within the context of their times.

The teaching of democratic values is reflected in the behavior of this pair of nineteenth- and twentieth-century presidential greats. They were guided by the democratic leadership of their predecessors, and the public rewarded them with reelection.

Successor generations pay tribute to the legacy of their democratic leadership through public monuments devoted to them. It is ironic that the special interest groups that push encapsulated agendas at the risk of undermining the national vision of these great leaders merely reflect their ignorance of American history.[4] Their agendas have much in common with the "multicultural" movement which, in the name of diversity, undermines the American political heritage.

We degrade America's unique political heritage when the contributions of our greatest leaders are minimized by according all other presidents equal recognition with them. Good intentions to compensate for imperfect policies of the past do not justify rewriting the American heritage.

The editors hope that this volume on comparative leadership will achieve several goals. An examination of Abraham Lincoln and Franklin D. Roosevelt contributes to better understanding of the values to which Americans as a nation subscribe and suggests how the personal and public lives of both leaders successfully championed these values, as well as revealing how the nation preserves their legacy not only in monuments but also through the living legacy of the classroom.

ENDNOTES

1. William D. Pederson and Ann McLaurin, eds., *The Rating Game in American Politics* (New York: Irvington Publishers, 1987).

2. Lloyd Ostendorf and Walter Oleksy, eds., *Lincoln's Unknown Private Life: An Oral History by His Black Housekeeper Mariah Vance 1850-1860* (Mamaroneck, NY: Hasting House, 1995).

3. For a similar treatment of Abraham Lincoln, see Frank J. Williams and William D. Pederson, eds., *Abraham Lincoln Contemporary: An American Legacy* (Campbell, CA: Savas Woodbury Publishing, 1995). Sherry L. Field, "Roosevelt's Army of Community Service Workers: Children and Their Teachers," *Social Education* 60 (5) (September 1995): 280-283.

4. C. Todd Stephenson, "Depicting Disability: The Franklin Delano Roosevelt Memorial in Washington, D.C.," *Social Education* 60 (5) (September 1995): 299-300.

"That's nothing, Franklin; you ought to read what they said about me."

(The Frank & Virginia Williams Collection of Lincolniana)

(The Frank & Virginia Williams Collection of Lincolniana)

I

DUAL GREATNESS IN THE WHITE HOUSE

1

Franklin D. Roosevelt's Abraham Lincoln

Ronald D. Rietveld

In one way or another, the Roosevelts have long been associated with the Lincolns, especially President Abraham Lincoln. Both President Roosevelts, Theodore and Franklin, became attached to the memory of Abraham Lincoln. Talking about statecraft in the White House, Theodore Roosevelt declared: "My experiences in all these matters gives me an idea of the fearful time Lincoln must have had in dealing with the great crises he had to face."[1] At the time of TR's swearing in as president on March 4, 1905, Secretary of State John Hay, Lincoln's young presidential secretary and his father's friend, gave the new president a ring with a locket of hair that he had taken from the head of the dead Lincoln.[2] TR's Lincoln was much more "direct."

Many years removed, and much more "indirect," Franklin Roosevelt's Abraham Lincoln was an example to be used, manipulated, and emulated. As Merrill Peterson so aptly declared in *Lincoln in American Memory*: "Lincoln . . . was an acquired taste which he indulged for calculated political effect." More than most presidents, FDR measured himself by his official ancestors who were instruments of historic change as they led the nation from one phase of development to another. As with most Americans, he had been taught to revere Abraham Lincoln. He thus appropriated the icon of the Republican Party—their sixteenth president—for his own purposes.[3]

By the time of his death, shortly before the end of another war, FDR achieved a popular stature equal to that of President Lincoln. Indeed, he ranked even higher than the martyred president in the public opinion polls of 1945 and 1946.[4] With great success, FDR had consciously wrapped himself in the Lincoln mantle in his presidential years and, using Lincoln's own words, told the 1944 Democratic national convention: "With firmness in the right, as God gives us to see the right, let us strive to finish the work we are in. . . ." These words FDR said were "as applicable today as they were in 1865." In October of his last presidential campaign, FDR reminded an audience that "we are holding a national election while the Nation is at war" for the first time since 1864, and then quoted Lincoln at the expense of his contemporary Republicans.[5]

Long before Pearl Harbor, Roosevelt was linked with Lincoln as a commander-in-chief as their careers converged. Both Lincoln and Roosevelt unified the nation behind a war defined in moral terms. Both inspired his fellow Americans with eloquence to self-sacrifice. Both conducted the struggle to a successful conclusion, though neither lived to see the end of war. And, indeed, both Lincoln and Roosevelt died in April on the eve of final victory.[6]

Lincoln's Influence on Young Roosevelt

The Oyster Bay Roosevelt, Theodore Sr., endeavored to serve the Union by using his philanthropic resources on behalf of its war effort, assuaging a guilty conscience for not serving in the war. He designed a program that encouraged soldiers to send home their pay and thus ease the sufferings of their families, a task which kept him months in Washington and involved frequent meetings with President Lincoln himself. Although physically shorter, Theodore Sr. was more than once mistaken for Lincoln while walking down the street with Lincoln's young secretary, John Hay. It was said that Theodore became a favorite of Mrs. Lincoln who asked him to escort her while shopping for bonnets.[7] With a clear and definite connection with the Lincoln White House, Lincoln became a hero to the six-year-old "Teedee." On April 24, 1865, TR watched the funeral cortege of the martyred president as it passed through Union Square area from the brownstone which belonged to his grandfather, Cornelius Van Schaack Roosevelt, a great grandson of Johannes, one of the two founding brothers of the Roosevelt clan and the most prominent member of the Roosevelt family when Lincoln died.[8]

The Hyde Park Roosevelt, James, a great grandson of Jacobus, the other founding brother of the Roosevelt clan, had chosen not to serve in the Civil War, like the first Theodore. Possessing wealth and a good name, and no guilt, he travelled extensively in Europe during and after the war years. While in Europe, James hobnobbed with fellow Americans, like General George McClellan, a fellow Democrat. James may have shared McClellan's bitter detestation of Lincoln and his emancipation policy for blacks.[9] Franklin's Lincoln heritage was in marked contrast to that of Theodore, his fifth cousin, much more "indirect." However, FDR, the future president, would link his distant relative with the great leaders of the Republic Washington, Franklin, Jefferson, Jackson, Wilson—and Abraham Lincoln.[10]

Young Franklin Roosevelt had his own impressions of Lincoln, especially the orator at Gettysburg. While at Harvard, the young man took a course in public speaking. This was in the closing days of the golden age of the Emerson school of oratory with "the bellowing, shouting, overdramatic technique." FDR enrolled in the public speaking course of Professor George Pierce, whose courses in drama were famous both at Harvard and Yale. Young Roosevelt and the professor differed in their interpretation of Lincoln's Gettysburg Address, enough to cause the young man to withdraw from the course after a few weeks. They could not agree on the way Lincoln delivered his famous address at Gettysburg that November day in 1863. FDR slouched to the rostrum and spoke the short address in a monotone without any gestures. Baker wanted rounded, resonant periods with gestures and all the other elocutionary tricks of oratory. That was not FDR's Lincoln.[11]

From the days when FDR was a young lawyer, he had forecast a bright future for himself and the presidency certainly was a plausible goal. For FDR, the White House was a familiar place, where his cousin had lived. TR was an example to follow. FDR's reason which he gave for *not* seeking the presidential office was that he had seen so much of presidents. He had personally known five, and the presidency was an office that he wished to have no part of. However, Ted Morgan writes in *FDR: A Biography* that "in fact, he felt he had been groomed for the job. It was the natural conclusion to having been taken to meet Grover Cleveland as a child, to having been a frequent guest of Cousin Teddy's, to having worked with Wilson during his two terms."[12]

Lincoln the Politician and Roosevelt's Ambition

As he drew on the usable past, FDR identified with former presidents who were links in a chain and were tutors, just like his boyhood tutors at Hyde Park. He admired Washington for governing in a time of crisis with difficult tasks and endless problems to overcome. But as a member of Wilson's cabinet during the attacks on the president in 1920, Roosevelt recalled from history that "most of our great deeds have been brought about by the Presidents who were not tools of Congress but were true leaders of the nation who so truly interpreted the needs and wishes of the people that they were supported in their great tasks. It seems to be written in our history that at some period in the lives of all of our great men they have been made the peculiar object of concerted attack and vilification," he said. "It was true of

Washington; it was true of Thomas Jefferson; it was true of Andrew Jackson." Then he added: "It was true of Lincoln himself. He was called a usurper, a traitor, and a tyrant. One of his own party accused him of treachery."[13] This Wilsonian Democrat found the Lincoln example a comfort. He would set about transforming Lincoln into a symbol for the "new" Democratic party.

It was "the reactionists in the Republican party" who had created sectionalism in the United States, Roosevelt boldly declared. "Before the first stone was laid for the first memorial to Abraham Lincoln his wise policy of forgiveness and forgetfulness had been superseded and the carpetbagger introduced into American national life," Roosevelt attacked these Lincoln traitors who called themselves Republicans. In fact, as far as he was concerned, the United States had no real leader between the death of Lincoln in 1865 and the rise of Theodore Roosevelt in 1901. By 1928, FDR believed that Wilson was the last great leader and that the present gray period might just last another ten years, unless a Democratic presidential aspirant were to be successful. Roosevelt was indignant that Lincoln belonged to that rival party. Anticipating the future use of Lincoln, the newly inaugurated governor of New York wrote the journalist and historian Claude Bowers on April 3, 1929: "I think it is time for us Democrats to claim Lincoln as one of our own. The Republican party has certainly repudiated, first and last, everything that he stood for." He added: "That period from 1865 to 1876 should be known as 'America's Dark Age.' I am not sure that we are not headed for the same type of era again." The ground work was laid for the Roosevelt claim to the Lincoln legacy.[14]

As the Great Depression began, the Republican party still claimed to be the party of Abraham Lincoln. Lincoln's birthday continued to be a Republican feast across the nation. On February 12, 1931, President Herbert Hoover delivered a nationwide radio address from the White House in which he spoke of Lincoln's invisible presence in the corridors of the executive mansion—the citadel of power. The southwest room where seventy years before Lincoln's office had been located now served as his own study. Above the mantel hung the engraving of *The First Reading of the Emancipation Proclamation*. He had found four chairs from the Lincoln era and had hung up a steel engraving of Lincoln which had accompanied him and Lou on all their overseas journeys.[15]

From the Lincoln office by radio, President Hoover praised Lincoln as a great builder and liberator. In the current economic crisis, he warned of the dangers which centralized government and the invasion of individual liberty would bring to the American people. As Hoover reviewed Lincoln's role as the Great Emancipator, he could not find any precedent for a major expansion of state power to fight the depression. Federal control would only destroy the "opportunity of every individual to rise to that highest achievement of which he is capable," and would ultimately lead to a "superstate where every man becomes the servant of the State and real liberty is lost." By no means was this the kind of government "Lincoln sought to build." President Hoover believed that President Lincoln had built a nation of villagers and the depression would be beaten, therefore, on the local level. Invoking Lincoln's image, Hoover dedicated the remodeled Lincoln tomb in Springfield that following June. On February 12, 1932, Hoover again spoke to the nation from Lincoln's White House office and pled with the American people to evidence the same kind of commitment, courage and resourcefulness as the people had given under Lincoln's leadership. After his electoral defeat, Hoover delivered his farewell address before the National Republican Club in New York City on Lincoln's birthday, 1933—still claiming Lincoln's support. The American humorist, Will Rogers, quipped that "If it hadn't been for Lincoln the Republicans ... would be short of a cause for celebrating."[16]

Hoover's understanding and use of the Republican president made it more difficult for FDR to use Lincoln. In addition to the fact that Lincoln was a Republican from Pigeon Creek, Kentucky and New Salem, Illinois, FDR was from Dutchess County, New York, and Hyde Park. But he chose to use Lincoln in his first campaign for the presidency in 1932. At a Jefferson Day dinner in St. Paul, Minnesota on April 18, Roosevelt drew on his tutors of the past. "We have had in our own history three men who chiefly stand out for the universality of their interest and of their knowledge—Benjamin Franklin, Thomas Jefferson and Theodore Roosevelt." All three of these men knew at first hand every crosscurrent of national and international life. And of the three, Jefferson was in many ways "the deepest student—the one with the most inquiring and diversified intellect and, above all, the one who at all times looked the farthest into the future, examining the ultimate effects on humanity of the actions of the present." This was the Jefferson "so big in mind and in spirit" who knew that the average man would understand. Jefferson had asked support against the errors of others who condemned what they would not, if seen in all its parts. This was the essential point of view that truly great leaders of every generation hold—including Lincoln. "Abraham Lincoln had it," FDR declared. "We could say today, as he said in 1861, 'physically speaking we cannot separate. We cannot remove our respective sections from each other nor build an impassible wall between them. A husband and wife may be divorced, and go out of the presence and beyond the reach of each other, but the different parts of our country cannot do this. They cannot but remain face to face, and intercourse must continue between them.'" And then FDR boldly concluded with Lincoln: "I say with Lincoln, 'Having thus chosen our course, without guile and with pure purpose, let us renew our trust in God and go forward without fear and with manly hearts.'"[17]

During this first presidential campaign, Roosevelt had carefully selected Lincoln metaphors as when he asserted that "no nation can long endure half bankrupt." He proceeded cautiously after his nomination. So much so that Walter Lippmann called him a master of the saddle, "a highly impressionable person, without firm grasp of public affairs and without very strong convictions," words which read strangely now. Lippmann's evaluation of Roosevelt seemed on the target for the electorate of 1932. "Franklin D. Roosevelt is no crusader. He is no tribune of the people," Lippmann posited. "He is no enemy of entrenched privilege. He is a pleasant man who, without any important qualifications for office, would like to be President." They voted against Hoover rather than for Roosevelt and he intended it to be so. For Roosevelt himself, the differences between the two were compounded of many different things. FDR's cousin, Theodore Roosevelt had once divided American presidents into "Buchanan" and "Lincoln" types. The first type were those who remained inactive in the middle of a national crisis and the Congress whittled away at executive power; the second type were those who had used their constitutional powers to the full in order to do exactly what the nation wished them to do. When FDR appraised Hoover, he had TR's presidential division in mind. Thus, tensions between the two men were never resolved.[18]

Lincoln the Politician, President Roosevelt's Example for Policy—1933-1939

The nation was in the midst of great crisis when Roosevelt became president. If a leader can associate a current crisis with the actions of a president like Lincoln, he can give an immediacy and a focus which sets the nation on the path to resolution. As Lincoln before him, FDR had a will to assume primary responsibility for events, and a will to make decisions regarding them. Lincoln once admitted that "I claim not to have controlled events, but confess that events have controlled me." FDR would claim the same thing. FDR's first inaugural address made full use of Lincoln the example. As early as September 1932, during the campaign, FDR had become impressed with the parallels to Lincoln in the present national crisis. Both men delivered their inaugural addresses in an atmosphere of national trauma. Roosevelt's oathtaking had a special symbolic meaning—a historical echo. The significance was greater, perhaps, than any other since

Abraham Lincoln had been sworn into the presidency on March 4, 1861 by Chief Justice Roger B. Taney, the author of the 1857 Dred Scott decision. As Lincoln had spoken of a nation's spiritual crisis in 1861, so now Roosevelt connected the depression to a crisis of the spirit which was affecting all of the nation. As one sportswriter recalled: "Then we turned to the radio and Franklin D. Roosevelt's inaugural address. It was a talk the nation had not heard in my lifetime . . . . I felt not merely the words—arousing, challenging, unexpected—but the tone and the great courage and strength of the man behind them. How fortunate are those of us who lived at that time and were touched, ever so lightly, by this gigantic force in our history." It was a crisis which a previous generation had known in 1861.[19]

Two years later, in his second Fireside Chat of 1934, FDR invoked the magic name of Lincoln to counter attacks on his New Deal recovery programs: "The course we have followed fits the American practice of courageous recognition of change. I believe with Abraham Lincoln, that 'The legitimate object of Government is to do for a community of people whatever they need to have done but cannot do at all or cannot do so well for themselves in their separate and individual capacities.'" These words of a Republican president seemed so pertinent for the New Deal programs that FDR repeated them at least on two other occasions. In his first administration, FDR pushed more the exemplar of Jefferson than Abraham Lincoln, it would appear, because the Jeffersonian seemed to "hit nerves" or roots in the New Deal vocabulary.[20]

Lincoln biographer Carl Sandburg wrote one of the early New Dealers, Raymond Moley: "I see many striking parallels between Lincoln and Franklin Roosevelt in political method, in decision amid chaos, in reading trends, in development of policy so as to gather momentum, in resilience and acknowledgment of hazards—and much else." Then he added: "If your magazine [*Today*] lasts through the Roosevelt term I may work out the parallel before the term is over, for you to print . . . ." In fact, Moley's magazine in February 1934, published Sandburg's article which drew a parallel between Lincoln's Emancipation Proclamation and the National Recovery Act 7A clause. Neither had proper authority in law and neither could be enforced, he said. But the announcement itself had far reaching results which were beyond calculation and was best estimated by the wrath of those who opposed them. Sandburg declared that for three years anyone who might ask him if he was for Roosevelt was answered that thus far Sandburg was amazed that "a President could get away with what he was putting across." And the Lincoln biographer declared that he would stay with FDR until he changed direction. In September of 1935, in the process of writing his fourth volume on *Abraham Lincoln: the War Years*, Sandburg planned to vote for Roosevelt for President in 1936.[21]

Vigorously supporting Roosevelt, Sandburg wrote the President on March 29, 1935 of his great admiration and the striking parallel between Lincoln and FDR. "All the time you keep growing—so it seems to some of us who read you from a distance," he averred. In the process of writing about Lincoln during the war years over a period of ten years now, he had his "eyes and ears in two eras and can not help drawing parallels." FDR was "the best light of democracy that has occupied the White House since Lincoln." Roosevelt had set in motion trends which were "banners of dawn" to many. It may be praise in his face, but it was also a recording of a hope and a prayer that the president would "go on as steadfast as you have in loyalty to the whole people, that in your difficult war with their exploiters your cunning may increase." "Your speeches like Lincoln's will stand the test of time," he wrote. Sandburg had gone through letters, diaries, speeches, and newspaper files of the time of Lincoln's administration and nothing stood out more strangely in that hour than that most of the utterance of that time now is touched with the pathetic or the ridiculous. As Sandburg put it, "Only a small remnant knew what was going on, had the clairvoyance to read what the deep underlying streams might shape across the future, with relation to decisions of the immediate moment." Contrary to Lippmann's 1932 evaluation of FDR, what many were seeing was that FDR had long preparation for what he was doing and "as with Lincoln there has been a response of the People to you: they have done something to you and made you what you could not have been without them, this interplay operating steadily in your growth." Sandburg was not the only one who saw parallels in FDR's turmoil and that in which Lincoln had been immersed. There were many others who saw the same thing.[22]

The 400th anniversary of the printing of the first English Bible was an event of great significance, as far as the president was concerned, and he prepared to address the occasion on October 6, 1935. He proffered that it would be difficult to fully appraise the far-reaching influence of the Myles Coverdale Bible which was produced in the vernacular in 1535, especially its impact, along with subsequent translations, on the speech, literature, moral, and religious character of the American people and their institutions. FDR believed that the richest and best in American literature could be traced to it, along with poetry, prose, painting, music, and oratory which the English Bible had offered guidance and inspiration. "In it Lincoln found the rounded euphonious phrases for his Gettysburg Address," a conviction he had held as a young Harvard student who left a professor's oratorical class many years before. And then he referred to the impact of the Bible on

Lincoln personally. He wrote, "Speaking of its place in his life, he [Lincoln] says: 'In regard to the great Book, I have only to say, it is the best gift which God has ever given to man.'" It certainly was apt to refer to the spiritual Lincoln in this context. The use of such occasions of discourse is a way that presidents may achieve some measure of self-understanding and Lincoln's thought was not only beneficial for exemplary use, but for FDR's own personal thinking. "At every critical hour, the deep current of religious sentiment in F.D.R's make-up came out in the open," Grace Tully noted of her boss. "Some people, of course, questioned the sincerity of this," but he respected all forms of religious belief as they were present in other men—especially Lincoln.[23]

Already in January of 1936, Roosevelt was thinking Lincoln. He penned a tribute to Lincoln which was to be read on his birthday before the Lincoln Association of Cleveland, Ohio. He congratulated the association's possession of a "Lincoln Shrine" and Ohioans for having such a symbol within their borders which served to "make more real the memory of him to whom you this day pay homage." And then FDR evaluated the Lincoln he so admired:

> Abraham Lincoln was not a son of the North or the South. Born in Kentucky and nurtured in the very heart of our land, the scope of his intellect and of his sympathies was co-extensive with the length and breadth of our domain. Nor could Abraham Lincoln have come from any class that did not know, through daily struggle, the grim realities of life. Self-sustained, self-educated, and grounded in common sense through contact with his fellow man, he developed that homely philosophy with which we have come to associate his name and with which he was to solve the problems of a distraught Nation.
>
> From such an origin and from such a school, there emerged a character destined to transfuse with new meaning the concepts of our constitutional fathers and to assure a Government having for its broad purpose the promotion of the life, liberty, and happiness of all the people.

On June 14, 1936, President Roosevelt made a pilgrimage to the birthplace of the Great Emancipator—a very distinctive thing for a Democratic president to do in those days. As he emerged from the restored cabin, he was deeply moved by the experience. He publicly declared that he had come to see the cabin in which Lincoln was born, "as one of millions of other Americans whose lives had been influenced for the good by Abraham Lincoln." "I live, temporarily, in the same house and the same rooms once occupied by him. The very window from which he gazed in the dark days is the same," he said. But the experience of seeing the cabin was even more personal than the scenes of his official life in the White House because "here was born and lived the child." Indeed, "here was the promise, later to be so splendidly fulfilled," a patrician's admiration. It was kind of a spiritual experience for FDR:

> I have taken from this cabin a renewed confidence that the spirit of America is not dead, that men and means will be found to explore and conquer the problems of a new time with no less humanity and no less fortitude than his.
>
> Here we can renew our pledge of fidelity to the faith which Lincoln held in the common man–the faith so simply expressed when he said: "As I would not be a slave, so I would not be a master. This expresses my idea of democracy. Whatever differs from this, to the extent of the difference is no democracy."

For Roosevelt, Abraham Lincoln was great *not* because he was born in a log cabin, but because he got out of it. In this presidential campaign year of 1936, Roosevelt led the Democrats in contesting the Republican title to Lincoln.[24]

By October, FDR was campaigning in earnest. Before his final campaign speech at Madison Square Garden, he spoke in Wilmington, Delaware, the home state of the DuPont corporation whose owners opposed the New Deal and hoped to defeat FDR's reelection. It was the perfect place to use Lincoln against the Republicans. He began by saying that it was appropriate that on the occasion he should not make any political speech because he thought he could better describe the kind of liberty which his administration had sought to continue to seek by just reading the simple words of "a great President who believed in the kind of liberty that we believe in—the great President who preserved the American Union." The words which FDR used were from Lincoln's speech to the Baltimore Sanitary Fair in 1864. "And I ask that you good people give heed to these words for, although they are three-quarters of a century old, yet I think you will find that they apply to 1936," he told his audience, quoting Lincoln:

> The world has never had a good definition of the word liberty, and the American people, just now, are much in want of one. We all declare for liberty; but in using the same word we do not all mean the same thing. With some the word liberty may mean for each man to do as he pleases

with himself, and the product of his labor; while with others the same word may mean for some men to do as they please with other men, and the product of other men's labor. Here are two, not only different, but incompatible things, called by the same name, liberty. And it follows that each of the things is, by the respective parties, called by two different and incompatible names—liberty and tyranny.

And then FDR used one of Lincoln's "homely examples." He said:

The shepherd drives the wolf from the sheep's throat, for which the sheep thanks the shepherd as his liberator, while the wolf denounces him for the same act, as the destroyer of liberty . . . . Plainly, the sheep and the wolf are not agreed upon a definition of the word liberty; and precisely the same difference prevails today among us human creatures . . . and all professing to love liberty. Hence we behold the process by which thousands are daily passing from under the yoke of bondage hailed by some as the advance of liberty. And the wolf's dictionary has again been repudiated.

And, in closing, FDR quoted Lincoln again:

Recently, as it seems, the people . . . . have been doing something to define liberty, and thanks to them that, in what they have done, the wolf's dictionary has been repudiated.

FDR then made his application: "My friends, today, in 1936, the people have again been doing something to define liberty. And the wolf's dictionary has again been repudiated." Clearly what Lincoln had said three-quarters of a century before was applied by Roosevelt as in Lincoln's own time. Roosevelt clearly laid claim to Lincoln for the Democratic party. He repeated this same speech, curiously, in the two successive times he closed his campaign in Wilmington in 1940 and 1944.[25]

Roosevelt defended his plan to reorganize the federal judiciary on March 9, 1937 in a Fireside Chat and reminded his listeners that some of his illustrious predecessors, including Lincoln himself, had also asked Congress to reform the bench. "The number of Justices has been changed several times before, in the Administrations of John Adams and Thomas Jefferson—both signers of the Declaration of Independence—Andrew Jackson, Abraham Lincoln and Ulysses S. Grant," as he gave the nation a lesson in its own history. This was a precedent worth emulating to control any abuse of the nation's Constitutional usage.[26]

The Democratic president made even greater use of Lincoln's image in 1938, a year when he intended to purge the Democratic party of conservatives. Generally speaking FDR believed that there are usually two general schools of political belief—liberal and conservative. In America, the system of party responsibility requires that one of its parties be the liberal party and the other be the conservative party. "This has been the division by which the major parties in American history have identified themselves whenever crises have developed which required definite choice of direction," he wrote in the introduction to his 1938 volume of public papers and addresses. "In Jefferson's day, in Jackson's day, and in Lincoln's, and Theodore Roosevelt's, and Wilson's day," he wrote, "one group emerged clearly as liberals, opposed to the other—the conservatives." The liberal party is a party which believes that it becomes the duty of the Government itself to find new remedies to meet the new conditions and problems which arise beyond the power of men and women as individuals. "The liberal party insists that the government has the definite duty to use all its power and resources to meet new social problems with new social controls—to insure to the average person the right to his own economic and political life, liberty, and the pursuit of happiness. This same New Deal theory of the role of government was expressed by Abraham Lincoln when he said, "The legitimate object of government is to do for a community of people whatever they need to have done, but cannot do at all, or cannot do so well for themselves, in their separate and individual capacities." He used this Lincoln quote at Marietta, Ohio on July 8, 1938.

Lincoln comparisons became a part of FDR's arsenal of attack as he interjected himself into the primaries with some unfortunate results. Roosevelt believed that the determination of the American people to continue the same liberal program of progressive reform was clearly expressed at the polls in 1938. The political struggle of 1938, which Lincoln could have fully comprehended, had not been in vain. In 1941, FDR believed that "Liberalism in Government was still triumphant." However, in 1938 many voters resented outside interference by the president in local political matters.[27]

At a Jackson Day dinner in the nation's capital on January 8, 1938, he began by denying Lincoln his Republican label. "In these recent years the average American seldom thinks of Jefferson and Jackson as Democrats or of Lincoln and Theodore Roosevelt as Republicans." Instead, Americans label each one of them according to the president's attitude toward "the fundamental problems that confronted him as President, when he was active in the affairs of government." These particular presidents stood out because of "the constructive battles they waged, not merely battles against things temporarily evil but battles for things permanently good—battles for the basic morals of democracy, which rest on respect for the right of self-government and faith in majority rule." With the wisdom of experience, these men knew that the majority often makes mistakes. They believed "passionately" that rule by a small minority class unfailingly makes worse mistakes. Class rule takes only counsel from itself and thus fails to heed the problems and the good of all kinds and conditions of men. "In the long run the instincts of the common man (like Lincoln), willing to live and let live, work out the best and safest balance for the common good." This is what FDR meant by "the battle to restore and maintain the moral integrity of democracy," which, of course, meant the New Deal programs.[28]

Then he said, "Let me talk history," he really meant let me show you where Lincoln and I stand together. When Lincoln emerged, he was "scorned for his uncouthness, his simplicity, his homely stories and his attitude for the little man." This man faced opposition far behind his battle lines from those who thought first and last of their own selfish aims. Gold speculators in Wall Street were the perfect example of those who cheered defeats of their own armies because the price of their gold would rise thereby. There were contractors who founded fortunes at the expense of the boys at the front. They were "a minority unwilling to support their own people and government unless the government would leave them free to pursue their private gains." As himself, "Lincoln too fought for the morals of democracy." Roosevelt believed that if Lincoln had lived, the south would have been allowed to rehabilitate itself on the basis of "those morals instead of being 'reconstructed' by martial law and carpetbaggers." FDR had certainly imbibed revisionist Reconstruction which labeled it "the tragic era," "the dreadful decade," "the age of hate," and "the nadir of national disgrace."

Roosevelt warned of the continuing menace of a comparatively small number of conservative people who honestly believed in their superior right to influence and direct government and would not admit that their actions were harmful to the nation. That same group asked Lincoln to let them alone. "Strangely enough, although they had no confidence in a people's government, they demanded that a people's government have confidence in them," he observed. Once again the "head of the Nation is working with all his might and main to restore and to uphold the integrity of the morals of democracy,"—himself. This was the heritage of the Democratic party from "the long line of national leadership—from Jefferson to Wilson—and preeminently from old Andrew Jackson himself." Although FDR had not yet listed Lincoln among the Democratic party "great," it was only a matter of time. But he had repeatedly listed Lincoln along with the customary Democratic stalwarts, which included his own dynamic cousin TR.[29]

Enthusiastically, Lincoln biographer Sandburg wrote President Roosevelt that he was about to finish his six-volume work on Lincoln possibly that year, 1938. "I may try my hand at a sketch of you," he proffered. "Meantime you may expect me some day at the White House door with a guitar, for an evening of songs and of stories from the hinterlands which may rest you on one hell of a job. You are on a spot where more personal passion, love, and malice concentrate than anywhere else in the USA," as he was fully aware in working with Lincoln and living with Roosevelt. President Roosevelt wrote back to Sandburg, "I am grateful to you for your thoughtful note of March ninth and appreciate the fine sense of justice which prompted you to write as you did. It was a delight to hear from you." In August, Sandburg dropped the president another shorter note which said: "Somewhat over two years ago I wrote to you that all the time you keep growing. This still holds." Just as Sandburg observed Lincoln's own growth during those difficult presidential years, so too now he was witness to that same phenomena in FDR. Emil Ludwig wrote a popular biography of FDR that same year and compared Lincoln and FDR. "The characters—profoundly different . . . . And yet, they are linked by two immense qualities, humor and friendliness," Ludwig wrote. When Ludwig asked Roosevelt what Lincoln meant to him, he answered without a moment's hesitation: "Lincoln? The greatest humanitarian!" And Sandburg wrote FDR that his "respect for Emil Ludwig ran higher on seeing the work he did with you." [30]

FDR continued to use Lincoln to bolster his New Deal defense that summer of 1938. In a fireside chat on June 24, 1938, he told the American people:

> Never in our lifetime has such a concerted campaign of defeatism been thrown at the heads of the President and Senators and Congressmen as in the case of this Seventy-fifth Congress. Never before have we had so many Copperheads–and you will remember that it was the Copperheads who, in the days of the War Between the States, tried their best to make Lincoln and his Congress give up the fight, let the Nation remain split in two and return to peace–peace at any price.

He could identify with Lincoln's experience because the "copperheads" of his own day were attacking him just as they had Lincoln before.[31]

President Roosevelt dedicated the Gettysburg Eternal Light Peace Memorial as the "shrine of American patriotism" on July 3, 1938, the seventy-fifth anniversary of the battle. A perpetual flame lights the top of the monument and an inscription reads, "Peace Eternal in a Nation United." Again, FDR boldly developed parallels between himself and President Lincoln. First, he evaluated the fullness of Lincoln's nature and the fundamental conflict which events had forced upon his presidency to which he and others could always turn for inspiration and encouragement. It was the very same issue which Lincoln restated at Gettysburg seventy-five years before that continued as the issue before the nation, and would do so "as long as we cling to the purposes for which the Nation was founded—to preserve under the changing conditions of each generation a people's government for the people's good." Lincoln had spoken "in solace for all who fought upon this field; and the years have laid their balm upon their wounds." Now men who wore the blue and those who wore gray were there, a fragment spared by time. They brought back memories of old divided loyalties, but they also met there in "united loyalty to a united cause which the unfolding years have made it easier to see." All were to be honored, irrespective of the flag they fought under—"thankful that they stand together under one flag now."

President Roosevelt developed Lincoln's democratic call for peace through unity before an audience of 150,000 which included that remnant of the old Civil War veterans:

> Lincoln was commander-in-chief in this old battle [undoubtedly an affront to some old diehard Confederates present]; he wanted above all things to be commander-in-chief of the new peace.

> He understood that battle there must be; that when a challenge to constituted government is thrown down, the people must in self-defense take it up; that the fight must be fought through to a decision so clear that it is accepted as being beyond recall.

> But Lincoln also understood that after such a decision, a democracy should seek peace through a new unity. For a democracy can keep alive only if the settlement of old difficulties clears the ground and transfers energies to face new responsibilities. Never can it have as much ability and purpose as it needs in that striving; the end of battle does not end the infinity of those needs.
> That is why Lincoln—commander of a people as well as of an army—asked that his battle end "with malice toward none, with charity for all."

To the hurt of those who came after him, Lincoln's plea was long denied. A generation passed before the new unity became accepted fact.

Then FDR made the application and drew the parallel between Lincoln and himself, telling "above all" what he wanted for himself:

> It is another conflict, a conflict as fundamental as Lincoln's, fought not with glint of steel, but with appeals to reason and justice on a thousand fronts—seeking to save for our common country opportunity and security for citizens in a free society.
>
> We are near to winning this battle [in 1938]. In its winning and through the years may we live by the wisdom and the humanity of the heart of Abraham Lincoln.

The task may take a different shape at different times, but the challenge always remained the same. And in the midst of the conflict, it was clearly Lincoln's humanitarian heart which moved FDR.[32]

Roosevelt believed that the Democratic Party would continue to receive the support of Americans as long as it remained a liberal party. In an address at Denton, Maryland, September 5, 1938, he evaluated his coming to the presidency with that of Washington and Lincoln. "When I became President I found a country demoralized, disorganized, with each of these groups [conservatives and liberals] seeking to survive by taking advantage of the others," he said. He boldly declared the crisis was the same:

> As in the time of George Washington in 1787, when there was grave danger that the states would never become a Nation—as in the time of Abraham Lincoln, when a tragic division threatened to become lasting—our time has brought a test of our American Union.

And as both Washington and Lincoln, FDR had risen to the challenge:

> A great part of my duty as President has been to do what I could to bring our people together again. That has been my unchanging purpose since March 4, 1933.

In this thinking, President Roosevelt's duty was identical with that of both Washington and Abraham Lincoln.[33]

In the middle of the 1938 primaries there was talk already of running FDR for a possible third term. It was certainly evident that FDR was consciously making an effort to link with the Lincoln tradition. Carl Sandburg wrote Governor Frank Murphy of Michigan, September 10, 1938:

> I belong to no party but all who know me are well aware that I am a New Dealer, that I agree with you it may be necessary to draft Roosevelt for a third term, that I rate you in any one of a number of contingencies as presidential timber, that I argue you were in the Lincolnian tradition in your handling of the sit-down strike crises.

Just over a week later, Sandburg wrote FDR that there had been other vehement times in the nation's history, as the bitterness in the campaign reminded him, and that the attacks on the president certainly were not new. "Shortly after Lincoln's assassination," he wrote, "you may be interested to know, one J. W. Phelps wrote to Senator Charles Sumner that in his opinion it was Lincoln's carelessness about his personal guards that resulted in the assassin's success." That was a minor point. But in connection with it, Phelps had written of Lincoln: "His goodness, benevolence, and magnanimity were as much out of place at the head of a people so truculently cunning as we are, as would be a human head upon a snake's body." As a verbal cartoon and metaphor, Sandburg averred, it was not true and correct, but for "grand vehemence in the American style," it surpassed General William Tecumseh Sherman's statement five days later that "Washington is as corrupt as Hell, made so by the looseness and extravagance of the war. I will avoid it as a pest house." The president replied: "To paraphrase the Old Testament we might say: There were giants (of invective) on the earth in those days." Roosevelt was encouraged.[34]

President Roosevelt's Thanksgiving Day Proclamation, November 19, 1938, was issued on the anniversary of Lincoln's Gettysburg Address. And the two occasions reminded him of the fact that "Abraham Lincoln set apart 'a Day of Thanksgiving and Praise to our beneficent Father who dwelleth in the heavens.'" Thus, from their earliest recorded history, Americans had thanked God for their blessings and, picking up the phrase first engraved on American coins in Lincoln's administration, he noted: "We turn to God in time of trouble and in time of happiness. 'In God We Trust.'"[35]

From the time of the first president of the United States, it was customary for the president to take with him, as his own personal property, all of his correspondence, documents, and papers which came during his term or terms in office at the White House. It was believed that many of the papers of such presidents as William Henry Harrison, John Tyler, Millard Fillmore, Abraham Lincoln, Ulysses S. Grant, and Warren Harding had been burned. By 1939, the Library of Congress had about 95 percent of the known surviving papers of the first president. But the presidential papers of John Adams and John Quincy Adams were not available to scholars and the papers of such presidents as Jefferson, Madison, Monroe, and Abraham Lincoln were widely scattered. Lincoln's papers were not available and would not be so until 1947 and the papers that did exist were scattered in numerous repositories because Mrs. Lincoln had given many away. Very few presidential papers were intact. Former presidents and their families who designated the Library of Congress as the depository for most of the presidential papers placed important restrictions on their use. President Herbert Hoover had already constructed a private library building at Stanford University in California for his own collection of papers and correspondence. Hoover was the first president who did not destroy a considerable part of the White House files at the time he left. But FDR wanted to do something not done before.[36]

Because of the sad history of destruction and dissipation of presidential papers, FDR gave serious thought to the best way to handle his own public papers and correspondence and documents. He came to the conclusion that as soon as he left the White House, they should all be turned over to the United States, as public property rather than as a private collection, as in the Hoover case. FDR was convinced that the commencement of his first term in 1933 began "a new period in American social, economic, and political history." Therefore, his presidential papers should be located in a spot generally accessible to the general public, and to scholars and students. In addition to his own papers, the collection should include also the papers of all the leading public officials of the United States during his administration who were willing to donate them. They should remain under the ownership, care and management of the U. S. government. And, the president added, they should be open to scholars and historians as soon as practicable, "with due concern for the interests of the United States and of the living personalities of our day." Thus, FDR decided to construct a public institution at Hyde Park, New York, because he believed that the collection of original historical documents in America should be decentralized instead of concentrating them all in the nation's capital. This would reduce the danger from fire, war, and other calamities. Just the sheer problem of storage in a few great repositories would change.[37]

The problem of Lincoln's papers was central in FDR's thinking. The fact that Lincoln's papers were scattered in numerous repositories, because Mrs. Lincoln gave them away, led to the problem that historians did not know where to turn to find information desired about Lincoln. As far as Roosevelt's adviser on the matter, Professor Samuel Eliot Morison, was concerned: "a great deal of the important evidence has been destroyed [about Lincoln], some purposely, some by mere neglect and accident." Thus, the tragedy of the scattered Lincoln papers directly impacted FDR's view of his own presidential collection and his desire to leave it to posterity.[38]

FDR's use of Lincoln increasingly irritated Republicans, long before the conclusion of his message to Congress on January 4, 1939, the beginning of a new year. However, Roosevelt repeated the Lincoln idiom in his annual message to the Congress on January 4, 1939. "Once I prophesied that this generation of Americans had a rendezvous with destiny," he reminded Congress. "That prophecy comes true." Paraphrasing Scripture, he said: "To us much is given; more is expected." Then drawing from Lincoln, FDR concluded: "This generation will 'nobly save or meanly lose the last best hope of earth . . . . The way is plain, peaceful, generous, just—a way which if followed the world will forever applaud and God must forever bless.'"[39]

By January of 1939, Abraham Lincoln had become a New Deal Democrat. On January 7, 1939, FDR delivered an address at the Jackson Day dinner in Washington, D. C. He talked about Jackson and the Democratic party and their legacy, of course. But then he used the occasion to lay claim to Abraham Lincoln as a "real Democrat." Picking up his history lesson following the Jackson era, FDR said that a full generation of twenty years passed by before Andrew Jackson's principle of true democracy came back to life in the White House. The principle of true democracy "came back to life in the White House with the next real Democrat, Abraham Lincoln." And, parenthetically, Lincoln was chosen president only by the founding of a new party. Then the president asked two obvious questions. First, did anyone maintain that the Democratic Party from 1840 to 1876 was by any wild stretch of the imagination the party of Thomas Jefferson or of Andrew Jackson? "To claim that is absurd," he declared. Secondly, did anyone maintain that the Republican Party from 1868 to 1938 (with the possible exception of a few years under his cousin Theodore Roosevelt) was the party of Abraham Lincoln? "To claim that is equally absurd," he boldly declared. Roosevelt's casual acquaintance, he observed, with political life for the last twenty-five years and his more serious reading of prior history led him to observe that the American people had greatly changed their attitude toward government in his generation. "We of this modern day take our politics less seriously," he said, "and we take our government more seriously." The voting public was influenced less and less "by the red fire and the hard cider ballyhoo of newspaper owners or political orators who adhere to the practices of a century ago." Indeed, the American voting public had learned to go behind headlines and behind leads and behind glittering generalities in order to analyze and reanalyze, using their own thinking processes and not those of someone else before coming to conclusions. "You remember what Abraham Lincoln said about fooling the people," he asked. "That was in the 1860's," in the old days. "I should say that no wise political leader of 1939 will take it as a safe working rule that you can fool many of the people any of the time," paraphrasing Lincoln's statement.[40]

Republicans were indignant with FDR's theft of Lincoln for the New Deal Democratic party. The New Deal's most redoubtable critic, former president Herbert Hoover, responded on February 12 at the Lincoln Day dinner held by the National Republican Club of New York. Hoover observed that every year at that time Americans expressed gratitude for the birth of Abraham Lincoln. He noted that recently Mr. Roosevelt had claimed him as a founder of FDR's faith. "I was under the impression he [Lincoln] was a Republican," Hoover groused. FDR's use of Lincoln had lowered the martyred president's esteem. Abraham Lincoln towered far above political partisanship, Hoover noted:

> He rests in the hearts of the American people not as a politician but as a great American who died fighting for the most precious possession of all American possessions—the liberty of men.

Americans were more sadly divided and confused than at any time since Lincoln's time and, if Lincoln could look down from the high stratosphere, he would see the nation "still professing liberty yet pursuing ideas which limit and endanger the freedom of men." However, Lincoln would also see another ray of light through all this confusion; he would see the American people steadily forcing a clarification of national thought. "Those who adhere to the traditional liberalism upon which the Republic was founded and which Lincoln sustained are crowding away from the pseudo-liberalism of the New Deal," Hoover opined. It was a paradox. The Republican party had become the conservative party in the sense of preserving true liberalism in America. And the spirit of true liberalism, according to Hoover, was to create free men; "it is not the coercion of men." Then Hoover declared: "Whatever this New Deal system is, it is certain that it did not come from Abraham Lincoln."[41]

Hoover responded to both Roosevelt's annual message to Congress and his Jackson Day dinner speech. Roosevelt had made a moving appeal for unity in the people, but "he smote the to-be-purged Democrats with hints to get out of his party" a few days later. Then FDR took in still more ground of combat when he observed: "Does any one maintain that the Republican party from 1868 to 1938 was the party of Abraham Lincoln?" In excepting his own cousin, Theodore Roosevelt, Hoover noted FDR wanted "to purge the Republican party also." This smear on the political faith of half the American people, did not add to unity. "Certainly Mr. Roosevelt's formula of appeasement does not follow Mr. Lincoln's method of 'with malice toward none, with charity for all,'" Hoover observed. No, no, "Mr. Lincoln would not be fooled by the notion that economic righteousness and social good burst upon the world with the New Deal," Hoover said. In fact, Lincoln would have seen that it was a Republican administration which *first* announced the responsibility of government aid in time of great depression. And it was the New Deal destruction of that energy, enterprise, and productivity which imperiled all the humanitarian work of the eighty years since Lincoln. Hoover admitted that the "followers of Lincoln" did not claim that the Republican party or any other party had always been perfect. As the Republican party had lagged in prompt action and faulty action in the past, so too the Democratic party had given great service in years gone by. But there was one thing for sure, declared Hoover: "With the millions of Americans with faith in this party and with the task now laid upon it to restore liberty in this land, it is certain that the spirit of Abraham Lincoln has not joined the New Deal." Indeed, the high purposes of the United States were being undermined by Roosevelt's policies pursued at home and abroad. The first great mission of the Republican party still remained the preservation of these principles of liberty for all people. But "we do not want to become entangled in another world war," declared Hoover. The Republican party mission included "peace for America." Lincoln was no New Deal Democrat, but a real Republican. Hoover concluded:

> We are the living custodians of the torch which fell from the hand of Abraham Lincoln. We may again rekindle the heart and mind of America with the glow of hope and promise for the future. Never since Lincoln has a political party faced such an opportunity for a service to a great nation.[42]

On March 8, 1939, Max Lerner published an article on "the Lincoln image" in the *New Republic*. He announced that there was "a new and revived Lincoln image in the making" as "almost providentially made for our present crisis." Lerner linked this revived Lincoln image with Roosevelt and, even before the party conventions of 1940, believed that FDR would be renominated and reelected in the time of national crisis. Franklin D. Roosevelt had always had a sense of history, Lerner wrote:

One thing Roosevelt has said clearly: he has no intention of being another Buchanan. Which implies that all the basic conditions that characterize a country on the eve of a civil war are true of our period. But to avoid being a Buchanan in the face of impending civil war one must be something of a Lincoln. How much of Lincoln does Roosevelt have in him? More, I am convinced, than any President since Lincoln or before.[43]

A new generation of students who had reached maturity since World War I were using "new cliches" and "new patter" to replace the old, according to Raymond Moley's evaluation of "The Class of 1939" in *Newsweek*, June 19, 1939. The new patter taught that capitalism had failed, that Americans must band together here and abroad to fight selfish men who wrecked the pre-depression world, and that Americans should believe that a dollar spent is a dollar earned. These students also said that Congress was terrible, and "that businessmen were curious beings, with myopic eyes in the backs of their heads, etcetera, etcetera." But this new generation of students were also "pattering" that "Roosevelt is greater than Abraham Lincoln."[44]

By 3:00 A.M., September 1, 1939, President Roosevelt received word that Hitler's forces had invaded Poland. World War II had begun. Grace Tully reached the White House before 8:00 A.M. to begin the first day of the pressure-packed years which continued until after President Roosevelt's death in 1945. While FDR retired for a brief rest after his all-night vigil, Grace moved into the Prince of Wales Room across the hall on the second floor where the "Lincoln bed" was located and took all the diplomatic messages which were coming in. At the news conference that day, FDR was asked, "Can we stay out?" The president answered that he not only hoped so, but he believed the United States could and that every effort would be made by his administration to do so. Roosevelt's use of the Lincoln idiom would now begin to change.[45]

While laying the cornerstone of the new Jefferson Memorial on November 15, 1939, FDR declared: "Today we lay the cornerstone of a third great shrine—adding the name of Thomas Jefferson to the names of George Washington and Abraham Lincoln." Washington represented abilities which had been recognized in every part of the nation, indeed, in every part of the civilized world of his own day. Washington had been many things, "a great military leader," "a great moderator," "a great executive," "a man of vision and accomplishments," "talented engineer and surveyor," "planner of highways and canals," "patron of husbandry," "friend of scientists" and "fellow of political thinkers." Lincoln, too, was a many-sided man, just like Washington. He was a "pioneer of the wilderness, counsel for the under-privileged, soldier in an Indian war, master of the

English tongue, rallying point for a torn nation, emancipator—not of slaves alone, but of those of heavy heart everywhere—foe of malice, and teacher of good-will." This was FDR's Lincoln in those closing troubled months of 1939.[46]

Earlier that year, Carl Sandburg had completed most of his manuscript of *Abraham Lincoln: The War Years*. It was ready to be turned over to Harcourt. For many years, Lincoln was Sandburg's companion. To a certain extent, he felt he had lost his own personality in the process. It was Lincoln who led Carl Sandburg back from the past to an active present. It was Lincoln who had rejuvenated Sandburg's interest in politics and his constant parallels between Lincoln and FDR. As a result of getting acquainted with Lincoln, the biographer's renewed faith in the American people and their president became a very important factor in the domestic and international turmoil of 1940. The publication date was December 1, with fifteen thousand sets of *The War Years* sold at $20 for each four-volume set. But before the printing date, there was a second printing for six thousand more sets for the Christmas holiday. Sandburg made the cover of the issue of *Time* for December 4, 1939. As reviewers and the press took note, historian Charles Beard wrote: "Never yet has a history or biography like Carl Sandburg's 'Abraham Lincoln: The War Years' appeared on land or sea." It was the apex in Sandburg's career, but it also had a great impact on Franklin D. Roosevelt.[47]

Lincoln the Statesman, Roosevelts' Example for Foreign Policy and National Survival—1940-1945

The Roosevelt administration began shifting its priority from domestic to foreign policy and President Roosevelt recovered his vigor with a renewed sense of purpose. However, FDR believed that his task was almost finished and, whenever talk of a third term came up, the president said he was not interested. FDR was still talking that way as late as May 1940. Certainly the outbreak of war in Europe in 1940 would be a good reason to seek a third term, as would, of course, saving New Deal policies from destruction. Besides, FDR believed that he would have much more trouble with Congress in a third term. "Did you ever stop to think," he asked in February, "that if I should run and be elected I would have much more trouble with Congress in my third term and much more bitterness to contend with as a result of my running for a third term than I have ever had before?" But if he did not run, where would all the Liberals go? He was tired. He replied: ". . . I am tied down to this chair day after day, week after week, and month after month. And I can't stand it any longer. I can't go on with it." A third term was a bad idea. It was a bad tradition.[48]

The Jackson Day dinner on January 8, 1940 was particularly important because of the fact that 1940 was an election year and so many were eager to know whether FDR intended to become a candidate for a third presidential term. Instead of giving any hints on his intentions, the president talked about the independent vote which had grown steadily during the past generation and warned that political parties must conduct their affairs in such a way as to win the votes of those who voted on principle rather than for a particular political party. He hoped that three leading invited guests from the Republican party had come in order to hear FDR talk about Andrew Jackson. They had not come. The president also intended to tell them about Abraham Lincoln. He wished to "tell them how much alike all of our great leaders have been, even to give them free—though unsolicited—advice as to how to reconstitute the Republican Party successfully along the lines on which Abraham Lincoln created it." As the Democratic Party leader, FDR said he was not reluctant to give them good advice because he was sure that they would not use it—"they of little faith," he joked. But seriously, the more Roosevelt had studied American history the more clearly he saw what the problems were. He believed that the common denominator of American great men in public life had not been mere allegiance to any one political party, but the "disinterested devotion with which they have tried to serve the whole country, and the relative unimportance that they had ascribed to politics, compared with the paramount importance of Government."[49]

Millions of unnecessary words and explanations and solemn comments were uttered and written year in and year out about the great men of American history, all written with ample quotations, including Lincoln, he said. All of them tried to prove what would have been said or what would have been done about some specific modern problem of government if they were alive. (He was also guilty of doing the same thing.) "Yes, the devil can quote past statesmen as readily as he can quote the Scriptures, in order to prove his purpose," FDR quipped. But those who are on the "actual firing line of the moment," like himself, attached major importance only to the motives of past leaders. "To them it matters, on the whole, very little what party label American statesmen bore, or what mistakes they made in the smaller things, so long as they did the big job that their times demanded be done," he noted. And then he claimed Lincoln again for the Democratic cause:

> I do not know which party Lincoln would belong to if he were alive in 1940—and I am not even concerned to speculate on it; a new party had to be created before he could be elected President. I am more interested in the fact that he did the big job which then had to be done–to preserve the Union and make possible, at a later time, the united country that we all live in today. His sympathies and his motives of championship of humanity itself have made him for all centuries to come the legitimate property of all parties—of every man and woman and child in every part of our land.

This was FDR's response to former president Hoover and all the other Republicans who laid exclusive claim to the Lincoln example. It was a fitting seizure of the symbol of the Republican birthright by a so-called reluctant candidate for an unprecedented third term.[50]

As early as January 24, 1940, FDR said: "I do not want to run unless between now and the convention things get very, very much worse in Europe." And FDR did not want to produce a violent isolationist reaction. "These are troubled times we of this generation are living through," he told the nation's farmers over radio on March 8, 1940. "Some of us, I know, are tempted to give way to doubt and fear, even to despair." he admitted. But when such thoughts beleaguer, "Let us remember how the nation has come through its dark hours of the past, and take courage." Think of Adams and Jefferson and Madison, he said, as they guided the nation through the confusion of the Napoleonic wars, with ships rotting at the docks and millions of dollars of farm products stored on the wharves of the Atlantic seaboard. And still nurturing the Lincoln comparison, he said: "Think of Lincoln as year after war-torn year he sheltered in his great heart the truest aspirations of a country rent in twain."[51]

In the spring of 1940 the Nazi high command launched its attack on western Europe. It would be one of the most successful military campaigns ever carried out. In April the Germans invaded Norway and Denmark. The Norwegians fought back fiercely for three weeks before they were defeated, while Denmark was occupied in even less time. In the second week of May the Nazi armies overran neutral Holland, Belgium, and Luxembourg. The next week they sped into northern France and to the English Channel. In the process the Germans trapped an Anglo-French army of nearly 400,000 on the beach at Dunkirk. The reversals in Norway and the Low Countries and the military crisis in France led to Neville Chamberlain's resignation, and Winston Churchill became prime minister of Great Britain.

The "Phony War" was over and a new phase in the Roosevelt presidency had begun. The New Deal revolution was sputtering and the nation seemed weary of reform. FDR's enemies on domestic issues had become his friends in foreign policy. In his speech before the Congress on May 16, 1940, FDR declared that the nation stood ready to spend millions for defense, but also to give service and even lives to maintain American liberty, as he renewed the courage and hope and faith of the American people. It was a united front which included former president Herbert Hoover as well. Lincoln's example as a statesman of Democracy now became Roosevelt's mentor.

During those months of gloom, Lincoln's presence seemed very close to the Roosevelt White House. In her sitting room, Eleanor Roosevelt spoke of "how the second floor of the White House seemed alive with historical presences." Sometimes she imagined she heard Lincoln walking about in the darkest hours of the night. She felt that Lincoln's ghost nightly prowled the halls of the second floor and haunted the room where Harry Hopkins slept, the room where the "Lincoln bed" was located—the very same bed and room in which young Willie Lincoln had died in February 1862. But others felt Lincoln's presence during that same time. Mary Eben, who was in charge of assembling and cataloguing the tremendous collection of books which poured in to FDR through his presidential years, had a shaking experience one day on the White House second floor. Stepping out of the elevator, Mary glanced into the opposite room where the Lincoln bed was located. According to Mary, Lincoln was at that moment sitting on the bed, leaning forward as if to pull on his boots. It was at that very moment that FDR rolled out of his bedroom door to find Mary reaching frantically for something to hold her up. She told Roosevelt her story and FDR just roared with laughter. "Child, you're a scream. What brand were you drinking last night?" "Whatever it was," he said, "I think I'd change it." FDR added, however, that he "rather liked the idea of Lincoln coming back to check up on things and ventured that he might find the world of today very interesting to him."[52]

On June 5, Roosevelt hosted the leaders of the American Youth Congress who perceived that he had abandoned the New Deal in the face of foreign threats. Fresh from campuses across the nation, they were disenchanted with FDR. In the East Room, they protested that he had subordinated social concerns wholly to those of national defense when the barest beginnings had been made in solving the nation's social problems. Roosevelt spoke frankly of the daily practical problems as he faced the totalitarian dictatorship abroad and blind selfish reaction at home—both powerful enemies of human freedom. While speaking, he was reminded of Lincoln who faced the responsibility of dealing with black slavery, an unmitigated evil, while attempting to save the dividing Union he had solemnly sworn to preserve. Lincoln postponed dealing with the slavery question in order to concentrate on saving the Union until a time when both became a part of the same problem—saving the Union by destroying human slavery in the United States. "Young man, I think you are very sincere," he said. "Have you read Carl Sandburg's *Lincoln*?" The "young man" admitted he had not. Then he continued, drawing from Sandburg's *Lincoln*:

> I think the impression was that Lincoln was a pretty sad man, because he could not do all he wanted to do at one time, and I think you will find examples where Lincoln had to compromise to gain a little something. He had to compromise to make a few gains. Lincoln was one of those unfortunate people called a "politician" but he was a politician who was practical enough to get a great many things for his country. He was a sad man because he couldn't get it all at once. And nobody can.

Everyone understood FDR's careful effort to identify his predicament with that of President Lincoln. Lincoln's top priority had been to preserve the Union and Roosevelt's was essentially the same.[53]

The swift fall of France and Britain's desperate condition placed the United States in grave danger, despite the college students' concern for New Deal policies. There was a need for an experienced leader in the White House who would do just what Lincoln had done when the nation's survival was at stake back in 1861. Who but Franklin D. Roosevelt could take a united nation into a possible war and preserve the New Deal social gains at the same time? "From the very beginning Franklin Roosevelt has been a crisis President, and there is little reason to suppose that he will cease to be President at a time when the crisis is deepest," wrote Max Lerner in *The Nation*, June 22, 1940 issue. Lerner's article appeared before the Democratic National Convention opened in Chicago on July 15. "The point is that, for the people's purposes today, Mr. Roosevelt is a good horse," he wrote, "and they know it." What kind of President would FDR be in his third term? Well, with his sense of history, he had once said in 1933 that "I shall be either America's greatest President or its last." Learner observed:

> I know that in externals they are poles apart. In the one an easy graciousness, in the other a clumsy grace; the one modern, alert, cosmopolitan, and the other a backwoodsman even for his own day; the one aristocrat, the other plebeian.
>
> Yet the resemblances are real. Each of them managed somehow to catch the accents and express the aspirations of events to complete an interior crisis out of which his real greatness emerged. Lincoln was a brooding man of thought whom the Civil War compelled to action.

Roosevelt is a man of action whom the crisis of the depression years and the international collapse have compelled to thought. The more memorable figure is undoubtedly Lincoln, the more effective President probably Roosevelt.[54]

Meeting in Philadelphia on June 15, the Republicans had already nominated Wendell Willkie who until recently had been a Democrat who voted for Roosevelt in 1932. Roosevelt's handling of the convention was a lesson in political strategy as he outmaneuvered opposition groups and avoided all discussion of the wisdom of a third term. FDR won his third presidential nomination on the Democratic ticket on the first ballot by an overwhelming margin.[55]

While the balloting began for the vice presidential part of the ticket, it appeared Wallace might lose. If Wallace went down, Roosevelt might yet refuse the nomination. A grim-faced Roosevelt laid aside his cards and took up a note pad and pencil and filled five pages with his scrawl. After it was revised and cleaned up, he wrote: "I cannot, in all honor, and will not . . . go along with the cheap bargaining and political maneuvering which have brought about party dissension. . . . It is best not to straddle ideals." Then echoing Lincoln's 1858 "house divided" speech, he wrote: "I wish to give the Democratic Party the opportunity to make its historic decision clearly and without equivocation. The party must go wholly one way or wholly the other. It cannot face in both directions at the same time."[56]

With Wallace nominated, FDR delivered his acceptance of the nomination before a cluster of microphones in the White House's Diplomatic Reception Room. Accepting this unprecedented third-term nomination, he told his party leadership and friends:

> Whatever its new trappings and new slogans, tyranny is the oldest and most discredited rule known to history. And whenever tyranny has replaced a more human form of Government it has been due more to internal causes than external. Democracy can thrive only when it enlists the devotion of those whom Lincoln called the common people. Democracy can hold that devotion only when it adequately respects their dignity by so ordering society as to assure to the masses of men and women reasonable security and hope for themselves and their children.

When World War II broke out in September of 1939, Roosevelt intended to announce clearly and simply, at an early date, that "under no conditions would I accept reelection." This was well known to his friends. But because of swift-moving foreign events and the necessity for swift action at home and abroad, he was persuaded not to refuse a forthcoming nomination under those circumstances. "Only the people themselves can draft a President," he said. "If such a draft should be made upon me, I say to you, in the utmost simplicity, I will, with God's help, continue to serve with the best of my ability and with the fullness of my strength."[57]

By September 1940 the presidential campaign had entered its final stages. The author of *Abe Lincoln in Illinois*, Robert Sherwood, joined the presidential speech writing staff as new blood. The First Lady had seen Sherwood's Lincoln play at its pre-Broadway premiere in Washington. Congratulating Sherwood, Eleanor Roosevelt commented: "Strange, how fundamentally people seem to have fought on much the same issues throughout our history!" She enthusiastically shared her view with the president. Roosevelt saw the film version of the play and then wrote Sherwood requesting a copy of the two Lincoln speeches which were delivered in the debate scene. Accompanying the transcripts, Sherwood wrote a letter. He told FDR: "I wish with all my heart to offer my services, for whatever they're worth, to you in this crucial year and to the cause which is yours as surely as it was Lincoln's." Thus, the playwright had received a call a few months later.[58]

After joining the staff in September, the stamp of Sherwood's presence and use of the Lincoln idiom did not seem to appear immediately. On the seventy-fifth anniversary of the ratification of the Thirteenth Amendment, FDR noted that there was "an irony of our day that three-quarters of a century after the adoption of the Amendment forever outlawing slavery under the American Flag, liberty should be under violent attack." And then he wrote:

> And yet over large areas of the earth the liberties which to us mean happiness and the right to live peaceful and contented lives are challenged by brute force—a force which would return the human family to that state of slavery from which emancipation came through the Thirteenth Amendment.[59]

Lincoln's name and words first appear in the fall campaign on October 23, 1940 when the president spoke from the rear platform of his campaign train. But it basically was the same address FDR had given in Wilmington, Delaware, on October 29, 1936. He introduced it, however by referring to his visit four years before when the famous Liberty League in Wilmington had intended to defeat the New Deal and drive it from office. He said:

In view of that fact I thought four years ago, and I still think, that Wilmington is a good place to read from a speech made by president Abraham Lincoln, his definition of the word "liberty." This year I think the definition is of even greater significance.

This same day, he formally opened the 1940 Presidential Campaign in Philadelphia with the words: "It is for peace that I have labored; and it is for peace that I shall labor all the days of my life."[60]

The following day, October 24, 1940, FDR gave a radio address to the New York *Herald-Tribune* forum. Sherwood's influence may be seen in this address. Closing the forum on the subject, "Saving Democracy," FDR began with an opening reference to Lincoln's Cooper Institute Address on February 27, 1860. Roosevelt observed that Lincoln was then speaking to an audience to whom he was a stranger. Represented in the audience, said the New York *Tribune* of that day, was the "intellect and moral culture" of New York City. FDR said that Lincoln warned them against the fear-mongers and the calamity howlers—the "appeasers" of that troubled time, appeasers who were numerous and influential. He said: "Neither let us be slandered from our duty by false accusations against us, nor frightened from it by menaces of destruction to the Government, nor of dungeons to ourselves." And then the president added:

We do well to repeat Lincoln's declaration of faith today. It gives the right answer—to the foreign propagandists who seek to divide us with their strategy of terror.

Roosevelt had confidence in the ability of the democratic system which gave men dignity and strength. And so he could echo, as all of Americans ought to, with Lincoln: "Let us have faith that right makes might, and in that faith let us to the end dare to do our duty as we understand it."[61]

In Lincoln's hometown of Springfield, Illinois, Republican presidential candidate Wendell Willkie used both the occasion and Lincoln to warn of "state socialism." Willkie challenged FDR's claim to Lincoln. Lincoln's "great experience and career and then the solemnity of his death made him the symbol, the hope and the purpose of America." Willkie recognized that it had become custom in the last few years for various public figures to choose the occasion of speaking either at the birthplace, or some memorial statue or shrine to the great dead, to draw comparison between these distinguished persons and the particular leader in his own interpretation of his viewpoint. He said:

> Within the last year and a half the candidate for the third term as President of the United States has made speeches in which he has inferentially described himself as Washington, Jefferson, Jackson, Lincoln, Cleveland, Wilson and Theodore Roosevelt. And, of course, his opponents were described always as the representative of what he has thought was the disadvantageous leader in American public life.[62]

After reviewing Lincoln's career as legislator, congressman, president, Willkie admitted that Lincoln "is recognized by all with Washington as the twin great Presidents of all time." "Neither of us has demonstrated any of the qualities of greatness demonstrated by Washington or Lincoln or those other great figures, because the greatest quality of all of those men was the quality of magnanimity." Roosevelt was not qualified to stand before the American people as a great man, nor was the Republican candidate. It does no good to draw on historical illusions or rush into hyperbole about the respective merits or demerits of candidates. The important question was: What does Roosevelt believe? What does Willkie believe? Not what does Lincoln believe! Willkie had read everything he could find on Lincoln and agreed with the martyred president's expression that "the people have the revolutionary right to change their form of government whenever they so desire." And then he concluded with Lincoln: "Lincoln, his brooding figure, had an expression for it and with that I leave you: 'We will nobly save or meanly lose, the last best hope on this earth.'"[63]

In the last days of the campaign, FDR portrayed the European conflict as a class war and returned to "the Lincoln model of national unity." In a speech entitled "What Lincoln Would Have Done," Carl Sandburg insisted that the martyred president would have done exactly what Franklin Roosevelt was doing. And, thus, on election eve, November 4, 1940, the Democrats went on the air from coast to coast, and gave the final climactic five minutes of their broadcast to the Lincoln biographer, the only politically independent speaker. Sandburg recalled Lincoln's critical 1864 presidential election. It was the independent voters who had come to Lincoln's rescue then. On the following day, election day 1940, independent voters would again speak as in 1864. He read a lengthy excerpt from an obscure Presbyterian minister, the Reverend Henry Fowler. In 1863, he had compared Lincoln with the prophet Samuel in Hebrew history. It was also Sandburg's assessment of Lincoln:

> The explanation of his every act is this: He executes the will of the people .... His wisdom consists in carrying out the good sense of the nation. His growth in political knowledge, his steady movement ... are

but the growth and movement of the national mind. . . . He stands before you. . . a not perfect man and yet more precious than fine gold.

"And for some of us," Sandburg concluded, "that goes, in the main, in the present hour of national fate, for Franklin Delano Roosevelt."[64]

A few days after Roosevelt's reelection to a third term, Sandburg wrote the president that he had enclosed the script of the speech with which he had closed the 1940 presidential campaign on the air. "The quotes in it are damned keen, vivid and human," he said. Then he counselled FDR: "You might read these quotes sometime in a dark hour when you are under compulsion to make a decision, not between right and wrong, but when your course must be for the lesser of two wrongs." Roosevelt responded later that "I have not had a chance since the election to tell you really and truly how much that broadcast of yours closing the 1940 campaign meant to me." Sandburg told FDR that he had a "flock of letters" which came after the broadcast and "most of them carry a deep love for you—a love joined with faith and trust. In these hours of ordeal you command loyalties that no one else could." "I am glad you are cunning—as Lincoln and Jackson were cunning," he wrote. Two little notes referred to "the Greatheart in the White House," D. W. Griffith's term for Lincoln in the 1915 silent film "Birth of a Nation." Ironically, Sandburg's letter was dated December 7, 1940–exactly one year to the day before the Japanese attack on Pearl Harbor which thrust the nation into war.[65]

As FDR fell asleep on the night of November 5, 1940, he had reached the apogee of his entire political career. The 1940 presidential election returns were not especially large in numbers. It was not considered a great election victory. Roosevelt had garnered 54.7 percent to 44.8 percent for Wendell Willkie. This was the smallest plurality of any election since 1916. Despite all the vituperative attacks of conservatives and isolationists, FDR had achieved something which Washington or Jefferson or Jackson or even Abraham Lincoln had never . . . done —a third term as president of the United States.

The 1940 presidential campaign began a turning point in the use of Lincoln by President Roosevelt. FDR and the New Deal Democrats had linked Lincoln and his policies with those of the New Deal. With the growth of fascism around the world and President Roosevelt's program to mobilize the nation for possible war, Lincoln's role as statesman for worldwide Democracy became more important than his political support for domestic New Deal programs.

In his third inaugural address, beginning an unprecedented third term, President Roosevelt spoke to the nation in "the face of great perils never before encountered." It was the strong purpose to protect and perpetuate the integrity of democracy. Each inauguration since 1789 served as a time for the American people "to renew their sense of dedication to the United States." "In Washington's day the task of the people was to create and weld together a Nation," he said. "In Lincoln's day the task of the people was to preserve that Nation from disruption from within." Equating the nation's current crisis with those of Washington and Lincoln, and his own task with the two examples, FDR declared: "In this day the task of the people is to save that Nation and its institutions from disruption from without." There had been three major crises under three American presidents, Washington, Lincoln, and Franklin D. Roosevelt. Most historians today agree with FDR's historical analysis.[66]

On behalf of the American people, President Roosevelt accepted the gift of the National Gallery and its collections on March 17, 1941. FDR was reminded that seventy-eight years before, in the third year of "the War Between the States," men and women gathered in the nation's capital to see the completed dome of the United States Capitol and to witness the bronze Goddess of Liberty set upon the top. The cost of completing the dome had been expensive and the task laborious in the midst of prosecuting a civil war. But there also were critics in 1863 and "certain critics found much to criticize," FDR noted. They criticized the new marble pillars in the Senate wing of the Capitol, the new bronze door for the central rotunda and other expenditures for more embellishments to the structure. Roosevelt observed: "But the President of the United States, whose name was Lincoln, when he heard those criticisms, answered: 'If people see the Capitol going on, it is a sign that we intend this Union shall go on.'" Borrowing Lincoln's words for his own, he believed that "we too intend the Union shall go on." "We intend it shall go on," he concluded, "carrying with it the great tradition of the human spirit which created it."[67]

The unity of the American nation was threatened. The chief weapon was propaganda disseminated within the nation's border by agents or innocent dupes of foreign powers and directed against all Americans whether they were Republican or Democratic, farmers or bankers, employers or employees, Roosevelt warned. These people were protected by American fundamental civil liberties while they preached "the ungodly gospel of fear," hoping to shatter the confidence of the American people in each other, as well as their government. The times called for courage and more courage—action and more action. Speaking from aboard the *U.S.S. Potomac*, FDR delivered what was to be his last Jackson Day dinner speech for the remainder of his presidency. The international crisis was deepening and Japan, in particular, was becoming more openly hostile to the United

States. The president needed unity among the American people to face the crisis, a kind of unity which finally did occur after Pearl Harbor. But the agents of Nazism, representing themselves as pacifists, exploited the natural love of the American people for peace, he told his fellow Democrats. They were really "the most brutal warmongers of all time." They preached "Peace, Peace!" in the same way that the devil quoted Scripture, he noted. "Of course, the purpose of all this has been to spread terror among us," he observed. "The effect of it has been only to fortify our determination." And then he called upon the great American leader Abraham Lincoln for support:

> When Abraham Lincoln became President, he had to face the awful reality of a war between the States. On July 4, 1861, in his first message to the Congress, he presented this vital question: "Must a government, of necessity, be too strong for the liberties of its own people, or too weak to maintain its own existence?" Lincoln answered that question as Jackson had answered it–not by words, but by deeds. And America still marches on.

The Americans of his day had been presented with that same question, and were also answering it with deeds. He concluded: "Our well-considered philosophy from the attainment of peace comes not from weakness but—everlastingly—from the courage of America."[68]

Roosevelt's competitor for the radio became Charles Lindbergh who believed the "real enemies" were those whose "prime objective is to get us into the war." By April 1941, Lindbergh's potent appeal brought an outcry from interventionists who turned to FDR for help. Perhaps the reserve colonel Lindbergh could be silenced by calling him into active duty, one reporter asked the president. Forewarned of the question, FDR skillfully played Abraham Lincoln to Lindbergh's Copperhead. Reminding the press, FDR said that a return to the roster of the Civil War Army would find that the nation called on "liberty-loving people on both sides . . . ; and from outside this country we had people fighting for us because they believed in it." On the other hand, he observed, the Confederacy and the North as well had let people go. "In other words, in both armies there were—what shall I call them?—there were Vallandighams." "Well, Vallandigham, as you know, was an appeaser," FDR declared. "He wanted to make peace from 1863 on because the North 'couldn't win.'" A reporter asked FDR if he was still talking about Lindbergh and he answered, "Yes."[69]

At a mass meeting, 24,000 people crowded into the Chicago Stadium on June 7, 1941 to hear a program of music and speeches for the cause of national unity. Carl Sandburg publicly condemned Charles Lindbergh,

Roosevelt's new "Copperhead." Lindbergh labeled interventionists who wanted to help Britain, like Sandburg, "hysterical." He was cool, he thought. Very well, then, Sandburg was hysterical, just as hysterical as the Declaration of Independence, the Constitution of the United States, the Bill of Rights, the Gettysburg speech, and the second inaugural address of Abraham Lincoln. So, too, were the men who fought and died to save those documents equally hysterical. As one who held theories of race discrimination and the color line, Lindbergh was opposite from Thomas Jefferson and Abraham Lincoln. Indeed, these same ideas linked Lindbergh the isolationist with the Know Nothing Party of Lincoln's own day which "gave Abraham Lincoln a troubled mind and a shaken soul"—something Lindbergh would call "hysteria." "Nowhere in speeches and writings of the one-time flyer do we find any hint of the passion for freedom and equality of opportunity that shook Lincoln . . . . ," he told the Chicago audience.[70]

In September, Sandburg picked up FDR's Civil War Copperhead analogy and went further with it than the president. Vallandigham said again and again that the war was wrong, the leadership false to the people, betraying the American people, and that, more than anyone else, the president had led the nation into war—and, if not stopped, the war would end in economic ruin and national suicide. Sandburg observed that Lincoln would have liked to let this congressman go on talking, because Vallandigham liked to hear himself talk. But such traitorous language from such a "wily agitator" might undermine troop morale. Lincoln asked in 1863, "Must I shoot a simple-minded soldier boy who deserts, while I must not touch a hair of a wily agitator who induces him to desert?" According to Sandburg, Lincoln added: "I think that, in such a case, to silence the agitator and save the boy is not only constitutional, but withal a great mercy."[71]

President Roosevelt sent a message to a special convocation held at Harvard on June 19, 1941 for his award of a degree of doctor of civil law. He talked of symbols which support truth and the search for truth. The American ambassador to Great Britain told Roosevelt that enemy bombs had destroyed the House of Commons room of the Parliament and had smashed the altar of Westminster Abbey. These hits seemed to symbolize the objectives of the dictator and the pagan. However, the American ambassador had noted that across the street from all this wreckage of state and church in London, still standing, was Saint Gaudens' statue of Abraham Lincoln. Roosevelt quoted the American Ambassador:

> As I looked at the bowed figure of the Great Emancipator and thought of his life, I could not help but remember that he loved God, that he had defined and represented democratic government, and that he hated

slavery. And as an American I was proud that he was there in all that wreckage as a friend and sentinel of gallant days that have gone by, and a reminder that in this great battle of freedom he waited quietly for support for those things for which he lived and died.

FDR concluded: "We, too, born to freedom, and believing in freedom, are willing to fight to maintain freedom. We, and all others who believe as deeply as we do, would rather die on our feet than live on our knees."[72]

During these difficult summer days of 1941, Lincoln's shadow (sometimes in the form of Sandburg's Lincoln biography) remained close by FDR. After FDR and Churchill formulated the Anglo-American postwar aims in the Atlantic Charter, the president held his first press conference on August 19, 1941. When you're winning, or when things look a little bit better, he told reporters, that's the time for you to redouble your efforts. "And—I wonder if I have got it—I have got an interesting thing—you might like to have it," he told them. Looking through papers in his work basket, he said: "It's a thing I dug out of Carl Sandburg's *Lincoln* [The War Years] the other day, something he said to some ladies who came in to see him at the end of the first year of the war, in 1862." Still looking, he said, "If you will bear with me for a minute, I will try to find this. Here it is." Then he read from volume one Lincoln's response to a delegation of sanitary commission women who begged words of encouragement from Lincoln during a dark period. "I have no word of encouragement to give!" Lincoln snapped. He continued on, after a painful silence, "The fact is the people have not made up their minds that we are at war with the South." Then Lincoln elaborated on the desperate unpreparedness of the people of the North. "That is rather an interesting parallel," FDR noted. "Lincoln's belief that this country hadn't yet waked up to the fact that they had a war to win, and Lincoln saw what had been going on." "Well, there are quite a lot of things for us to think about in this day and age," he said. Roosevelt believed that there were a lot of people who had not awakened to the danger around them. A reporter piped up, "If you were going to write a lead on that, how would you do it?" There was laughter. FDR said: "I'd say, 'President Quotes Lincoln"–(more laughter)–"And Draws Parallel."[73]

That same August, Sandburg wrote a piece called "The Job of Chief Magistrate," in which he concluded that Lincoln would have understood the pressures which Franklin Roosevelt was experiencing. In fact, he might even repeat some of Lincoln's quaint quips. And in November, Sandburg reminded his readers how Lincoln dealt with Vallandigham, now associated with Lindbergh because of FDR's allusion back in April. Sandburg concentrated on lessons from Lincoln as he persistently urged the issue of national unity.[74]

Representatives of more than thirty-three nations met in the White House on November 6, 1941 for the final session of the International Labor Organization, a kind of parliament for the justice of all people. President Roosevelt said that there were some words which had been written in that same house by a president "who gave his very life for the cause of justice." He said:

> Nearly eighty years ago, Abraham Lincoln said: "The strongest bond of human sympathy, outside of the family relation, should be one uniting all working people, of all Nations and tongues, and kindred."

The essence of the struggle for his own day was that all people should be free. He declared: "There can be no real freedom for the common man without enlightened social policies. In the last analysis, they are the stakes for which democracies are today fighting."[75]

Fatally unprepared for war, the United States Pacific Fleet at Pearl Harbor, Hawaii, was attacked by Japanese forces shortly after 7:30 A.M. Sunday, December 7, 1941. The United States was at war. At 8:30 that Sunday evening, the cabinet began to gather in the president's study on the White House second floor, the room that was the Lincoln family parlor during the civil war years. He expressed thankfulness that they all had arrived and then he pointed out that this was the gravest meeting of such a body since President Abraham Lincoln had called his advisers to him at the outbreak of the Civil War in April 1861.[76]

Like Lincoln, President Roosevelt now had to cope with the problems of internal security which war brings. During Lincoln's prosecution of the Civil War, he faced the problems of civil liberties which were not as clearly defined in 1861 as they were in 1941.

By the close of 1941 Roosevelt had become a war president, just like Lincoln, the leader of the nation in a deadly war for survival. On January 5, 1942, *Time* magazine placed him on its cover as the "Man of the Year." The United States had five war presidents in its history, "and for Lincoln, the greatest of them, the war was civil war," the editor noted. In the wars with foreign foes, Madison, Polk, McKinley, Wilson—predecessors of President Roosevelt—faced no such task as he faced. The editor observed:

> Never before had a U.S. President faced so great a task in unifying the country that had made him President, of summoning up the spirit that

would make the factories produce on a scale equal to the needs of the world's worst war.

FDR was the man of 1941 because the nation he led stood for the hope of the world.[77]

No longer was Lincoln a partisan figure, nor even a national figure alone. By December of 1941, Abraham Lincoln had become a symbol for freedom, for democracy, for national unity, and a symbol for charity, national and international. Lincoln and the survival of both the United States and democracy in the world had become one. The martyred president, now the statesman of democracy, was an important legacy not only as an example to the nation, but to help the United States and her allies save democracy for the world. The Lincoln image became an important vehicle to rally Americans behind a nonpartisan foreign policy to conduct an international war for the survival of both the United States and democracy.

In the middle of conducting war in April 1942, President Roosevelt studied the White House filing system, with special emphasis on his own personal files which were to be preserved upon leaving the White House and placed at Hyde Park. His personal files contained some letters from the King of England, others from King Haakon VII of Norway, Queen Wilhelmina of the Netherlands, and innumerable other letters from worldwide prominent people. Some of the letters would have to be sealed for at least twenty-five or thirty years, he said, when some of those correspondent names would be forgotten, "If they are lucky." Then he talked to William Hassett, his friend who would become press secretary in 1944, about Lincoln's papers, or what was left of them, which were sealed in the Library of Congress. FDR believed that no one would know what Lincoln's son, Robert, had destroyed of his father's papers. Hassett asked FDR why Robert Todd Lincoln maintained what seemed such indifference toward his father's memory. The president replied that he thought RTL took after his mother, "truly a dreadful inheritance which would account for any unlovely tendency." And then FDR fell to musing about wives of the presidents from Lincoln onward.[78]

In July 1942, FDR was concerned that the trial of Nazi spies in Washington before the military commission be a long drawn out affair. Talking with his close friend Hassett, FDR asked: "What should be done with them? Should they be shot or hanged?" "Hanged by all means," said Hassett—shooting was too honorable a death for them. Hanging would teach a lesson to Nazis—to Germans—and particularly to American traitors and near traitors . . . nothing else would do. Then FDR queried: "What about pictures?" Hassett responded "by all means." Anyone who had ever looked at the photographs of the hanging of the Lincoln conspirators would not be likely to forget them, pictures of Mary Surratt and the rest of them swinging in the air under a hot July sun. Hassett said: "Such a picture [was] worth more than a million words in driving home the lesson the country needs without further delay." For FDR, these pictures were all the more horrible because of the possible innocence of Mary Surratt. He said he always thought her guilt had been proved, however. Hassett had a different view after "rather scrappy reading on the subject" and from talking to people years before who remembered Lincoln's assassination. "We had a long talk, pro and con, on Mrs. Surratt and the others, particularly Dr. Mudd," he wrote in his diary.[79]

President Roosevelt was in high spirits in those early weeks of 1943 as he left on January 9 for the first of four major conferences which he would hold that year on three different continents with Britain's prime minister, Winston Churchill. He began the first leg of a seventeen thousand mile top-secret journey to Casablanca for a ten-day meeting with the prime minister. FDR was the first president to leave the nation in wartime, the first since Lincoln to visit his troops in an active theater of war. He revealed the decisions made at Casablanca to the nation by radio on Lincoln's birthday and reported a complete understanding and accord among the allies on their war efforts. The only terms of peace acceptable to any of the Allies would be unconditional surrender, and FDR said he looked forward to the day when United Nations forces would march "in triumph through the streets of Berlin, Rome and Tokyo." "Today is the anniversary of the birth of a great, plain American," he told the American people:

> The living memory of Abraham Lincoln is now honored and cherished by all of our people, wherever they may be, and by men and women and children throughout the British Commonwealth, and the Soviet Union, and the Republic of China, and in every land on earth where people love freedom and will give their lives for freedom.

Then he used a quote from Lincoln's message to the nation in 1862, the first year of another American war:

> Fellow Citizens, we cannot escape history. We of this Congress and this administration will be remembered in spite of ourselves. No personal significance or insignificance can spare one or another of us. The fiery trial through which we pass will light us . . . . in honor or dishonor, to the latest generation.

Eighty years after Lincoln delivered that message, "the fires of war are blazing across the whole horizon of mankind"—from Karkov to Kunming—from the Mediterranean to the Coral Sea—from Berlin to Tokyo. Then he closed:

> Again—we cannot escape history. We have supreme confidence that with the help of God honor will prevail. We have faith that future generations will know that here, in the middle of the Twentieth Century, there came the time when men of good will found a way to unite and produce and fight to destroy the forces of ignorance, intolerance, slavery and war.[80]

The spirit of Lincoln seemed to hover in Sandburg's *Home Front Memo* which was published in 1943. Saturated by Lincoln lore and even Lincoln's thought pattern, the Lincoln biographer opened the work with five Lincoln pieces. He drew "a strong parallel between the Civil War President in his years of travail, and Roosevelt today, but Lincoln constantly recurs in the book as a kind of theme with variations." Sandburg continued to merge Lincoln and Roosevelt in both his thinking and writing in the middle of war.[81]

From the president on down, war was on the lips and on the minds of Americans everywhere in 1944. American soldiers were still to experience some of the worst fighting ahead. It was also another campaign year for the political parties and their selected presidential candidates.

On Lincoln's birthday, February 12, 1944, President Roosevelt transferred to France the destroyer escort *Senegalais*, built by American hands in an American navy yard. Symbolizing the ancient friendship between France and the United States, it was transferred under the lend-lease law, typical of the thousands of transfers of American-made weapons of war which the United States had given to the Allies. This was another effort "to drive from the soil of France the Nazi invaders who today swagger down the Champs Elysees in Paris," as FDR put it. President Roosevelt said: "No day could be more appropriate for this ceremony than the anniversary we now celebrate of the birth of that illustrious American who, in his time, struck such might blows for the liberty and dignity of the human race—Abraham Lincoln." Lincoln the international Democrat apparently approved FDR's lend-lease support of the Allied cause. The president's remarks were broadcast through facilities which had been installed in his official car.[82]

By March of 1944, Roosevelt was still noncommittal regarding a possible fourth presidential term. His poor health would undoubtedly have some bearing on his fourth-term plans. In March, he was diagnosed with acute bronchitis, cardiac failure of the left ventricle, high blood pressure, and heart disease. Here was a seriously ill president whose declining health was not revealed to the nation. The political machine that FDR built was finally going to run him for president in 1944. The Democratic National convention met in Chicago on July 19. The next day, FDR addressed the convention to accept the presidential nomination for a fourth term, after Harry Truman joined him on the ticket as the vice presidential candidate. The president gave his address over the radio from San Diego where he was about to leave for Pearl Harbor for a visit with General Douglas MacArthur. He closed his acceptance address with Abraham Lincoln. He said:

> The greatest wartime President in our history, after a wartime election which he called the "most reliable indication of public purpose in this country," set the goal for the United States, a goal in terms as applicable today as they were in 1865—terms which the human mind cannot improve.

And then he finished his remarks with the peroration of Lincoln's second inaugural:

> With firmness in the right, as God gives us to see the right, let us strive on to finish the work we are in; to bind up the Nation's wounds; to care for him who shall have borne the battle and for his widow, and his orphan—to do all which may achieve and cherish a just and lasting peace among ourselves, and with all Nations.[83]

The 1944 presidential campaign was different from the three preceding campaigns. This one was in wartime and President Roosevelt was campaigning as commander-in-chief. It was a unique campaign in that the nation was not told of the president's ill health, and the president genuinely despised the Republican presidential candidate, Thomas E. Dewey, as he had no other previous opponent. In Wilmington, Delaware where he traditionally spoke in the closing days of each presidential campaign before, he referred to Lincoln again. "Somebody tells me that we are holding a national election," he said, "but remember that we are holding a national election while the Nation is at war–and this is the first time that an election has been held under these conditions since 1864—eighty years ago." And that reminded FDR of a remark Lincoln had made when he was campaigning for the senate in 1858, a remark he thought was "particularly timely and applicable in this campaign." Lincoln had said, about something that Stephen A. Douglas had said, "In every way possible he tried to prove that a horse chestnut is a chestnut horse." Roosevelt added:

> It seems to me that that applies very neatly to some of the Republican political oratory that has lately been agitating the air waves . . . I think you all know the difference between a chestnut horse and a horse chestnut. You know a great deal about the size and the quality of the effort that has gone into the performance of our great job of production.[84]

A near record of 48 million voters went to the polls on November 7, 1944, but it was FDR's most slender victory with 53.4 percent of the popular vote. However, Roosevelt still had a mandate to continue his efforts on behalf of a new world order.[85]

Lincoln and Roosevelt: The Symbolism of Death

Franklin D. Roosevelt breathed his last breath at 3:31 P.M. on April 12, 1945. On April 14, 1945, Roosevelt's body lay in the East Room of the White House, the eightieth anniversary of the assassination of President Lincoln. Lincoln had died on April 15, 1865. Exactly on the anniversary of Lincoln's death, FDR was buried at his childhood home in Hyde Park, New York. Press Secretary Hassett spotted a lilac bush in bloom and was reminded of Whitman's tribute to the martyred Lincoln, eighty years before: "When Lilacs Last in the Dooryard Bloom'd." "Like Lincoln, his work is done," Hassett wrote in his diary. "God grant that those who follow will not make the mess of things that followed Lincoln's death."[86]

Eleanor Roosevelt and others were also reminded of Lincoln's death and funeral train, and of Whitman's poems, in those days following FDR's death. As the Roosevelt train travelled north from Warm Springs, Georgia, in the Ferdinand Magellan, Eleanor was thinking other thoughts:

> I lay in my berth all night with the window shade up, looking out at the countryside he had loved and watching the faces of the people at stations, and even at the crossroads, who came to pay their last tribute all through the night. The only recollection I clearly have is thinking about 'The Lonesome Train,' the musical poem about Lincoln's death. (*A lonesome train on a lonesome track/Seven coaches painted black/A slow train, a quiet train/Carrying Lincoln home again...*) I had always liked it so well—and now this was so much like it.

In her column, *My Day*, Eleanor Roosevelt noted that any man in public life is bound to create certain enemies over the course of years. But so often when he is gone, his main objectives stand out more clearly and there is the hope that "a spirit of unity may arouse the people and their leaders to a complete understanding of his objectives and a determination to achieve those objectives themselves." "Abraham Lincoln was taken from us before he had achieved unity within the nation, and his people failed him," she observed. "This divided us as a nation for many years." And then referring to her own dead husband, she wrote:

> Perhaps, in His wisdom, the Almighty is trying to show us that a leader may chart the way, may point out the road to lasting peace, but that many leaders and many peoples must do the building. It cannot be the work of one man, nor can the responsibility be laid upon his shoulders, and so, when the time comes for peoples to assume the burden more fully, he is given rest.[87]

The similarity between Lincoln and Roosevelt was very quickly underlined by Harvard professor H. Buck in his American history class the next day when he quoted Walt Whitman's tribute to Abraham Lincoln:

> Hush'd be the camps today;
> And soldiers let us drape our war-worn weapons,
> And each with musing soul retire to celebrate
> Our dear commander's death.

Then Professor Buck went on:

> As one studies history, the stature of a man is judged by what he does to build or destroy the faith by which men live . . . . Mr. Roosevelt was great because he, like Lincoln, restored men's faith. . . .[88]

Carl Sandburg recorded the nation's loss in a poem, "When Death Came April Twelve 1945," in which he remembered another wartime April and the death of another wartime president:

> And there will be roses and spring blooms flung on the moving oblong box, emblems endless flung from nearby, from faraway earth corners, from frontline tanks nearing Berlin unseen flowers of regard to The Commander, from battle stations over the South Pacific silent tokens saluting The Commander . . . Can a bell ring in the heart in time with

the tall headlines, in the high fidelity transmitters, the somber consoles rolling sorrow, the choirs in ancient laments–chanting: "Dreamer, sleep deep, Toiler, sleep long, Fighter, be rested now, Commander, sweet good night."[89]

On April 14, in London, Harold J. Laski wrote an article "Not Since Lincoln" for the April 21, 1945 issue of *The Nation* in which he said that the sudden death of President Roosevelt had stunned and grieved the American people more than that of any great public figure in his memory. In Great Britain, "From King and Queen and the Prime Minister on to the ordinary man and woman the President's death seems a personal loss as in the case of no other foreign statesman since men and women in the cotton towns of Lancashire wept openly at the death of Mr. Lincoln," he wrote. Not since the death of Lincoln in 1865 had the British felt more close to America, more eager for mutual understanding. Laski concluded: "We pledge ourselves before him—our dead, too—that the work he wrought so nobly shall not have been in vain."[90]

Following the funeral, three major national periodicals, *Time*, *Newsweek*, and *Life* (all issued on April 23, 1945) used the Lincoln connection in their editorials commemorating the death of another wartime president. The *Time's* editorial entitled "World's Man," called FDR a "people's man":

> Not Lincoln as a legend, nor Wilson, beyond his brief hour of triumph, had been known so well to the plain people of the earth. They felt they had lost a friend, the American who to them was all that they wanted America to be, and they feared the times to come without him.

Newsweek also used the same theme, "the world citizen," for their editorial headline. The editor called FDR "an aristocrat by birth," "a great democratic leader of a great democracy," "a man of wealth, "a cripple throughout most of his career," "a man of action as well as words," "a supreme politician," "a leading statesman of his time," "an advocate of peace," and "the leader of the greatest army of free citizens ever to wage a war." Then the editor declared:

> No man of his time was more beloved. No man since Abraham Lincoln endured more calumnies. . . . No President ever made more use of the powers of his office than Roosevelt did in peacetime. In wartime he was—by deed as well as by title—Commander-in-Chief.[91]

The *Life* magazine editorial was simply entitled: "Roosevelt."

The most striking thing about President Roosevelt's death was that millions and millions of people had felt a personal sense of loss and shed tears for it. "I'd been depending on him in such a personal way," they said; or, "I feel as though I'd lost my father." This reminded the editor of how Walt Whitman expressed the nation's grief at the time of Lincoln's death; he called him "my father." "Like great shafts driven into the national consciousness, these two deaths struck a stratum of grief which had lain untouched by an event in the 80 years between," the editor noted. But there was still a difference between the two deaths, "unlike Lincoln's, our 'fearful trip' is *not* done." "The captain died barely within sight of shore."[92]

The Lincoln-Roosevelt Legacy

During the era of the New Deal and World War II, Abraham Lincoln's image was revitalized with the new scholarship of Carl Sandburg and other Lincoln scholars. But the revitalization process also included the political use of Lincoln, both as a pragmatic politician and as a statesman of democracy. Franklin Delano Roosevelt who admired Lincoln when he was a young man, later claimed his words and deeds to bolster New Deal policies, as well as enlisting the earlier war president's support on behalf of preserving democracy both in the United States and in the world at war. Lincoln's memory after his death never failed the nation, but the lessons of his life and presidential career brought personal encouragement and political support for FDR, as he consciously wrapped himself in the mantle of Lincoln during the last days of the New Deal and those years of war which followed. Lincoln's intellect and skills were genuinely appreciated and consciously used by FDR. But this use of Lincoln changed from political purpose mainly to the challenge of saving the nation and democracy from its enemies, both within and without.

Franklin D. Roosevelt also loomed large in death. The timing of his death and funeral with that of Lincoln's death and funeral eighty years earlier helped place his memory with that of two great American presidents before, Washington and Lincoln. His secretary Grace Tully saw this and commented:

> It cannot be without significance that the men who stand foremost and in undisputed places in our history—Washington and Lincoln to take the most obvious examples—were men who saw far beyond the vision of the petty intolerant. This will be one of the many reasons, in my opinion, for Franklin Roosevelt taking a comparable place in history.

After 1945, historians ranked FDR consistently with both George Washington and Abraham Lincoln.[93]

In a recent biography of Franklin Delano Roosevelt, *The Roosevelt Presence*, Patrick J. Maney critically evaluated Lincoln and Roosevelt. He wrote:

> Yet Roosevelt's greatness was specific to a particular time and place in history. One imagines that Lincoln, with his commanding intellect, moral vision, and superior political skills, would have distinguished himself at almost any time. Roosevelt did not have Lincoln's great gifts. He was highly intelligent, to be sure; but he lacked the intellectual range and speculative cast of mind not only of Lincoln but of a half-dozen or so other presidents, including his mentors, Theodore Roosevelt and Woodrow Wilson, and his unhappy immediate predecessor, Herbert Hoover. . . . He lacked the moral fiber of Lincoln, Washington, or his immediate successor, Harry S. Truman.[94]

Other historians differ in evaluating the Lincoln-Roosevelt legacy. Frank Freidel, writing of the legacy of FDR, noted that a more significant monument to Roosevelt than any massive memorial is the vast number of books and articles devoted to him; more has been written about Roosevelt than even Lincoln, he claimed. Historians have ranked FDR as one of the most outstanding of U.S. presidents in several different polls. In two recent polls Roosevelt is ranked third among all presidents, following only Lincoln and Washington. Even FDR's denigrators grant him significance and political leaders of both major parties continue to court voters by invoking his name.[95]

Franklin D. Roosevelt was very confident about his place in history, just as he was confident about everything else he did. He would have been pleased with his posthumous reputation. Because he, himself, consciously made an effort to place himself and his labor on the nation's behalf on equal status of his previous presidential colleagues, George Washington, and most especially Abraham Lincoln.

ENDNOTES

1. Peter Collier and David Horowitz, *The Roosevelts: An American Saga* (New York: Simon and Schuster, 1994), 127.
2. Ibid.

3. Merrill D. Peterson, *Lincoln in American Memory* (New York: Oxford University Press, 1994), 320.

4. Alfred Haworth Jones, *Roosevelt's Image Brokers* (Port Washington, NY: Kennikat Press), 112-113.

5. Ibid.

6. Ibid.

7. Collier and Horowitz, *The Roosevelts: An American Saga*, 33.

8. Ibid., 33-34; 27-28.

9. Ibid., 49.

10. William E. Leuchtenburg, *In the Shadow of FDR* (Ithaca and London: Cornell University Press), 279.

11. William D. Hassett, *Off the Record with F.D. R.* (New Brunswick, NJ: Rutgers University Press, 1958), 159.

12. Ted Morgan, *FDR: A Biography* (New York: Simon and Schuster, 1985), 365.

13. Ibid.; Donald Day, *Franklin D. Roosevelt's Own Story* (Boston: Little, Brown, 1951) (September 14, 1920), 58-59.

14. Day, *Franklin D. Roosevelt's Own Story* (October 5, 1920), 62-63; 100; (April 3, 1929), 120.

15. Richard Norton Smith, *An Uncommon Man: The Triumph of Herbert Hoover* (New York: Simon and Schuster, 1984), 29.

16. *The State Papers and Other Public Writings of Herbert Hoover*, ed. William Starr Myers (Garden City, NY, 1970), 2:500-505; 587-590; *New York Times*, February 13, 1921, January 14, 1933; Will Rogers, *Weekly Articles* (Stillwater, OK, 1980), 5:235.

17. "A Concert of Action, Based on a Fair and Just Concert of Interests." Address at Jefferson Day Dinner, St. Paul, MN. April 18, 1932, *The Public Papers and Addresses of Franklin D. Roosevelt*, ed. Samuel I. Rosenman, 13 vols. (New York: Random House, 1938), 1:629-630; 639.

18. Philip Abbott, *The Exemplary Presidency: Franklin D. Roosevelt and the American Presidency* (Amherst: University of Massachusetts Press, 1990), 66-67; "The Forgotten Man Speech, Radio Address, Albany, NY, April 7, 1932," *Public Papers and Addresses of Franklin D. Roosevelt*, 1:625; Herbert D. Rosenbaum and Elizabeth Bartelme, *Franklin D. Roosevelt: The Man, The Myth, The Era, 1882-1945* (New York: Greenwood Press, 1987), 5; Grace Tully, *F.D.R.: My Boss* (New York: Charles Scribner's Sons, 1949), 59.

19. Abbott, *The Exemplary Presidency*, 66; "To Albert G. Hodges, April 4, 1864," *The Collected Works of Abraham Lincoln*, ed. Roy P. Basler, 9 vols. (New Brunswick, NJ, 1953), 7:282; Rosenbaum and Bartelme, *Franklin D. Roosevelt*, 6.

20. Second Fireside Chat of 1934, "We Are Moving Toward a Greater Freedom, to Greater Security for the Average Man," September 30, 1934, *Public Papers and*

Addresses of Franklin D. Roosevelt, 3:422; Abbott, *The Exemplary Presidency*, 50, 75.

21. Herbert Mitgang, *The Letters of Carl Sandburg* (New York: Harcourt, Brace & World, Inc., 1968), 297-298; "To Bruce Bliven, September 12, 1935," Ibid., 333-334.

22. "To Franklin D. Roosevelt, March 29, 1935," Ibid., 317-319.

23. "The President Hails the Four Hundredth Anniversary of the Printing of the First English Bible, October 6, 1935," *Public Papers and Addresses of Franklin D. Roosevelt*, 4:418-419; Abbott, *The Exemplary Presidency*, 13; Tully, *FDR: My Boss*, 66-67.

24. "A Tribute to Abraham Lincoln to Be Read on His Birthday, January 25, 1936," *Public Papers and Addresses of Franklin D. Roosevelt*, 5:222.

25. "Campaign Address at Wilmington, Delaware on "Liberty,' October 29, 1936," *Public Papers and Addresses of Franklin D. Roosevelt*, 5:557-558; *The Collected Works of Abraham Lincoln*, 7:301-302; 8:578.

26. "A Fireside Chat Discussing the Plan for Reorganization of the Judiciary, Washington, D.C., March 9, 1937," *Public Papers and Addresses of Franklin D. Roosevelt*, 6:129.

27. Introduction, *Public Papers and Addresses of Franklin D. Roosevelt*, 7:29-30; Morgan, *FDR: A Biography*, 495.

28. "We In Turn Are Striving to Uphold the Integrity of the Morals of Our Democracy." Address at the Jackson Day Dinner, Washington, D.C., January 8, 1938, *Public Papers and Addresses of Franklin D. Roosevelt*, 7:38-39.

29. Ibid., 7:39-42; 45; Jones, *Roosevelt's Image Brokers*, 66.

30. "To Franklin D. Roosevelt, March 9, 1938," Mitgang, *The Letters of Carl Sandburg*, 360; "To Franklin D. Roosevelt, August 24, 1938," Ibid., 368; Emil Ludwig, *Roosevelt: A Study in Fortune and Power* (New York: Viking Press, 1938), 341; Mitgang, 360.

31. "I Have Every Right to Speak . . . Where There May Be a Clear Issue Between Candidates for a Democratic Nomination Involving . . . Principles, or . . . a Clear Misuse of My Own Name." Fireside Chat. June 24, 1938, *Public Papers and Addresses of Franklin D. Roosevelt*, 7:395.

32. "Avoiding War, We Seek Our Ends Through the Peaceful Processes of Popular Government Under the Constitution." Address at the Dedication of the Memorial at the Gettysburg Battlefield, Gettysburg, Pennsylvania, July 3, 1938, Ibid., 7:419-421; Peterson, *Lincoln in American Memory*, 67.

33. "The Democratic Party Will . . . Continue to Receive the Support of the Majority of Americans Just So Long as It Remains a Liberal Party." Address at Denton, Maryland, September 5, 1938, *Public Papers and Address of Franklin D. Roosevelt*, 7:520.

34. "To Frank Murphy, September 10, 1938," Mitgang, *The Letters of Carl Sandburg*, 369-370; "To Franklin D. Roosevelt, September 21, 1938," Ibid., 370-371.

35. "A Thanksgiving Proclamation," November 19, 1938, Ibid., 7:608.

36. "The Five Hundred and Eighth Press Conference, December 10, 1938," Ibid., 7:636-639-641.

37. Ibid., 7:641-642.

38. Ibid., 7:635, 637.

39. "Annual Message to Congress, January 4, 1939," Ibid., 8:12.

40. "On Jackson Day Every True Follower of Jackson Asks That the Democratic Party Continue to Make Democracy Work." Address at Jackson Day Dinner, Washington, D.C., January 7, 1939, Ibid.

41. *New York Times*, February 14, 1939.

42. Ibid.

43. Max Lerner, "The Lincoln Image," *The New Republic* 98 (March 8, 1939): 135; "Men Who Would Be President: IX. Franklin D. Roosevelt." *The Nation*, 101 (June 22, 1940): 753-754.

44. *Newsweek*, June 19, 1939.

45. Morgan, *FDR: A Biography*, 511; Tully, *FDR: My Boss*, 234-235.

46. "He Believed, As We Do, That the Average Opinion of Mankind is in the Long Run Superior to the Dictates of the Self-Chosen." Address at the Cornerstone Laying of the Jefferson Memorial, Washington, D.C., November 15, 1939, *Public Papers and Addresses of Franklin D. Roosevelt*, 8:577-578.

47. Penelope Niven, *Carl Sandburg: A Biography* (New York: Charles Scribner's Sons, 1991), 528-534.

48. Morgan, *FDR: A Biography*, 502, 516, 520, 527.

49. "The Future Lies With Those Wise Political Leaders Who Realize That the Great Public is Interested More in Government Than in Politics." Address at Jackson Day Dinner, January 8, 1940, *Public Papers and Addresses of Franklin D. Roosevelt*, 9:26-27.

50. Ibid., 9:29-30.

51. Morgan, *FDR: A Biography*, 520; "Radio Address to Anniversary Farm Dinner Held Throughout the Country," March 8, 1940, Ibid., 9:99.

52. Eleanor Roosevelt to Joseph P. Lash, June 10, 1940, quoted by Lash in *Love, Eleanor: Eleanor Roosevelt and Her Friends* (Garden City, NY: Doubleday and Co., Inc., 1982), 303; Tully, *FDR: My Boss*, 346.

53. *Complete Presidential Conferences of Franklin D. Roosevelt* (New York: Da Capo Press, 1972), 15:508-509.

54. Max Lerner, "Men Who Would Be President, IX. Franklin D. Roosevelt," *The Nation* 101 (June 22, 1940), 752-754.

55. Morgan, *FDR: A Biography*, 529.

56. Kenneth S. Davis, *FDR: Into the Storm, 1937-1940. A History* (New York: Random House, 1993), 600-603.

57. "The President Accepts the Nomination for a Third Term," Radio Address to the Democratic National Convention in Chicago, Illinois, from the White House, Washington, D.C., July 19, 1940, at 12:25 a.m., *Public Papers and Addresses of Franklin D. Roosevelt*, 9:301.

58. Jones, *Roosevelt's Image Brokers*, 71-73.

59. "A Greeting on the Anniversary Celebration of the Thirteenth Amendment," October 16, 1940, *Public Papers and Addresses of Franklin D. Roosevelt*, 9:471-472.

60. "Rear-platform Remarks on 'Liberty,' at Wilmington, Delaware," October 23, 1940, Ibid., 9:483-484; 485-495.

61. "We Have Confidence in the Ability of the Democratic System Which Gives Men Dignity to Give Them Strength," Radio Address to the New York *Herald-Tribune* Forum. October 24, 1940, Ibid., 9:495-498.

62. *New York Times*, October 19, 1940.

63. Ibid.

64. Carl Sandburg, *Home Front Memo* (New York: Harcourt, Brace, 1943), 29-30.

65. "Carl Sandburg to Franklin D. Roosevelt, November 9, 1949," Mitgang, *The Letters of Carl Sandburg*, 390; "Carl Sandburg to Franklin D. Roosevelt, December 7, 1940," Ibid., 392.

66. "The Third Inaugural Address—In the Face of Great Perils Never Before Encountered, Our Strong Purpose is to Protect and to Perpetuate the Integrity of Democracy," January 20, 1941, Ibid., 10:3.

67. "The Freedom of the Human Spirit Shall Go On," Address at Dedication of National Gallery of Art, March 17, 1941, Ibid., 10:74-75.

68. "The Time Calls for Courage and More Courage," Radio Address from the *U.S.S. Potomac* to Jackson Day Dinner, March 29, 1941, Ibid., 10:86-87.

69. Jones, *Roosevelt's Image Brokers*, 92-93; *Complete Presidential Press Conferences of Franklin D. Roosevelt*, 17:293-294.

70. Sandburg, *Home Front Memo*, 34-37; 73.

71. Ibid., 94-96.

72. "The President Sends a Message to the Special Convocation of the University of Oxford, Held at the Harvard Commencement on the Award of a Degree of Doctor of Civil Law, June 19, 1941, *Public Papers and Addresses of Franklin D. Roosevelt*, 10:226-227.

73. "The Seven Hundred and Sixty-Second Press Conference (Excerpts), August 19, 1941," Ibid., 10:328-329.

74. Sandburg, *Home Front Memo*, 83-86; 114-117.

75. "The American People Have Made an Unlimited Commitment that There Shall be A Free World," Address to the Delegates of the International Labor Organization, November 6, 1941, *Public Papers and Addresses of Franklin D. Roosevelt*, 10:474-477.

76. Tully, *FDR: My Boss*, 257.

77. *Time*, January 5, 1942.

78. William D. Hassett, *Off the Record With F.D.R., 1942-1945* (New Brunswick, NJ: Rutgers University Press, 1958), 40.

79. Ibid., 90.

80. "The Peoples of All the United Nations . . . See the Utter Necessity of Our Standing Together After the War to Secure a Peace Based on Principles of Permanent." Address to the White House Correspondents' Association, February 12, 1943, *Public Papers and Addresses of Franklin D. Roosevelt*, 13:71.

81. Jones, *Roosevelt's Image Brokers*, 117; August Derleth, *The Chicago Sun Book Week* 1 (September 26, 1943), 4.

82. "Remarks on the Transfer of the Destroyer Escort Senegalais to the French," February 12, 1944, *Public Papers and Addresses of Franklin D. Roosevelt*, 13:71.

83. "Address Broadcast from a Naval Base on the Pacific Coast to the Democratic National Convention in Chicago, July 20, 1944," Ibid., 13:206.

84. "I Think You All Know the Difference Between a Chestnut Horse and a Horse Chestnut"—Campaign Remarks at Wilmington, Delaware, October 27, 1944, Ibid., 13:354-355.

85. Morgan, *FDR: A Biography*, 740.

86. Hassett, *Off the Record With FDR*, 1942-1945, 345.

87. Bernard Asbell, *When FDR Died* (New York, Holt: Rinehart & Winston, 1961), 160-161; Eleanor Roosevelt, *My Day, 1936-1945*, (New York, 1988), 390.

88. Morgan, *FDR: A Biography*, 740.

89. Niven, *Carl Sandburg: A Biography*, 558.

90. Harold J. Laski, "Not Since Lincoln," *The Nation*, April 21, 1945.

91. *Time*, April 23, 1945; *Newsweek*, April 23, 1945.

92. *Life*, April 23, 1945.

93. Tully, *FDR: My Boss*, 35.

94. Patrick J. Maney, *The Roosevelt Presence: A Biography of Franklin Delano Roosevelt* (New York: Twayne Publishers, 1992), Introduction, xiv.

95. Rosenbaum and Bartelme, *Franklin D. Roosevelt, The Man, The Myth, The Era, 1882-1945*, 7-8.

2
Two Wartime Elections: The Presidential Elections of 1864 and 1944

David E. Long

In 1864 Abraham Lincoln was reelected to his second term as president of the United States. In 1944 Franklin Delano Roosevelt was reelected to his fourth presidential term. Probably no two elections in American history separated by four score years were characterized by so many common features. This in spite of the fact that both events were in themselves unique among national elections occurring in their respective eras. These were the only two elections that occurred while the nation was in a state of total wartime mobilization. At no other time in American history, but for the Civil War and Second World War eras, have a majority of American men of military age been in the service. In 1864 and 1944, the United States was preparing to initiate offensive military operations which would bring those respective conflicts to final and victorious conclusions. At no other time in American history, though true to a lesser extent in 1917-18, had the nation's economy been so totally focused on the production of the goods necessary to wage war.[1]

Abraham Lincoln in 1864 and Franklin Roosevelt in 1944 both faced challenges in their respective wartime reelection campaigns from challengers who were considerably younger and more attractive than the incumbents. George McClellan in 1864 and Thomas Dewey in 1944, were extremely well-qualified and popular nominees, and at times in the campaigns they appeared to be favorites, or at least even-money bets, to win. Both incumbent candidates campaigned strongly on platforms calling for national unity necessitated by wartime emergency, and both of them received a strong crossover ballot from voters who in peacetime would have supported the opposition party. Lincoln and Roosevelt were buoyed in their respective presidencies by popular support attributable to the national crises.

Both were able to remain above the partisanship of a political campaign while reaping the benefits of the widely held belief that it is not wise to metaphorically change horses while in midstream.[2]

Then, after benefiting from that principle of leadership continuity which swayed untold numbers of votes, both presidents died unexpectedly shortly after beginning new terms and while the military enemies of their administrations still had armies in the field. Lincoln and Roosevelt both suffered sudden, fatal injuries to their brains that resulted in the immediate loss of consciousness and death soon afterward. Neither regained the use of their senses before dying. Both were struck down, Lincoln by a bullet and Roosevelt by a stroke, during the second week of April. Both were the subjects of widespread mourning and thousands of eulogies and sermons delivered during the Easter weekends of 1865 and 1945.[3] These parallels in the deaths of Lincoln, the sixteenth president, and Roosevelt, the thirty-second, are merely coincidences that spawn folklore and popular myth. The similarities threaded through their 1864 and 1944 elections, however, merit attention from scholars for the lessons that they may contain about the political realities, and more importantly the inherent integrity of the democratic election process even in time of national crises precipitated by wars.

At the Republican, or Union, Party convention in 1864 the major and most controversial issue concerned the nomination for vice president. The convention dropped the incumbent, Hannibal Hamlin, for Andrew Johnson, a nomination that moved the ticket closer to the middle of the political road. At the Democratic Party convention in 1944 the major and most controversial issue also concerned the nomination for vice president. The convention dropped the incumbent, Henry Wallace, for Harry Truman, a nomination that moved the ticket closer to the middle of the political road. Both Lincoln and Roosevelt sought reelection in these two wartime campaigns, with running mates they barely knew, and with whom they had had little occasion to work in the past.[4]

In the 1864 and 1944 campaigns, in a manner unmatched in any other presidential elections in American history, the question of the absentee ballot for soldiers away from home became a dominant issue, one which the incumbent administrations and their supporters pushed strongly during the period leading up to the election. As a result of absentee ballot legislation enacted by various states in 1863 and 1864, hundreds of thousands of Union soldiers and sailors stationed away from home had the chance to vote in the presidential election of 1864. As a result of absentee ballot legislation enacted by the various states in 1943 and 1944, millions of American soldiers and sailors stationed overseas had the chance to vote in the presidential election of 1944.

In the summer of 1864, the president's prospects for reelection depended, more than anything else, on the success of Union armies in the field. In the summer of 1944, the president's prospects for reelection depended, more than anything else, on the success of Allied armies in the field.[5]

Abraham Lincoln and Franklin Delano Roosevelt have come to be regarded as the strongest symbols and most towering figures of their respective parties in American history. Though this is due in large part to their reelections in 1864 and 1944, there were many similarities in their presidencies before those elections. Abraham Lincoln was first nominated for the presidency in 1860 at a convention held in Chicago. He was nominated by a party that was virtually assured of victory in the November election due to the failure of the incumbent party to resolve the great debate over the expansion of slavery into the territories. Franklin Roosevelt was first nominated for the presidency in 1932 at a convention held in Chicago. He was nominated by a party that was virtually assured of victory in the November election due to the failure of the incumbent party to resolve the Great Depression and its resultant problems of unemployment, starvation, and despair. Both Lincoln and Roosevelt won nomination at those conventions after three ballots when some delegates changed their votes and put the candidates over the top.[6] Between Lincoln's election in November and his inauguration the following March, seven states had seceded from the Union, seizing nearly all of the federal facilities and property located within those states. On his first day in office he faced a crisis so unprecedented in American history that he had to rely almost entirely on instinct and first-impression judgment. Between Roosevelt's election in November and his inauguration the following March, thousands of banks closed in a panic that resulted in the shutdown of more than 80 percent of the nation's banks by inauguration day, inflicting virtual paralysis and portending imminent collapse of the country's economy. On his first day in office in 1933, Roosevelt faced a crisis of such magnitude that, with the sole exception of the secession crisis that Lincoln faced in 1861, no previous national emergency compared as a threat to the national security in 1933. Roosevelt had to rely almost entirely on instinct and first-impression judgment. Lincoln replaced a president who decried secession as unconstitutional and unlawful, but refused to undertake military action to prevent it. Roosevelt replaced a president who agonized over the depressed economy and the resultant misery experienced by millions of Americans, but refused to undertake radical or experimental measures to alleviate it.[7]

In their first months in the White House both Abraham Lincoln and Franklin Roosevelt were called upon to take, and each willingly undertook, unprecedented and seemingly extreme measures because of the national emergencies that confronted them immediately upon assuming the presidency. In 1864, Abraham Lincoln faced a stiff challenge to the continuation of his presidency, a challenge mounted from the left wing in his own political party. In 1934 and 1935, Franklin Roosevelt faced a stiff challenge to the continuation of his presidency, a challenge mounted from the left wing in his own political party.[8]

During the Civil War, Congress enacted the Revenue Act of 1862, the first federal income tax in American history. It was levied to pay the tremendous and rapidly burgeoning costs of the war. It was an unpopular measure challenged by many as unconstitutional. It would hurt Lincoln's reelection prospects in 1864. During World War II, Congress enacted the Revenue Act of 1942, which greatly expanded the number of Americans required to pay income taxes. It also resulted in the treasury department, for the first time in American history, imposing payroll deductions to withhold money from the paychecks of American workers to be applied toward their income taxes owed at the end of the calendar year. Previously, taxpayers had simply paid their taxes in January based on their gross earnings of the previous year. It was a very unpopular measure that hurt Roosevelt's reelection prospects in 1944.[9]

Ultimately, however, after considering all of the circumstances and relationships which constitute parallels between these two distant and distinct elections, the most salient similarity was that in both important changes were made in the choices of running mates. Those changes resulted in new and unseasoned vice presidents being suddenly catapulted into the presidency during times when critical circumstances required them to make difficult choices. As a result of the assassination of Abraham Lincoln, Andrew Johnson became president and commander-in-chief at a time when a critical tug-of-war over control of the reconstruction process was about to be played out. Because of the way he performed his duties and his conduct as the president of the United States, Andrew Johnson was impeached by the House of Representatives, the first president to be impeached in the nation's history. The Senate came within one vote of the two-thirds majority necessary to remove him from office.[10]

Because of the death of Franklin Roosevelt, Harry Truman became president and commander-in-chief at just the moment when a number of very difficult choices had to be made. Because he chose to drop the atomic bombs on Hiroshima and Nagasaki, Harry Truman has been second-guessed and criticized ever since, an exercise in hindsight that reached a new intensity during the fiftieth anniversary celebrations of the end of the Second World War. Also, a number of critical decisions were required during his presidency regarding the character and shape of postwar Europe, the reconstruction of nations devastated by the war and the Holocaust, and the posture of the United States with regard to a paranoid and aggressive communist regime in the Soviet Union, and, before the decade was out, another even more dogmatic communist dictatorship in China.[11]

Because of the deaths of both Lincoln and Roosevelt very early in their terms after these elections, the question of the choice of vice president assumed extraordinary importance, more so than in any other presidential elections in American history given the crucial junctures the nation faced and the critical decisions that new presidents would have to make. But an even more intriguing issue arises when considering recent scholarship with respect to the 1944 election that reveals, or purports to prove, that virtually everyone connected with the process of choosing FDR's 1944 running mate was aware that his health was so poor that he would not live to the end of another term. That "everyone," of course, does not include Roosevelt himself, who refused to consider the possibility of his own mortality. Thus, the decision was not simply a choice of running mate for the president, but a much weightier choice, a man who would accede to the presidency for part, if not most, of the term.[12]

Of course, such factors were not considered in the selection of the running mate for Lincoln, who apparently was the only person who predicted his own demise. Harriet Beecher Stowe met with Lincoln that winter of 1864-65 following his reelection and was impressed by his suffering. In addition she was taken aback by his pronouncement that he didn't expect to survive long after the end of the war. Though this might have seemed apocryphal had only Ms. Stowe reported it, the incident was consistent with conversations with Lincoln reported by others even before his 1860 election. There was no reason to believe the president's life was in imminent danger, certainly not that second week in April after the primary Confederate army in the field had surrendered and the war was quickly winding to an end. Judging by the actions of each of those in the best positions to protect him, and vested with that specific responsibility, the evening of April 14 apparently gave no cause for alarm.[13]

Thus, the question of Lincoln's health was never an issue in deciding who the nominee for vice president would be in 1864. What did become the subject of a contentious and even acrimonious debate in the years following Lincoln's death, was the issue of his role in selecting Andrew Johnson as the 1864 vice presidential nominee. The principal antagonists in this controversy were John G. Nicolay and A. K. McClure. Nicolay, one of the two young men who served as Lincoln's primary secretary during his presidency, later coauthored a ten volume history, one of the principal primary sources about the White House during the Civil War years.

Nicolay was at the Baltimore nominating convention in 1864. Because he was there and the president was not, the Bavarian-born secretary was regarded by some of the delegates as the person in attendance most intimately acquainted with Lincoln's wishes. As such he was treated deferentially while in Baltimore.[14]

The controversy arose some twenty-six years later when, after the death of Lincoln's first vice president, Hannibal Hamlin, the Philadelphia *Times* editor, A. K. McClure, reported that Lincoln had favored Johnson's nomination by the convention in 1864. This claim was disputed by Nicolay who said that the president's "personal feelings" were for Hamlin's renomination, but that he carefully avoided doing or saying anything which might influence the convention. Nicolay's assertion was emphatically contradicted by McClure who criticized the former secretary for his "ignorance" and for purporting to speak for Lincoln. McClure claimed that Nicolay's presence at the convention meant nothing, that he "was dress-parading at Baltimore and knew nothing of the president's wishes." McClure further wrote of Nicolay that "He saw and knew President Lincoln: the man Abraham Lincoln he never saw and never knew." Nicolay responded that McClure was venting his "rage and wounded vanity at being exposed in a gross historical misstatement." He produced Lincoln's written statement composed while the convention was taking place which said, "Wish not to interfere about V.P. Cannot interfere about platform. Convention must judge for itself." This brief note by Lincoln was actually an endorsement on a letter which Nicolay had written to Hay from Baltimore the previous day. McClure responded that Nicolay did not know fully what was going on in June 1864, and that some of his statements were "flagrantly. . . false." McClure also claimed that John Hay, the other half of the Lincoln secretarial tandem, refused to sustain Nicolay's interpretation of the president's brief and noncommital note. McClure's position was supported by Ward Hill Lamon's biographer, Clint Clay Tilton. According to Tilton, Ward Lamon was present when two of the leading Republican political pundits, Leonard Swett and A. K. McClure, met with Lincoln and discussed the issue of the vice presidential nomination. According to Tilton, both Swett and McClure personally favored the renomination of Hamlin, but yielded when Lincoln insisted that they should work for the defeat of the vice president in favor of Andrew Johnson. At the convention Swett and McClure promoted the candidacy of Joseph Holt of Kentucky, but according to both Tilton and Lincoln biographer James G. Randall, this was only a "smoke screen" behind which they could maneuver for the nomination of Johnson.[15]

Much of the discussion about the subject in the years after the war was influenced by radical Republican hatred of Andrew Johnson during the Reconstruction years. Those who most wanted to discredit and dismiss Johnson would have liked to have shown that the martyred president had stated a preference for somebody, anybody other than the despised Tennessean. If Lincoln had been prescient enough to see in 1864 just what a terrible choice Andrew Johnson would be for vice president, it would certainly have suited the radicals' purposes in 1868 when they were trying to impeach him.[16]

This position fares better when viewed in retrospect from a postwar radical Republican perspective than it does when the circumstances and popular perceptions of 1864 are considered. Lincoln was a political pragmatist, particularly so in an election year when faced with an uphill battle for re-election in a contest that might very well shape the destiny of the country. Whether considered from the perspective of 1864, or in hindsight after Lincoln's death, it is impossible to argue that Hannibal Hamlin added as much to the ticket as Andrew Johnson did. And yet in a recent article published in *Civil War History*, Lincoln scholar Don E. Fehrenbacher has provided a very comprehensive overview of the entire controversy. He has concluded that McClure's assertion, though accepted as established fact by many historians over the past century, has never been proven either conclusively or even presumptively. Fehrenbacher argues convincingly that McClure's credibility and reliability were suspect, that his account of events was laced with absurdities, and that his bold assertion that "Lincoln nominated Johnson" was implausible. He concludes that "the story of Lincoln's deliberate, conspiratorial intervention in the vice-presidential contest should be put aside until such time as the weak evidence supporting it is greatly strengthened and the strong evidence against it is somehow explained."[17]

There was another incident regarding the vice presidential nominee in 1864 which McClure later dredged up in support of his position. In McClure's recollections, and later in an article in the *Mississippi Valley Historical Review* written by Louis Taylor Merrill, the writers claimed that Lincoln's first choice for a vice presidential running mate was General Benjamin F. Butler. According to McClure, Lincoln stated this to Simon Cameron in making Cameron his agent to go to Fort Monroe and to broach in confidence the subject to the general. In *Lincoln the President: The Last Full Measure*, Randall and Current speculated that it would have been unlikely for the president to employ Simon Cameron, of all people, on such mission. They pointed out that there was no verification from anybody close to Lincoln.[18]

There was, however, confirmation from another, seemingly unlikely, source. In an article published in the *North American Review* in October 1885, Butler wrote: "A gentleman who stood very high in Mr. Lincoln's confidence" came to see him at Fort Monroe to convey the message that the president wished Butler to serve as his vice presidential running mate. According to the article, written twenty years after Lincoln's death and characterized by an irreverence that may suggest it was true, Butler had responded: "Please say to Mr. Lincoln that I must decline. Tell him . . . I would not quit the field to be vice president, even with himself as president, unless he will give me a bond with sureties, in the full sum of his four years' salary, that he will die or resign within three months after his inauguration." Even Butler, a man not known for good taste in either his public utterances or private dealings, had to recognize how inappropriate such a claim was—unless it were true. If it were true, then his refusal to accept Lincoln's invitation meant he had forsaken the only opportunity he would ever have to be the president of the United States. It is difficult to imagine how different the Reconstruction period in American history would have been with Benjamin Butler rather than Andrew Johnson as president.[19]

This claim, if true, would certainly have made it more likely that Lincoln would have been willing to play an active part in unseating the incumbent vice president and replacing him with another man. However, Fehrenbacher finds this claim even more incredible than the one McClure made regarding the president's role in adding Johnson to the ticket. Both arose many years after the election, and became important only because of the venomous and vituperative exchange that took place between Nicolay and McClure following the story's appearance in 1891. According to Fehrenbacher "it is difficult to believe that the self-important Butler would have remained silent for two decades about so flattering a proposal." The account was belated in its announcement and was totally unsupported by Butler's voluminous Civil War papers. In addition, this most political of generals was notoriously unreliable. Viewed from any angle, the story lacks credibility. Even if Lincoln had been willing to preempt the power of the convention in such fashion, the controversial "beast" of New Orleans would have been a poor choice, offensive to the very elements whose allegiance the president wanted most to secure.[20]

Thus, the part that Lincoln played with respect to the vice presidential nomination in 1864 was subtle at most, and Nicolay's account must be accepted as established fact in the absence of anything more credible than what has been presented up to this time. If Lincoln played a role at all it was through the agency of others, while carefully cloaking himself against any appearance of partisanship or advocacy in the selection process. As had been characteristic with so many of Lincoln's wartime actions, he did not permit someone's status as a Democrat to cause him to treat that person negatively. If it influenced him at all, it was to the benefit of that individual. He was accused by some Republicans of favoring generals who had been antebellum Democrats. With regard to politics, he knew that establishing a Union coalition which included as many prowar Democrats as possible, won his administration the broadest possible consensus in support of prosecuting the war to a successful conclusion.

If he ever stated preferences for running mates in 1864, all of the people who were the objects of that support had been lifelong Democrats who had nevertheless vigorously supported the government's war effort. Lincoln was honest, even if subtle, and never resorted to prevarication on the subject when discussing the matter with anyone. In this regard his handling of the matter was significantly different from the way Franklin Roosevelt dealt with a similar matter in 1944.

One of the first conclusions among most Democratic insiders in the spring of 1944 was that Henry Wallace had to be dropped as the running mate. Wallace could cost Roosevelt too many votes in a national election in which the country had made a major conservative shift during the previous four years. The controversial secretary of agriculture, who was farther to the left politically than any other New Deal insider, would never have gotten the nod for the vice presidency in 1940 had FDR not threatened to decline the nomination unless the convention made Wallace his running mate. Wallace was favored by Roosevelts other than the president; Eleanor contributed her considerable political pull by addressing the delegates and strongly endorsing the populist from Iowa as "the man to carry on best in times such as we are facing." Even then, Wallace only narrowly defeated William Bankhead of Alabama, and so great was the convention's antagonism toward him that he was unable to deliver his acceptance speech. During the nominating and seconding speeches for Wallace in 1940, the delegates and crowds in the galleries had booed and hissed at every mention of his name. The scene was humiliating to Wallace and embarrassing to Roosevelt and party leaders. It was a scene that no Democrat wanted to see repeated in 1944.[21]

Nevertheless, even though the president, influenced by the advice of virtually every important party leader, had concluded that he was too weak politically to carry Wallace through another campaign, Roosevelt would not directly ask Wallace to withdraw his candidacy. Instead, FDR assigned

Harold Ickes and Samuel Rosenman to meet with Wallace early in July 1944, following the vice president's return from an extended visit to the Soviet Union and China. They were to inform him that somebody else was needed on the ticket. But Wallace, who very much wanted to continue as vice president, would not accept his fate without hearing it personally from Roosevelt, something FDR was not likely to do. The two men were together shortly thereafter at a White House meeting during which the vice president spent several hours reporting to his chief about the trip to China. Then, according to Wallace's oral history, Roosevelt said: "I am now talking to the ceiling about political matters." The president told his second-in-command that he was Roosevelt's personal choice as a running mate and that FDR was willing to make a statement to that effect. According to the vice president, FDR went so far as to indicate his preference by saying: "If I were a delegate to the convention," which of course he wasn't, "I would vote for Henry Wallace."[22]

If he did say that, it was an example of Roosevelt at his most duplicitous. All indications were that he had already decided that his incumbent vice president was too great a liability and must be sacrificed. At a meeting of Democratic leaders held at the White House on July 11, Wallace already had been eliminated as a potential running mate. However, in the days which followed the president continued to indicate to Wallace that he was Roosevelt's personal choice. On that basis, the vice president attended the convention in Chicago believing he could win in a floor fight over the nomination. Many of Wallace's supporters attended the convention fully expecting FDR to throw his support to the incumbent vice president and defeat the "dump Wallace" movement. On the evening that the president was to speak to the delegates by radio, "the Wallace-ites, undetected, packed the convention hall, readying themselves for the stampede." Thousands of the vice president's supporters filled the Chicago Stadium to its eaves and spread banners throughout proclaiming "We Want Wallace," "Keep the Winning Team, Roosevelt and Wallace" and "The People Want Wallace." According to Ferrell "the hall resembled a Wallace rally rather than a convention." The President's radio address concluded at 10:35. After several minutes of cheering, the convention chairman began a rendition of the national anthem.[23]

It was at this point that the Democratic convention came very close to being stampeded by this "spontaneous" floor demonstration. "The convention organist . . . perhaps paid by someone, maybe in ignorance, took up the theme, playing the Iowa state song, 'Iowa, Iowa, that's where the tall corn grows.'" Wallace parades began inside the convention hall, and Roosevelt-Wallace banners appeared everywhere. Party leaders were furious. It was a classic confrontation between political professionals, who were watching their most important quadrennial gathering get completely beyond their control, and grassroots populism, whose masses were becoming more exuberant as their demonstration grew in intensity and volume. Attempts were made to secure an ax to stop the organ, presumably by cutting the cable which supplied it with power, and Mayor Edward J. Kelly of Chicago declared that he had the "right to declare an overcrowded hall a fire hazard." By 10:54 PM the convention chairman was ordered to close the convention. A motion was made to adjourn and after a quick call for ayes and nays, he ruled that the motion carried and the mikes and spotlights were cut.[24]

Roosevelt actually attempted throughout the preconvention season to create the impression that, like Lincoln in 1864, he wanted to have no part in the selection process for the vice presidential nominee. Unlike Lincoln, however, he was more than willing to engage in discussions with virtually every Democratic political pundit within earshot and speculate as to whom would make the best candidate in what would prove to be Roosevelt's most difficult run for the presidency. And, in even greater disregard of his self-proclaimed neutrality, he stated orally or in writing to no fewer than four different potential candidates, his preference for, if not outright support of, their individual candidacies (in addition to Truman and Wallace there were also William O. Douglas and James Byrnes). Roosevelt knew full well, just as Lincoln had in 1864, what his endorsement of an individual's candidacy would mean. Although it would not assure that candidate of winning the nomination, it would be the single most important factor weighed by the convention.[25]

Lincoln and Roosevelt were the two giants of American politics during their respective centuries. They led the nation through the two greatest crises in its history and cloaked themselves in honor and glory in the process. Probably no two national leaders so changed the face and character of the nation as these men did during their stewardships as chief executive. During their presidencies the relationships between the federal and state governments, and between the national authority and the citizens, changed dramatically. And yet they were very different. In their respective wartime reelection campaigns both would presume to take the same position regarding the nominations of vice presidential candidates. In the case of Abraham Lincoln the best evidence was and is that he lived up to his stated position, that he did not actively intervene in the process of selecting a vice presidential candidate. The only apparent part he played was to let it be known that he would not object to any of the certain contemplated candidates about whom he was asked. Franklin Roosevelt, however, despite his rhetoric that the vice presidential nominee was the convention's decision and that he did not want to interfere, played an active role in choosing his running mate. It was a role in which he was less than honest with the various prospective candidates, and that duplicity generated a near stampede for the incumbent vice president at the Democratic convention in Chicago. If the Wallaceites had prevailed, it would have resulted in the nomination of the one man that both Roosevelt and most party leaders regarded as least acceptable. Lincoln ended up heading a ticket which included a vice presidential candidate who, if not necessarily his first choice, was more than acceptable to him, for he understood the realities of electoral politics and the strength that Andrew Johnson brought to the ticket. Franklin Roosevelt ended up with a running mate who, if not necessarily his first choice, was more than acceptable to him, for he, too, understood the realities of electoral politics and the strength that Harry Truman brought to the ticket.

Though the results of this nominating process in 1864 and 1944 were very similar, the behind-the-scenes activities and the roles played by Abraham Lincoln and Franklin Roosevelt were very different.

ENDNOTES

1. David E. Long, *The Jewel of Liberty: Abraham Lincoln's Re-election and the End of Slavery* (Mechanicsburg, PA: Stackpole, 1994), 179; Emerson D. Fire, *Social and Industrial Conditions in the North during the Civil War* (New York: 1910); Allan Nevins, *The War for the Union: The Organized War to Victory 1864-1865* (New York: Scribner's, 1971), 196-99; Richard Polenberg, *War and Society: The United States, 1941-1945* (Philadelphia: Lippincott, 1972), 1-4; Thomas L. Livermore, *Numbers and Losses in the Civil War in America 1861-1865* (Boston, 1901), 1-63; E.B. Long, *The Civil War Day by Day: An Almanac* (Garden City, NY: Doubleday, 1971), 705; *War Production Board Minutes*, October 6, 1942, 141-42.

2. Barry Keith Beyer, *Thomas E. Dewey, 1937-1947: A Study in Political Leadership* (Unpublished Ph.D. dissertation, University of Rochester: 1962), 438, 426; Long, *Jewel of Liberty*, 56-58, 39-40; James McPherson, *Battle Cry of Freedom: The Civil War Era* (New York: Oxford University Press, 1988), 771; John Morton Blum, *V Was For Victory: Politics and American Culture During World War II* (New York:: Harcourt Brace Jovanovich, 1976), 289-300; Polenberg, *War and Society*, 212.

3. William Hanchett, *The Lincoln Murder Conspiracies* (Urbana, IL: University of Illinois Press, 1986), 56; Thomas Reed Turner, *Beware the People Weeping: Public Opinion and the Assassination of Abraham Lincoln* (Baton Rouge, LA: Louisiana State University Press, 1982), 44; Lloyd Lewis, *The Assassination of Lincoln: History*

and Myth (Lincoln, NE: 1929), 68-80; Blum, *V Was for Victory*, 4-6; Hugh Gregory Gallagher, *FDR's Splendid Deception* (Arlington, VA: Dodd Mead, 1994), 208-10.

4. Harold Dudley, "The Election of 1864," *The Mississippi Valley Historical Review* 18 (March 1932), 509; Andrew McClure, *Our Presidents and How We Make Them* (New York: 1900), 184-85; James H. Glonck, "Lincoln, Johnson and the Baltimore Ticket," *Abraham Lincoln Quarterly* 6 (March 1951): 255-71; Robert H. Ferrell, *Choosing Truman: The Democratic Convention of 1944* (Columbia, MO: University of Missouri Press, 1994), 50-82.

5. Long, *The Jewel of Liberty*, 215-34, 195-214; Blum, *V Was for Victory*, 255-99; Polenberg, *War and Society*, 195-97.

6. David Herbert Donald, *Lincoln* (New York: Simon and Schuster, 1995), 246-50; Phillip Shaw Paludan, *The Presidency of Abraham Lincoln* (Lawrence: University Press of Kansas, 1994), 3-14; William E. Leuchtenberg, *Franklin D. Roosevelt and the New Deal* (New York: Harper and Row, 1963), 1-16; Frank Friedel, *Franklin D. Roosevelt: A Rendezvous with Destiny* (Boston: Little, Brown, 1990), 63-65.

7. Allan Nevins, *The War for the Union: The Improvised War 1861-1862* (New York: Scribner's, 1959), 3-4; Freidel, *Roosevelt*, 80-91.

8. Donald, *Lincoln*, 296-301; Long, *Jewel of Liberty*, 179-88, 193-94; Leuchtenberg, *Franklin D. Roosevelt*, 41-62, 179-83.

9. Allan Nevins, *The War for the Union: War Becomes Revolution 1862-1863* (New York: Scribner's, 1960), 214; Polenberg, *War and Society*, 27-29, 197-99.

10. Eric Foner, *Reconstruction: America's Unfinished Revolution 1863-1877* (New York: Macmillan, 1988), 333-36.

11. David McCullough, *Truman* (New York: Simon and Schuster: 1992), 345-62.

12. Ibid., Ferrell, *Choosing Truman*, 1-3.

13. Harriet Beecher Stowe, "Abraham Lincoln" (reprinted from *Littell's Living Age*, February 6, 1864), essay contained in Herbert Mitgang, ed., *Abraham Lincoln: A Press Portrait* (Athens: University of Georgia Press, 1956, reprinted 1962, 1971, and 1989), 378: William H. Herndon, *Herndon's Life of Lincoln* (Cleveland: 1949), 390; Stephen Oates, *With Malice Toward None: A Life of Abraham Lincoln* (New York: Harper and Row, 1977, reprinted 1994), xv, 29, 66, 69, 70-71, 425-31.

14. J.G. Randall and Richard N. Current, *Lincoln the President: Last Full Measure* (Urbana: University of Illinois Press, 1955, reprinted 1991), 162-63.

15. Philadelphia *Times*, July 6, 1891; the text of the McClure-Nicolay exchange appeared in many newspapers beginning July 6, 1891, and was reprinted in the appendix to Abraham McClure, *Abraham Lincoln and Men of War Times: Some Personal Recollections of War and Politics During the Lincoln Administration*, 4th ed. (Philadelphia: 1892), 474-75; Don E. Fehrenbacher, "The Making of a Myth: Lincoln and the Vice-Presidential Nomination in 1864" in *Civil War History* 54, (4) (December 1995): 273-90.

16. J.G. Randall and Richard Current, *Lincoln the President: Last Full Measure*

(Urbana: University of Illinois Press, 1955, reprinted 1983), 133-34.

17. Don E. Fehrenbacher, "The Making of a Myth," in *Civil War History* 41, (4) (December 1995): 273-90.

18. Randall and Current, *Last Full Measure*, 134-36.

19. Benjamin F. Butler, "Vice-Presidential Politics in '64," *North American Review* 141 (October 1885): 333.

20. Fehrenbacher, "Making of a Myth," 283.

21. Graham White and John Maze, *Henry A. Wallace: His Search for a New World Order* (Chapel Hill: University of North Carolina Press, 1995), 135-37; Ferrell, *Choosing Truman*, 3.

22. Ibid., 22-25.

23. Ibid., 3-14, 73-80.

24. Ferrell, *Choosing Truman*, 79-80.

25. Ferrell, *Choosing Truman*, 22, 28-34, 50-51, 80-82.

3

Abraham and Mary, Franklin and Eleanor: Their Growth From Private to Public Comprehension

James Chowning Davies

Introducing Equal Dignity to Politics

In this chapter, I will consider the backgrounds of Abraham and Mary Lincoln, and Franklin and Eleanor Roosevelt, with hopes of accomplishing more than a rearranging, a recital of well-known and often disputed facts. Next, I will set these backgrounds in the matrix of the moral and political issues of the two eras. And then I will suggest why political leadership that truly is based on movement toward equality, on equal respect for all human beings, endures even for centuries in the active memory of citizens. The implication is that, in the modern world, leadership which is based on hierarchized values, even when it professes equalitarian values, is as durable as any demagogy: that is, not very durable at all.

It seems remarkable that these two presidents can even be considered by common criteria. Lincoln was overly tall (almost 6 ft. 4 in.) and ungainly. Only when his total presence, his personality, became an object of awe after his death did his physical appearance become some new kind of definition of handsomeness. FDR was tall (a bit over 6 ft. 1 in.), well proportioned, and very handsome. FDR did not need Lincoln's redefinition. However, he made it necessary for people to redefine how and in what ways a president must be healthy: he had to make clear to himself and then everyone else that paralysis was not necessarily crippling. Lincoln's dark melancholy and Roosevelt's bright optimism will be considered near the end of this chapter.

What Lincoln began learning in childhood—empathy with people as human beings rather than as members of higher or lower status—FDR could not really begin to learn until he was thirty-nine years old, when he was quickly and permanently crippled by polio. Roosevelt could learn human empathy on a solid foundation of affection and self-confidence; Lincoln had to acquire reciprocal liking for people outside his immediate ken and self-confidence, as he moved from childhood to maturity. As he grew up, he had to learn that people liked him, even when he was unsure of their affection, as he was at first of Mary's; Roosevelt was assured of this, almost from birth; Eleanor merely reassured him.

It seems increasingly clear that neither Lincoln nor Roosevelt would have given history such a large nudge, but for their spouses. Their wives shared their husbands' beliefs, though their roles were very different and will be considered in light of their respective times. As influence goes, Abraham and Mary Lincoln and Franklin and Eleanor Roosevelt were almost uniquely influential.

My judgment on the basic reasons for the immortality of Lincoln and Roosevelt is three-fold: that they both identified with people as human beings and trusted them; that both very strongly believed in the inherent worth, the equal dignity, of human beings; and that both acted successfully on this belief. I believe that Lincoln and Roosevelt remain such vital figures because they were able to do something about equality in modern times. It was no random, impulsive act to build a memorial to Lincoln, so soon after his death, or to put Roosevelt's image on the American dime, so soon after his.[1] And citizens in not just the United States but increasingly throughout the world admire these men, not just because they identified with people as equals but also because they acted on their belief. In the modern era, when massive wealth has been slowly emancipating ordinary people all over the world from poverty and degradation, people all over the world are now demanding moral equality.

Neither man invented moral equality. It was advocated by Buddha, Jesus, and Mahomet long before modern societies started producing massive wealth as they become economically and politically integrated; and long before Lincoln and Roosevelt did something about equality in the modern world. The desire to be regarded and treated as equals is, I believe, an innate characteristic of the entire human race. Buddha, Jesus, and Mahomet brought the desire to the surface, morally and socially. Aristotle wrote that the best state is "a community of equals [similar individuals] aiming at the best life possible"[2] but what he said and what he did were different things. His major political deed was training the young Alexander, who did not help establish democracy in Athens or Macedonia but conquered and made an empire of a big part of the world. Lincoln and Roosevelt did some very significant things about it, morally and politically.

The Late Blooming of Lincoln

Lincoln's life history up to adulthood reads like that of millions of people whom we know or believe to be disadvantaged or victimized or overwhelmed by their environment. Millions are indeed overwhelmed and we may avoid investigation by concluding that it was some supernatural miracle that Lincoln was not. It is little noted that his father was not overwhelmed, nor were his two mothers.

Lincoln's grandfather Abraham moved the family from Virginia to Kentucky when Lincoln's father Thomas was four. Two years after the Anglo-American family got there, some native Americans raided their clearing. They killed the father Abraham and were about to kidnap the six-year-old Thomas when the eldest brother Mordecai killed the man who had seized the child.

Witnessing the death of his father could have shattered Thomas Lincoln's soul. The terrified boy could have grown up a drifter. He may have had the genetic potential to sire some remarkable progeny but he might not have taken the trouble to acknowledge them if he did. Instead, he married and named his and Nancy's son after his murdered father. Experiencing the death of Nancy could have done in Thomas Lincoln as a person. But Thomas did not fall apart or give up, nor did he encourage an attitude of hopelessness in his one and only son. For a time, in either Indiana or Illinois, deaths in his extended family kept him busy making coffins and burying one family member after another. Once when he sent Abraham with the old mare to a grist mill, Abraham treated the horse meanly and she kicked him in the head. As Lincoln later put it, he was dead for a short while. His father hurried to the mill to rescue his son, as his brother Mordecai had rescued Thomas when he was a small boy.

Thomas had serious flaws from which flowed failures that were predictable if not avoidable. He was not good at starting enterprises, even as basic as getting good title to land he intended to cultivate. In his partnership in a general store, Lincoln failed as badly as his father had. But giving up or abandoning his familial responsibilities were not among the faults of Thomas. There are few more elemental virtues than facing up to familial responsibilities; the father's example stuck with the son. A commonly mentioned flaw in Lincoln was his refusal to visit his father when he was dying. But Lincoln always remembered how long he lived: "seventy-three years and eleven days," he told his law partner Billy Herndon.[3] Lincoln's father was always with him.

Community responsibility, in the form of social security, aid to dependent children, head-start programs, health insurance, and retirement insurance did not exist in the nineteenth century, in the United States or so far as I know anywhere in the world. Family values then were prominent and strong, but that does not mean they were always adhered to.[4] Thomas did stick to them. The elemental familial stability that Lincoln experienced—despite the numerous deaths—made it possible for Lincoln to develop rather than stagnate or disintegrate as a person. Later, he had to test it, on his own and to his own satisfaction, because of his very strong need to be liked and to be loved and respected, by those immediate and remote from his day-to-day life. If he had not had this childhood background, it seems doubtful that he would even have bothered trying as an adult.

In Greek mythology, Athena was born fully grown as she emerged from the head of her father Zeus. Some admirers of Lincoln seem to suppose the same thing happened with him. The nonmiraculous quality of his development becomes visible once one clears away the sentiment from accounts of Lincoln's supposedly independent, unsupported, innate ability to stand on his own. It seems self-evident that every child needs not just physical but also mental nurturance to grow. Lincoln did grow in his first two decades. He got help not just from his stepmother, his "angel mother"[5] as he called her, but also from his demanding, cantankerous father. Abraham may have been the master of his own fate and the captain of his own soul more than almost any other individual in the political world, but there was a loyal, supportive crew in his lifeboat, from his birth to his death.

The major spurts in his later growth stemmed from his realization that people not only liked him but also respected him, as both a person and a leader. From his first political ventures, he was popular among townspeople, fellow soldiers, and fellow lawyers and legislators. So he felt free to pursue that which he loved and that which he was good at: formulating and carrying out programs that his fellow citizens wanted but could not achieve on their own.

As his public and private life developed, his self-confidence strengthened so firmly that he took increasing political risks, with the confidence of being ultimately successful. When he was thirty-seven he was elected to Congress, just after war had broken out with Mexico. He opposed what he considered a little imperialist war.[6] He was strongly criticized in Illinois. After serving his one term, Lincoln went back to Illinois to think things over. The Kansas-Nebraska Act of 1854 proposed leaving the issue of free versus slave territory to whatever decision the territorial majority might come to. This manifestation of popular sovereignty reduced the economic issue of competition between free farmers and slave owners to majority rule. It reduced to majority rule the moral issue of whether any class of human beings had the right to own others. Lincoln got reactivated to politics, in a goal-oriented course of action that headed him toward the presidency.

His motives in opposing the extension of slavery were a mixture, as they were for those around him—and for his father. In 1787, the Northwest Ordinance and in 1820 the Missouri Compromise, had forbidden slavery in most of the territories. Northerners wanted this prohibition continued and they wanted to expand the area in which each individual was regarded as being of equal value, equal worth, equal dignity, and meriting equal opportunity to prosper. Lincoln shared this high evaluation of equality and, even more intensely, valued the Union as a unique political institution that allowed wide diversity, but was not neutral on huge moral issues like slavery. With these two values and his powerful political ambition, he reentered politics after only a four-year dormancy, when the 1854 Kansas-Nebraska Act made moral equality a matter of majority rule.

The road from a preliminary acceptance of these values to leading his fellow countrymen toward their political realization was a long one. When he first ran for office, in 1832, he was just twenty-three and proposed a set of local improvements (roads, bridges, and canals) that would make it easier for people to move goods from field to market. Such proposals were consistent with the belief Lincoln expressed, that government should do for people only those things that they cannot do or that the government can do for them better. But such proposals were a long shot from proposing and effecting the idea that a large and diverse society could be maintained as a political union. And then proposing that a large and diverse society could be maintained only under the equality principle guaranteeing equal opportunity to all. In the short run, of course, white men were regarded as more equal than everyone else, so black people and women had to wait their place in line. But Lincoln began in the mid-nineteenth century insisting that no one could have such total control over other human beings as slavery permitted. It was an enormously significant position, because, if it succeeded, it would insure that neofeudal hierarchy and sanctified ownership of some human beings by others would not to be reimposed and sanctified.

It would ensure that the hierarchized societies in Europe would not be reestablished in America. The young man who ran first on a platform of local improvements grew into the man who gets the most credit for saving the Union and freeing the slaves. He was closer to his father than to his wife on the issue of slavery. In the White House she became a strong abolitionist and close friend of Senator Charles Sumner, the ardent abolitionist from Massachusetts.[7] She kept the heat on her husband to end slavery. In putting pressure on her husband on abolition in 1862, Mary Lincoln was doing what Eleanor Roosevelt did so insistently to her husband on a wide variety of issues.

Ann Rutledge and Mary Todd

Not long after getting out on his own at the age of twenty-two, in 1831 Lincoln settled in New Salem, Illinois. He became attached to the place after the townspeople watched him free a flatboat stuck on the local mill dam and cheered. He boarded at the inn and fell in love with Ann Rutledge, daughter of the innkeeper, who was well educated, owned many books, and founded a debating society. Directly or through her family, Ann thus helped fill several of Lincoln's needs. He was at last, in a place where people liked him, free from parental domination, free to develop his normal interest in women, and free to feed his voracious appetite for intellectual stimulation.[8] Lincoln started courting her, read as many books as he could get hold of, and got involved in the debating society meetings. He deeply impressed his listeners. The future was looking bright for the young, awkward, ill-schooled, but extraordinarily sensitive, intelligent, and ambitious young Lincoln.

The attraction between Ann and Abraham probably was mutual but it didn't last. A year after Lincoln got to New Salem, she died, in August 1832.[9] Her death bereft Lincoln terribly. Whether this was because she was so attractive to him or because Lincoln didn't think he could be attractive to anyone cannot be known. But the fact of their being in love is not easily questionable. Some biographers have belittled or ignored what is the evident fact of their love, implying that, since there is no documentary evidence, not much could have been there. People do not always leave a paper trail about their loves, even their true loves.[10] If Ann had become his wife, possibly Lincoln would have survived in politics, the occupation he had already chosen. But Ann may not have had the strong hunger to be the nation's First Lady that Mary had.

The attachment between the two may have encouraged his first run for office.[11] After launching his candidacy in March 1832, he volunteered for a little war against native Americans, got elected captain by his fellow soldiers, and reenlisted. He lost the election when he got back from the Black Hawk War. Her death did not stop him from continuing his self-education, his interest in politics, nor his interest in women.

Four years later a friend asked him if he would marry a woman from Kentucky. Lincoln thought it worth having a look. Mary Owens came to Springfield to see this promising young attorney who had just got his license to practice. Things warmed up a bit, but Lincoln kept protesting to her how unpromising a relationship with him would be. His protest was successful: she left town.

With Mary Todd, it started out much the same. Mary's sister Elizabeth was married to Ninian Edwards, a man of rather widely recognized local distinction. His father was the former governor of Illinois, both before and after it was admitted to the Union. The Todds of Kentucky were also distinguished: the father was a prominent banker in Lexington. He had finished his daughters off well enough that Mary was pretty good at the French language. Senator Henry Clay was a good friend of the family and was Mary's idol. And she was ambitious for a successful marriage, defining that term politically.

Her life before Lincoln was not particularly smooth. Born in 1818, she was the fourth child in the Todd family. Her older brother Robert Todd died in infancy and her mother died in childbirth when Mary was only six. Her father remarried within two years; he and his second wife produced nine more children. Mary and her stepmother did not get along.[12]

By the time they met, in December 1839, Lincoln was nearly thirty-one; she was almost a decade younger. He must have already set his sights on the political heights, and after he had been in Congress from 1847 to 1849, she was telling people that her husband would some day be president of the United States.[13] But his political aspirations did not convince him that he could attract a woman. He was very tall, not because of being well proportioned but because he had very long legs and arms. He looked rough hewn and he was very ill at ease with women. He was not sure he could keep a woman as a wife. But they had long talks in her sister's home and fell in love and became publicly engaged.

Lincoln's engagement did not resolve his doubts about being accepted. The distinguished Edwards' were unimpressed: it was well enough that Mary should befriend this young politician, but should she marry a man who lacked family and schooling? His father was neither a banker nor a former governor. Lincoln came to question that Mary could love him against her family's objection. That is, could she love him despite his shortcomings and apart from the political ambition they both had? On the first of January 1841, now almost thirty-two, he broke off the engagement. She had reason enough to be at least humiliated and perhaps also devastated. He went into a period of profound depression. His closest friend, perhaps his closest lifetime friend, Joshua Speed, and some others took precautions to see that he didn't use a knife or other instrument to take his own life. Lincoln wrote to Mary's cousin John Todd Stuart, his early mentor and law partner,[14] that "if what I feel were equally distributed to the whole human family, there would not be one cheerful face on the earth. Whether I shall ever be better, I cannot tell; I awfully forbode I shall not. To remain as I am is impossible. I must die or be better, it appears to me."[15]

For the months after the break, Lincoln was in the midst of a session of the legislature. He attended his legislative duties, gloomily but steadily. In 1841 he was absent seven days in two months. That is to say, it wasn't just concerned friends but also politics that helped to save his life. Working in the legislature gave Lincoln two elemental assurances: that people liked and esteemed him and that he could still be effective as a maker of public policy

Some eighteen months after he broke off their engagement, a friend of Mary's and Lincoln's got them back together. They became engaged again, this time privately and on November 4, 1842 Mary and the diffident, ambitious giant were married—in the Edwards' parlor. From that point on they were never really separated mentally, till death on the twelfth of April 1865 did them part.

In August 1842, during their second and secret engagement, the two of them conspired to do dirt to the state auditor, James Shields. They published in a newspaper the scurrilous "Letters from a Lost Township." Lincoln wrote some of them and Mary others. Shields was not only the state auditor in a time when there was some question of financial skullduggery; he was also a reputed womanizer of sorts; and, even more immoral, he was a Democrat.

Understandably, Shields was offended, so offended that he proposed a duel to Lincoln. The custom of dueling was illegal in Illinois but still lawful in Missouri. He seemed willing to forget the whole thing if Lincoln would tell the state auditor who was the author of the most offensive letter. Lincoln accepted the challenge but refused to reveal whether it was he or Mary who wrote the most offensive letter.[16] Lincoln would not betray his fiancée.

So the duel was arranged, the challenged person by dueling custom having the choice of circumstances. Lincoln, with his six-foot-four-inch frame and powerful build, proposed broadswords at a distance that would have made it difficult even for Lincoln to get in a good cut and impossible for the diminutive and rotund Shields. The duelists and their seconds got together on an island in the Mississippi near St. Louis; had a concentrated discussion; Lincoln made a dignified apology, still without revealing the letters' authorship; and the duel was called off. Long after the event, Mary said they both were ashamed.[17] She now knew that he would not betray her. Again, as in discussing Lincoln's father, there is a tendency to emphasize the negative in discussing Mary Todd Lincoln. She was not mentally as stable as her husband, but her moodiness was understandable in an emotional woman who lacked support from her stepmother. There were at least mild mental problems in her extended family.

In Springfield this high-strung, energetic, emotional woman went into occasional rages directed at housekeepers and husband. Their second son, Eddy, died in February 1850 in Springfield, less than a year after her father died in Kentucky.[18] She was devastated, but the two of them got pregnant with their third son very soon after Eddy's death. Some of the problems may have been both cause and consequence of Lincoln's perpetual tendency to be out on the circuit, arguing cases in court while Mary was left at home with the children and had nobody to talk to or sleep with. In the "Victorian" nineteenth century, one did not talk about such things, but the verbal silence did not quiet the glands.

For a decade before the Lincolns made their final move to Washington, they had a loyal and intelligent housekeeper, Mariah Vance. She was very warmly liked by both husband and wife, and they treated her with dignity. In her memoirs, as they were recounted orally to a woman who knew her some decades later,[19] Mariah Vance reported conditions in the Lincoln household that make it sound like a marriage that was not rapturous but was very close. Mrs. Vance did relate numerous fights and rages; she was quite sure Mary was on laudanum, opium as it is now known. She was sure both parents dearly loved their children, and in their own distinct, different ways loved not only politics but also each other.[20]

Would Lincoln have been able to become and to remain president, were it not for Mary? Long before meeting her, Lincoln had the example of his father, who survived the trauma of his first wife's death. Lincoln survived his own mother's death and the death of his beloved Ann, who might not have pushed him to aim for national politics. Whereas Ann was a local girl and innkeeper's daughter, Mary knew Clay, a national figure and minor hero of Lincoln. She was born into the ruling class that Lincoln aspired to, and she wanted to be First Lady.

In the complex process by which people form their judgments, their attachments, and their actions it seems very clear, in the social and moral context of the times, that Mary was indispensable to Lincoln. She did not desert him when he deserted her in 1841, nor ever thereafter. Perhaps she became indispensable from the time they became secretly engaged and had their tiff with the Democrat, James Shields. Part of her loyalty to him derived from her own political ambitions: She fancied being the cynosure as First Lady of the land. She had seen through this rough-hewn giant to his core. She regarded him more highly than another possible mate, Stephen Douglas. That is, she established and maintained in him a measure of self-confidence. Mary, with her affection, status, and charm, in loving Lincoln re-enforced intimately the feeling of being admired and loved that he got from townspeople, the fellow soldiers who elected him their captain, and fellow legislators. Quarrels and hysterics aside, she was there every day to assure him that he was not alone and was loved and respected. She stuck with him, because she had faith he would realize their dream. And by admiring but not idolizing him, she continuously helped him remember that he was not God and that his vaulting ambition should not o'erleap itself.

Lincoln's route to the White House and his tasks there stretched him to the utmost. Mary's fragile mind was a strain on Lincoln both before and during the four White House years. The year 1862 was perhaps the most agonizing one for Lincoln. The war was not going well. Abolitionists were demanding immediate emancipation. And in February they lost their beloved Willie. Lincoln cried uncontrollably but public problems compelled him to regain control. Mary did not respond to these problems and came unglued. Mrs. Elizabeth Keckley, the seamstress who made Mary's clothes and became a close friend and confidante of Mary, reported that Lincoln took her to a window in the White House and pointed to the asylum for insane. He told her that if she did not control herself, they might have to take her there.[21] She did regain control.[22] From the perspective of the late twentieth century, it seems that it was easier for Lincoln to bear living with and supporting a wife whose behavior verged on the psychotic than it would have been not to have her there. She avoided going into an asylum while in the White House because they were so strongly committed to each other, and she did manage to recover for the three remaining years of their life together. Mrs. Keckley reported that Mary Lincoln was a "peculiarly constituted woman."[23]

The Early Blooming of FDR

In the formation of his personality Franklin Roosevelt is almost a reversed image of Lincoln. Roosevelt's mother Sara was in labor with him for close to twenty-four hours. If the year had been 1809, it seems likely that either the child or the mother or both would have died. In 1882, it came to the point when the attending physician concluded he must try to save the mother's life and sacrifice the oversized fetus. He gave her chloroform to relax her before removing the fetus. She relaxed, and on the 30th of January a ten-pound boy emerged.

As a child, he had few traumas, was never kicked in the head by a horse, and the ones he owned were for recreation only. Once he badly cut his head while outdoors playing. He put his cap over the wound so that his parents would not see it, because they had stressed that Franklin was not to complain about or even to have, little physical problems.

Both Sara Delano and James Roosevelt were devoted to the child. Whether deliberately or by the passage of time, they did not have another. They concentrated their affection on their very winsome, very handsome, very gifted boy. Unlike Lincoln, whose mother died when he was nine and whose affection for his father was mixed with enormous resentment, FDR had two parents who nicely blended affection, strict discipline, and indulgence. Members of the moneyed aristocracy of late-nineteenth century America, Franklin's parents brought him up with the aid of nannies and tutors, who gave him much more attention than he would have gotten in public schools. When guests came, they found it easy to admire the boy.

Franklin had found when he was a child that he could get his own way fairly easily by his gracious, warm amiability. When he was eight, he looked upset to his mother, who asked him what he wished for. Clasping his hands, he said: "Oh, for freedom."[24] So his mother let him do just what he wanted, without either supervising or hovering over him. That is, she let him be free—for a couple of days. But his parents didn't always hover. When he was just eleven and they were visiting in England, he went quite by himself on a train trip, out of London. He grew up with a dominant but deeply affectionate mother who let him take risks, and with a companionable and affectionate father. He grew up with virtually no ambivalence in his parents' affection for him and his for them. But his parents did more than indulge and hover: they kept close control over his growth. He was so strong minded that he didn't allow the hovering attention of his mother and the strong companionship of his father to smother or soften him. Sara's devotion was accompanied by strong discipline, and not just by admonishing him not to be a complainer. And he must not think only of himself. Once when he was playing a game with his mother, she won a round with the critical token turning up in her favor. Franklin got angry. She gave him the critical token and it did not turn up in his favor. He got angrier. She closed the game and quietly told him that he must learn to be a good loser.

It was apparent at an early age that he always had to be in command. As a child he and a friend were building a fort, Franklin telling the friend exactly how to do it. Sara watched and told her son he should let the other boy give some of the commands. Franklin said to his mother: "Mummie, if I didn't give the orders, nothing would happen."[25] When FDR was a senior and (of course) editor-in-chief of the Harvard Crimson, one of his associates said that "in his geniality, there was a kind of frictionless command."[26] The geniality and frictionless command were with him for his entire life.

Franklin developed his skill at getting what he wanted by nicely conjoining amiability and occasional deception. Getting his way with a strong-minded mother sometimes meant not fighting her but deceiving her. But he did not let his deviousness become the end, which was to do well and to do good to people whom he needed and they themselves wanted his affection. This amiable, affectionate, and sometimes convoluted path to gaining and maintaining control became a pattern he followed habitually in public office: FDR always, always felt that means must be separated from ends, and he was more than just flexible about means. He used warmth, amiability, and deviousness when necessary, in order to gain people's affection, respect, and loyalty—as he did good for them in his pursuit of power.

Sara kept him home for two years beyond the time when an aristocratic boy would normally enter preparatory school, prolonging the time that he was present as the center of her attention but at most the center of attention of his agemates, usually when their parents came for a visit. So when Franklin headed for preparatory school, he was headed for social adjustments he had not anticipated. At Groton, his classmates had had two years to establish a closed little society. His fellow students at first rejected him, particularly his classmates. He was puzzled, because he was the social center of attention at home, and he did try to charm them as he had his parents and family guests. He was too skinny for sports competition but he served as manager in sports and in nonacademic events. He did these with skill and with charm that elicited enthusiasm, particularly from lower classmen. In letters home Franklin did not mention his problems in getting adjusted: He reported that studies and friendships were going well.

He became strongly, permanently attached to the head of the school, Endicott Peabody, an Episcopalian minister who had founded Groton shortly before developing a clientele among America's aristocracy and who served very well as a fair-minded and affectionate surrogate father. He dignified and nurtured this young Roosevelt but did not spoil him. He presided at the marriage of Franklin and Eleanor Roosevelt in 1905, and conducted a prayer service in Washington for his former student, two hours before his 1933 inauguration.

Two things are clearly contrasted in the gradual fixing of the personalities of Lincoln and FDR: Lincoln as a child was often alone, not just solitary but also bereft of the kind of companionship he needed. He worked alone a lot, in woods and fields, and he continually had to rely on himself. Roosevelt was always able to rely on the support of others. But even though he was not often alone, if he were to discover and uncover his enormous potential, FDR as a child could not do it simply by ingratiating people. And as an adult, if he had been merely ingratiating, in politics he would have established an image of emptiness—the stereotyped image of the "politician." He had to get people to appreciate what he did for them. He was nearly always charming and disarming, whether or not he was being devious and deceptive. But the striking factor in this part of his longtime reputation is that he did things for the people he charmed and deceived.

FDR very early in his life showed his strong will. His mother did indeed dominate him; she was the formidably strongest influence on Franklin's character formation. But she loved him, as well as one domineering person can love another, and reluctantly she did let him grow up. When his strong-minded mother finally was reconciled to her beloved only child marrying another strong-minded woman, Franklin spent the rest of his life resolving or avoiding conflict between the wishes of his mother and his wife. But he developed early and his personality was well established—more fully than Lincoln's—when he left home.

Three events in Franklin's adulthood helped to establish the goal-oriented direction toward which his genes impelled him and for which his parents had provided nearly ideal nurturance. These events had starting points but not endings: they were active throughout his life. The first gets separate attention below: his marriage in 1905 to the niece of the president of the United States. The second came thirteen years later: his affair with Lucy Mercer. The third, the attack of polio that paralyzed him from the waist down, came three years after that.

Marriage to Eleanor helped to deepen and strengthen FDR's personality. FDR knew he was marrying a very strong-willed person who might overlook some of his deceptions despite seeing them more clearly than his mother. The fact that she didn't let these destroy their marriage told him of the strength of their common interests and commitments. Both were close to their families, and Eleanor with very mixed feelings established manageable ways of sharing her husband with her mother-in-law. And the distinct but complementary political careers of Franklin and Eleanor strengthened their marriage as they had the marriage of Abraham and Mary.

The affair with Mercer had a toughening affect. Eleanor told him he could have his freedom but in no event could abandon his children. His mother told him she would disinherit him if he left Eleanor. FDR considered his priorities: His political ambitions were more important than surrendering to his strong need for physical and mental attention. He decided that he would put the affair behind him and continue the existing familial arrangements. In addition, with his childhood-established gift of deceptive charm, he told Eleanor he'd never see Lucy again. He did see her again and may have had affairs with other women, but he was at least more circumspect. No later than when he was elected governor of New York in 1928, he established very close ties with at least two other women: his secretary Marguerite LeHand (Missy) and a distant cousin of his, Margaret Suckley. Neither of them ever married; both maintained their strong bond to FDR for as long as they lived. But, like Lincoln, he never with them or anyone else violated his commitment to himself to put his political career first.

The third part of his character formation came with his polio, which hit FDR in 1921. It was a terrible blow to the intensely ambitious thirty-nine-year old New Yorker. Three years after the affair with Lucy, it offered again the prospect of an end to his political career. Thus far his career had followed in the footsteps of his ideal, Theodore Roosevelt. From the state legislature he had become assistant secretary of the navy. He had served as the Democratic vice presidential candidate in 1920, as TR had served as vice president to McKinley in 1896. His next step in 1920 was to work toward governorship of New York. Then the agonizing pain of polio, and its paralysis. He moved—from the impossible question: Why me? that the Biblical Job had asked of God–to a sense, as Frances Perkins put it, "that Divine Providence had intervened to save him from total paralysis, despair, and death."[27] When it became clear that Eleanor and others would stay with her very gifted, very ambitious husband, the paralysis that could have permanently crippled him became an event in his life, without which he might never have become president. From sensing perhaps that he was fated to fail, he now became calmly confident that he could not fail.

True to his parents' aversion to whining, he did not use polio as an excuse to feel sorry for himself. At first he tried to regain his ability to walk. Missy LeHand related a sad story. He was in Warm Springs, Georgia, which he bought for the use of crippled people about 1924. When he was beginning at least to gain better use of his body by swimming in the warm spring water, he decided to make another attempt to walk. He stood up in a room and in the presence of Missy tried to walk unaided across the room. Sweat came out of his face as he concentrated totally on the task. He made two or three steps and gave up. Missy cried. When he stopped, he decided, at least for now, that he would not be able to walk again[28]; and he was evidently deciding that he would not let that disability stop his political career.

FDR's upbringing steered him in the direction of changing the disaster to a challenge. He did not whimper, less from his upbringing than from the interaction between his very powerful will and the engulfing pain. Polio put him in ineluctable, direct contact with exquisite pain and near helplessness. The inescapable pain and his triumph over it made it possible for him to identify with people as human beings—not as a feudal squire, benign in his aid to the long-suffering poor. He now could identify with people as a human being who had himself experienced elemental suffering and was not destroyed by it. Eleanor put it thus: "Anyone who has gone through great suffering is bound to have a greater sympathy and understanding of the problems of mankind."[29] And the polio catastrophe reinforced his liking and his trust in people: Neither his wife nor his mother nor his closest friends, nor his political friends in New York deserted him as he worked his way out of the catastrophe.

His mother wanted him to retire to Hyde Park and become a country squire like his father, but FDR continued his prior course, moving from triumph to triumph. With the support of a newspaperman, Louis Howe (a physically tiny man with enormous vision who had attached himself to FDR when FDR was a young state senator), Eleanor concentrated her efforts not only moving him beyond his polio but also on keeping him from being absorbed by his mother—keeping him politically active. Now Eleanor and Louis worked to keep him at shooting for their ultimate aspiration: his presidency.

Eleanor Roosevelt (and Lucy Mercer)

As a child, probably few people had stronger negative feelings about Eleanor than Eleanor herself. Her mother called her "Granny," in the presence of others, and was very busy bobbing about on the bubbly waters of New York society—and very busy trying to figure out what to do with and about her engaging, errant husband. With these concerns, mother could not or did not pay much mind to her daughter, who was too tall and had too many teeth. She was shipped off as young teenager to a finishing school in London, a school run by a French spinster. Mlle. Souvestre clearly saw the extraordinary emotional-mental gifts of this tall young woman from the distinguished Roosevelt family. She was perhaps even more important in Eleanor's finding herself than Endicott Peobody had been for FDR. She encouraged her to become a leader among her fellow students. Eleanor became the person to whom her fellow students turned for advice and encouragement. They came to admire and even adore her. She was entering her lifetime vocation: building self-confidence in others and helping them to find and realize themselves. Throughout her life, in that kind of service, Eleanor realized herself.

During his first year at Harvard, Franklin met and later proposed marriage to Alice Sohier, a beautiful sixteen-year-old woman. Once when visiting at the home of her family, he said that he intended to go into politics and might some day be president. Somebody asked: "Who else thinks so?" and the Sohier family laughed.[30] It isn't clear whether Alice was impressed with Franklin's political ambitions, but on some occasions she clearly understood another ambition and slapped him—"hard," as she put it—for getting fresh with her.[31]

Alice went abroad and Franklin turned his attention to his distant cousin Eleanor. She had come back from Mlle. Souvestre's London finishing school in the summer of 1902, made her social debut, and entered the closed society of the very rich. Her father was the younger brother of Theodore Roosevelt, who was president of the United States when Franklin was a student at Harvard and the idol of Franklin.[32] TR called her his favorite niece. She was the object of attention of many young men who might want to take advantage of the connection.

Eleanor evidently did not laugh at Franklin's ambition, but she was puzzled that such a very handsome, self-confident young Harvard student would pursue such a plain young woman. He persisted and with his charm convinced her that he loved her. She finally said yes and fell pell-mell in love. She was reassured, we can suppose, that Franklin did not ask for his mother's approval and did not break their secret engagement when redoubtable Sara told her "boy" that he shouldn't be so hasty. This indicator of primary loyalty to Eleanor was like Lincoln's to Mary in the Shields affair. Eleanor was making a decision as politically portentous as the decision of Mary Todd to marry Lincoln—and I'd guess consciously so. She too, like Mary Lincoln, helped to keep her husband's ambition from o'erleaping itself, reminding him not of his divinity but of his humanity and of his well-hidden imperfections.

Eleanor eased her fiancé into contact with people outside the landed gentry that formed his background and hers. During the year 1903-1904, when the Harvard student was in his fourth year and they were first privately and then officially engaged, she took him with her to visit a settlement house in New York where she was working. One of the children was ill at school; Eleanor invited her fiancé to help her take the child home. After helping Eleanor take the girl into the dank, dark, foul-smelling tenement where she lived, he said to Eleanor: "My God, I didn't know anyone lived like that."[33] In 1961, sixteen years after her husband died, Eleanor told a friend that she had planned the whole thing: "I wanted him to see how people lived. And it worked. He saw how people lived, and he never forgot."[34]

Eleanor thus introduced her prospective husband to poor and ordinary people, as Mary Todd—in another mirror image—had introduced her visibly poor, uncouth, and very ordinary prospective husband to high society in Springfield. Lincoln thus looked up the social scale; FDR looked down.

Eleanor and Franklin were married in March 1905, and her uncle, who was starting his second term as president of the United States, gave away the bride. They honeymooned in Europe; he flirted with one woman after another; and then they returned. Like his ideal, TR, but for additional reasons, FDR started law school at Columbia. In New York he was closer to Eleanor as she vigorously pursued both child-bearing and social work among poor people, and closer to his affectionate, domineering mother. Starting in 1906 and running until 1916, they had six pregnancies. While the Lincolns lost two of their four children, the Roosevelts lost only one of their six.

They left New York when Roosevelt was appointed assistant secretary of the navy in 1913, and she moved the site of her social work to Washington. It grew to include helping soldiers and sailors when the United States entered the war in 1917. All these activities she loved. To organize dinners and parties, which she didn't love, in 1914 she hired as secretary a beautiful and dignified twenty-three-year-old woman named Lucy Mercer. Eleanor, who was then thirty-one, began to hear about her husband and Lucy, but in gossip-rife Washington she was too busy to heed the rumors. In the fall of 1918 she read letters Lucy had written her husband and so discovered that the rumors of an affair with Lucy were indeed true. Still in love with her husband, Eleanor now felt so plain and unloved that she reverted to the low level of self-confidence she had before going to Mlle. Souvestre's finishing school.

In America before the First World War, marriage had very strong moral recognition and hypocrisy was an amoral, ill-recognized reality. Eleanor might have gained sympathy for being wronged by her husband but not for "giving him his freedom," as she put it. A divorce would have accomplished little more than destroying the careers of both. And she remembered her beloved father: she had to recognize that he had repeatedly been less faithful to his beautiful wife than Franklin had been to his "plain" wife.

Eleanor felt grievously wronged in the Victorian era when adultery was seldom heard of but often gossiped about, often on a solid factual basis. And she was inhibited by the fact that Victorian correctitude, her promiscuous father, and her own unloving mother made her contain her humiliation. She made herself continue as her husband's collaborator in gradually evermore widespread political concerns. And she evidently slept alone, telling her daughter Anna that sex was a duty one had to put up with in marriage. How much that comment was sour grapes and how much it was implicit recognition of her own shortcomings as a spouse is not known. What is very certain but much less mentioned is that, with all her ego strength, she was also an intensely emotional person. During her long life she had very close and affectionate relationships with several individuals.

The resolution in 1919 of the conflict over Franklin's affair with Lucy was probably the most critical event for what followed: the mutual support of Eleanor for Franklin and of Franklin for Eleanor. She then decided that what she wanted in her life could be most surely achieved if she were her husband's wife: she had in him a solid base that she would not otherwise have had, for doing so much good for so many people. He must then have decided that with her he could indeed do more good as president of the nation if he had her as a redoubtable, reliable source for knowing who needed what help, how much, and where.

Long after the affair was history and after her husband could no longer see Lucy because he was dead, she said she thought the reason he did not walk away from the marriage was that he wanted to continue pursuing his political ambitions. This was certainly part of the picture, but there were other reasons: FDR did not want to be disinherited, he knew his mother was a strong-minded person and might disinherit him, and he knew Eleanor complemented politically his engaging and easy charm with people. And they both had enormous energy in addition to their enormous need for affection.

Eleanor herself had found ways to combine her energy and affection: it was to do good, to help people of poor or distorted lives. If she never really had her mother's love and lost her husband's, at least she could gain the gratitude of the troubled people she helped. She could do this in a very large way if her husband held high public office. Well before the Mercer affair, she knew that he did indeed care about poor people and that she could go further in her chosen career by being his wife rather than becoming a divorced woman.

Many people who admired the strong and often successful domestic programs of the New Deal became what Gore Vidal called himself, "Eleanorites."[35] She got out into the country, seeing people in all walks of life, even visiting a coal mine at one point. During the war this awesome woman, near the age of sixty, climbed through the cramped quarters of a B-17 bomber. In her efforts to realize her desire to help people, she never gave up. During the 1940s she hounded and badgered her husband to keep economic and social reforms from being dissolved when the all out war effort turned her husband's attention to world problems. There were problems that she did not adequately appreciate at first: Nazism was expanding butchery and mechanizing it in Europe, and Japan was doing the same thing in the Pacific and Asia. At times she importuned too much and he would lose his patience, telling her to let him alone.[36] And she found that she could get her husband's goat by making a comparison with her uncle Theodore that was invidious to Franklin. She later said that she had made life a bit too hard for him during the war.

Eleanor, Franklin, et al.

Both Franklin and Eleanor had to have people around them to whom they were closely attached. FDR always had one or more women to whom he was close in ways that he no longer was to Eleanor, after the affair with Lucy. That went on for the rest of his life, if not physically, then at least emotionally. His beloved secretary, Missy LeHand, joined his staff when he was campaigning for vice president in 1920. She was with him when he was recuperating from his polio, on occasional boat trips off the Florida coast, and she lived in the White House up to the time she had a stroke in June 1941.[37] Two months later Lucy Mercer Rutherfurd, his mistress during the First World War, evidently started coming to visit FDR in the White House. FDR's son Elliott believed Missy LeHand was his mistress; his son James believed not.[38] As to that and other relationships that both FDR and ER had, the truth doubtless lies somewhere in between.

It has been said that it's impossible to overestimate the importance of sex in human relations, and that Freud achieved the impossible. I think people are too ready to suppose that if people love each other, they go to bed—or, if they don't, they should. Parents love their children, usually; and the overwhelming majority of them don't sexually abuse them. High-energy people seek out leadership positions, including politics. What is relevant to understanding political leaders is that their energy is truly enormous, and in some cases it finds sexual outlet.[39] It seems to me that the sex life of people in politics is important as an indicator of their promiscuity or loyalty and their willingness to lie and cheat. But it is not directly an indicator of their political effectiveness.

During a long railroad trip across the country in the summer of 1942, FDR asked Eleanor if she would be willing to resume their marriage as it had been before Lucy. She said she'd think about it awhile. She did and in October indirectly told him "no" by responding enthusiastically to his offer that she go abroad to see how the war was going. Eleanor had gone to Europe with him at the end of the First World War and very much wanted to go with him in January 1945 to the Yalta Conference with Churchill and Stalin. FDR took Anna instead.

FDR had very close, affectionate relationships with many male associates, with no indication that the relationships were physical. Louis Howe, the newspaperman who early on apparently wanted to attach himself to a political star, became a close member of the Roosevelt political household. He worked with Roosevelt when he was in the New York state senate in 1911, during the 1920 campaign for vice president; he was with FDR at Campobello when he got polio in 1921; with him during his governorship of New York from 1928-1933; and with him in the White House until he died in 1936. Like others to follow him, Howe became a family intimate.

Many others were for short or extended times very close to FDR. Felix Frankfurter, professor at the Harvard Law School, was a close adviser, before and after he was appointed to the Supreme Court. Particularly in the first term, two protégés of Frankfurter were much in the White House group: two young lawyers who drafted legislation and helped move it through Congress (Ben Cohen and more particularly Tommy Corcoran, inevitably dubbed Frankfurter's two "Hot Dogs"). William O. Douglas, another young lawyer, was another close adviser who became a rather steady visitor to Hyde Park, passenger on the presidential yacht, and poker player—both while Douglas headed the Securities and Exchange Commission and after he was appointed to the Supreme Court.[40] Henry Morgenthau was also a steady poker player, in addition to being secretary of the treasury. After Howe's death and Missy's stroke Harry Hopkins became a live-in adviser to FDR. When he remarried and moved out of the White House, Hopkins was succeeded by Anna, the daughter of FDR and ER. She settled in at the White House, as a comfortable replacement for Missy and Hopkins, for the last year of his life. Hopkins, grievously ill, nonetheless remained very close to the president through the Yalta Conference in January and February 1945. When the conference was over, except for postmortem assessments, Hopkins, now mortally ill, left to go to the Mayo Clinic in Minnesota. FDR, also mortally ill, was more than nettled at Hopkins' early departure, seeming to feel that he was being deserted by a man with whom his affection was reciprocal and who was supposedly no more fragile than The Boss. A longtime crony and adviser, General "Pa" Watson, died aboard the warship on the way home from the Yalta conference. FDR was very, very upset; it was said that Watson's death cast a pall over FDR's remaining two months of life. FDR was very curt in refusing to see Rosenman promptly during the return from Yalta, to draft the report the president would make to Congress. The dauntless adult for awhile was briefly replaced by the spoiled child. Roosevelt always needed people, particularly these people, both to be with him and to help in tasks whose purposes they shared.

Eleanor likewise had a series of friends, working either for her or with her, to whom she was very closely attached. Unlike her husband, she was quite open about herself, so that there is a fuller picture of her inner self than of FDR. Among her many longterm friends were her longtime bodyguard Earl Miller, Lorena Hickcok, and Joe Lash. Whether or not Eleanor had sex with any of these individuals is relevant only as critical evidence that she, like her husband, had an enormous need for affection. She may have realized the strength of the need in both of them when she found out in 1918 about Lucy Mercer.

In any event, FDR's very strong need for affection was a major ingredient of his public relationships with individuals and the public that showed up at rallies, speeches, and along railroad tracks. These interactions tended to be reciprocal. The need for affection could be seen in the ways FDR would warmly greet visitors in and out of his office and in his look for approval and response from audiences at public gatherings. In Eleanor it was evident in her need to see people who needed help: the relationships were mutual. It is somewhat curious that she got it from those who guaranteed to her that she would be appreciated, that they would be grateful to her, even though they could not reciprocally love her. One of the sound bytes of the time was that Eleanor had no time for you unless you had a grievous problem.

Whether she ever in her entire life enjoyed the really deep love that evidently prevailed in her husband's affair with Lucy is still to me very doubtful. If she did not, her strong need for love was probably never fulfilled. She once told Joe Lash, to whom she was very close for years, that only very rarely did two people love each other equally. She seemed to have given up experiencing equal love.

Eleanor and Franklin had started concentrating on their separate but parallel careers almost before their children were born. It is false to say that only their parallel careers kept Eleanor and Franklin together, but the times for being together diminished as the nation moved from domestic to world problems. After his mother's death on September 7, 1941, just three months before Pearl Harbor, there was an empty space in his psyche that Eleanor could have filled but she did not, perhaps by choice of each spouse. Yet she was very touchingly and magnanimously sensitive to her husband, immediately after her redoubtable eighty-six-year-old mother-in-law died.

Eleanor had long since become used to her husband's eager eye. During the war years, she had ample opportunity to observe the mutual attraction between her husband and Crown Princess Martha of Norway, who was welcomed at Hyde Park when she came as an exile to the United States during the German occupation of her homeland. Eleanor was evidently silent about this flirtation. But when her husband died in April 1945 in Warm Springs, she was appalled to learn that Lucy had been with him and that Anna, the daughter to whom she had at last become very close, had arranged several visits for Lucy to the White House.

What she may not have appreciated was that not just she but also her husband had a strong need for love. They both got it from their respective and overlapping publics and from close friends rather than spouse. What's more, perhaps she realized that her children were more closely attached to her husband.[41] Like her own mother and unlike Sara with Franklin, Eleanor left their upbringing to nannies while she pursued satisfying her own needs for love and respect in the slums of New York, the poor people in Washington, young men away from home in military service, and poor people everywhere in the country.

In one of her many frank comments on herself, Eleanor told how being miserable during her pregnancies made her more tolerant of physical ailments. She wrote: "I never let anything physical prevent my doing whatever had to be done. This is hard discipline, and I do not recommend it either as training for those around one or as a means of building character in oneself. What it really does is kill a certain amount of the power of enjoyment. It makes one a stoic, but too much of a thing is as bad as too little, and I think it tends to make you draw away from other people and into yourself."[42]

Whether Abraham Lincoln and Mary Todd Lincoln were oversexed or undersexed, what is of basic political significance is not their libido but the love that each had for the other and that they had for people generally. Without this love—sharply focused between themselves and in diffuse focus onto people generally—Abraham could not have made the great contributions that he did. That is, his success in furthering the process of equalizing people politically was in critical degree the product of his very close bonding to Mary.

It may be that FDR and ER were oversexed, but it seems more likely to me that both were so intensely and broadly emotional that, with or without sexual contact, they always needed to have people around to whom they were passionately attached. Without this love that each of them, in very complementary ways, focused on each other and diffused onto people generally, both Franklin and Eleanor could not have made the great social and political contributions that each did.

If they were to be judged on the basis of their spousal perfection, Lincoln perhaps would be downgraded. He was a faithful but not an unfailingly devoted husband: he enjoyed the legal profession and its members and didn't always come home from litigating on the circuit when he could have. Roosevelt certainy would be downgraded: he was unfailingly an unfaithful husband. His lifelong deviousness was indeed a flaw, and duplicity seems to have become more common in American public life since Roosevelt. But it is hard to fault either Franklin or Eleanor Roosevelt for seeking affection outside their marriage when they got so much respect and so little affection in it.

Intelligence, Empathy, and Comprehension

Intelligence is a term so loosely used that appraisal of the present four may be helped by distinguishing it from some other mental attributes that are relevant here. The commonest use of the term denotes the kind of ability that has been measured for the last century by academic intelligence tests. To avoid increasing definitional muddle, I stick to this commonest usage here. Some well-educated guesses have attributed extremely high intelligence to some unmeasured prominents: Newton, Goethe, John Stuart Mill, and Einstein. Less educated guesses have attributed lesser intelligence to politicians. On the other hand, it is hard to imagine political problems being addressed and dealt with by Newton,[43] Goethe, Einstein, or Pauling. This doesn't mean these people were stupid but that they worked with problems and concepts involving far fewer variables and were judged as involving, if any, few social and political variables. Einstein and Pauling both wanted peace and harmony among the human race. However, neither is remembered for having developed any specific practicable programs that have been adopted by the international community. The skill specialization of intellectual immortals suggests that politicians need more than conventional IQ to gain immortality. The ability of ordinary citizens, of the general public, to distinguish between immortal scientists and immortal politicians suggests that intellectuals need to be more modest in their evaluations of their own work.[44]

Empathy is a mental attribute close to but distinct from conventional IQ. It is defined here as the ability to identify with other individuals, objects, or beliefs. It is distinguishable from the term sympathy by suggesting that empathy puts one individual mentally inside another, whereas sympathy leaves the individuals mentally separate.

Comprehension is a third term. It helps to consider the total range of individual's behavior, because to describe such behavior as being empathetic or intelligent omits the fact that all behavior, all action, of any individual, ranging politically from ordinary citizens to chiefs of state, contains both intellectual and empathetic ingredients. The term comprehension is used here to indicate the ability of individuals to embrace both the intelligence and the empathy aspects of relationships or interactions. It is extended here to denote the ability of people—both ordinary citizens and their leaders—to understand public problems, and to understand themselves and others as citizens of the same communities. By using the term comprehension, we can more easily look at the consistencies and the connections between individuals in a one-to-one relationship (private comprehension) and individuals as members of a public, ranging from neighbors to fellow citizens of a nation (public comprehension).[45] And of course it's a two-way street: if publics, if citizens, are inclined to comprehend but their leaders are not, little progress is made in solving public problems; if leaders comprehend but their citizens do not, progress is similarly inhibited.

Comprehension, particularly in politics, has to be evaluated in the context of time, in the context of the era in which it is examined. If ordinary citizens lack empathy or apply it parochially, that is, in constricted context, they contribute to producing the chaos and disintegration that showed up in the sixteenth century in Europe during the Protestant Reformation and in the twentieth century in newly decolonized nations in Asia and Africa and the Balkans. If people sense but cannot articulate what they want and don't want, the challenge to politicians is to express these wants.

Societies in chaos suffer from a constricted sense of common identity and a failure to appreciate that wants—expectations—tend to be generally shared. If politicians understand what people want and how it can be got, they can do an effective job of verbally articulating these ends and means. More important, they can help people use *nonviolent* political means to achieve realization of community-wide, even species-wide, ends.

Now for a look at the ability of our foursome to comprehend. Lincoln was good enough at teaching himself that, after studying relevant mathematics and its application to surveying, he was able to map much of the land area in central Illinois. He read voraciously both before and after he left home when he was twenty-two: classics, notably the Bible, Shakespeare, and more recent English literature. Robert Burns was one of his favorite poets. The breadth and voracity of his interests stimulated his self-education, and he used them in his chosen occupation. His literary interests were not an escape but a means of understanding and effecting public policy. In his second inaugural address, he expressed in Biblical terms the dialog in his mind between fatalism and voluntary action. The endless anecdotes that he told and retold were an indication of his ability to see connections between seemingly discrete events and between abstractions about events and actual events themselves.[46] This latter is what natural and social scientists are supposed to be particularly good at.

He taught himself law and was admitted to the bar without really serving an apprenticeship. When he served in the Illinois legislature, he taught himself how to draft legislation; he gained a reputation for drafting and was very often called on for this difficult work. He became outstanding in his ability to present and argue cases in court, both orally and in writing. He got to the heart of legal issues and in the courtroom would keep the focus on central issues. In his forties he was one of the most distinguished lawyers in the state. He did not have the quickness or the voracious reading habits of his younger partner, Billy Herndon, but Lincoln almost always prepared the overall argument in his cases and Billy studied precedents in earlier caselaw and garnered evidence for the case at hand.

Perhaps the most renowned case involved his questioning the evidence that was convincing as to the guilt of a client charged with murder. He found that the person who said he had seen the defendant by the light of the moon would have had a hard time doing so, because the almanac showed there was no moon that night.

Less well known are two other cases. One was the McCormick reaper case, which was argued in court in Cincinnati in 1855 and involved big money. Lincoln had come east from Springfield, to serve as sort of associate counsel and had been designated by his client to give the closing argument. Edwin Stanton, who had come west from Pittsburgh to serve as cocounsel, appointed himself head counsel. He ignored Lincoln and took over presentation of the closing argument.[47] Lincoln was very disappointed at the waste of all his work and he was depressed by the insult of Stanton's snubs but he stayed in the courtroom to listen and learn by observing the Eastern attorneys. He understood not only the substance of the reaper case but magnanimously also the underlying rivalries among the lawyers. He comprehended.

Two years later he was the attorney in a case involving a railroad bridge across the mighty Mississippi river. A new and mighty river steamboat had run into one of the newly constructed bridge piers and been badly damaged. The owners of the great boat sued the bridge builders for wrongful, indeed immoral, interference with the free flow of river traffic on the Mississippi. From his knowledge as an old river hand (experienced with the hundreds of miles of river from Illinois down to New Orleans), from his training in surveying, and from his interest in mechanical devices, Lincoln made a brilliant presentation. The case was critical for opening up transportation from east to west and thus for opening up the West to rapid settlement.[48] Victory for the bridge builder overthrew the special protection that had been accorded to river traffic. He won the case and made a lot of money. He had progressed a long way from the young man who understood how to get an oar- and water-powered flatboat, which he had helped to build, over a mill dam at New Salem; he had moved from understanding the physics and geometry of river transport to seeing the long-range public need for railroads. Lincoln explained—perhaps defended—his mind to his partner Billy Herndon by saying it was like a large knife: it did not cut so quickly as a small one, but it cut longer and deeper.[49] Lincoln's comprehension was broader than the big jackknife to which he compared it. He had an ability to understand himself and others. It was the product of probably innate and certainly extraordinary sensitivity to others, that was refined by decades of interactions, starting with everyone from his "angel mother" and his demanding father (who sometimes drank too much but never deserted the family or his very gifted son), to his friends in the town and in the army and in the legislatures in Springfield and Washington. He understood what was involved in these interactions—and often condensed them to anecdotes. He comprehended.

He did this with great political significance when he saw his attack on the 1854 Kansas-Nebraska Act as the platform from which he could launch his national political career. In choosing the issues on which to speak, he constantly looked inside himself. He appraised the kind of society he wanted to be a part of and what kind of society his fellow citizens wanted. He then called for their collaboration with him in maintaining and strengthening it. Lincoln did not just guess right; he did not simply evaluate what would sell politically. Rather, when the time was ripe—when the contest over control of the territories had become the issue on which people were both intensely involved and divided—he comprehended.

His decisive success in the 1858 debates with Stephen Douglas made public his understanding of what he wanted and what others wanted. When he became president in 1861, Lincoln had to move with exceptional care to maintain contact with public opinion and therefore public support. The Congress and the public were able and willing to go only so far. He made progress in the realization of equality, but only to the point of emancipating slaves. The times would not have tolerated establishing full equality—recognition of the intrinsic equal worth—for either black people or women, let alone equalizing the dignity of people who had the most and the least of wealth.

Lincoln's ability to keep basic goals in sight, as he worked from day to day, is reflected in his public writings. They established him as one of the most masterful users of language in public life that has ever lived. When he was first getting underway as a politician at the age of thirty-three, speaking to the Washington Temperance Society in 1842, the substance of his speech was solid but his style was conventional and flowery.[50] At its best, his writing was Biblical, Shakespearean. He had the ability to sense what was fundamental and to say it simply.

At the dedication of the cemetery in November 1863, commemorating the most decisive battle in the war, just four months after it ended, one of the famous orators of the nineteenth century and the former president of Harvard, Edward Everett, gave an address at Gettysburg. He spoke mellifluously, brilliantly, seriously, and scholarly for two hours, to a rather awestruck audience. He was followed by Lincoln, who spoke for a couple of minutes. The audience of some 15,000 gave Everett an enthusiastic and Lincoln a mixed reaction. As Randall put it, "humans cannot always be expected to hail a classic at birth." The day after the ceremony Everett wrote the president: "I should be glad if I could flatter myself that I came as near to the central idea of the occasion in two hours as you did in two minutes."[51] Soon, Everett's learned Gettysburg address was little noted and not long remembered; Lincoln's sometimes raspy tenor voice uttered what in time became known as the Gettysburg Address.

Mary Todd Lincoln was well schooled, and her extensive letter writing, notably after her husband died, makes it hard to deny that she was intelligent. She went to Europe with her son, Tad, where she supposedly used the French she had acquired in the finishing school in Kentucky; and she continued writing to people on both sides of the Atlantic. Her writing is clear and coherent, but it is marked often by an introspection of a sort that was almost the opposite of her husband's: She kept telling about how much she had suffered and how much people she thought loved or at least liked her turned against her. Her son Robert, who helped get her put away for awhile, is a notable example.

She did not have the ability to see herself very well as others saw her and she generally lacked any hint of her husband's self-deprecating humor. She was not notably prejudiced against black people: Their housekeeper in Springfield, for a decade, Mariah Vance, spoke well of her.[52] When her close friend and companion in the White House, Mrs. Keckley, came to New York after the war and couldn't get a room at Mrs. Lincoln's hotel, she and Mrs. Lincoln shared a room in the hotel attic, and when the hotel restaurant refused service to Mrs. Keckley, Mary offered to go with her to a public restaurant. Mrs. Keckley refused. Vance was a freeborn black and Keckley a freed slave. But her views on the Union were not noteworthy. Her strong support of emancipation seem to have been derived from the friendship she established with Senator Sumner, the distinguished Harvard graduate who used her as a bridge to the president in expressing his demands for emancipation—now (that is, in 1862).

Roosevelt's intelligence has been depreciated by many, perhaps more by citing his scholastic record at Harvard and the sound byte that Oliver Wendell Holmes so wittily uttered after Roosevelt visited him shortly after taking office in 1933: "second-class intellect, but first-class temperament." And he had speech writers, whose contribution to his many memorable addresses is hard to separate from his own. Nonetheless, in discussing what should be said with his speech writers, he took the leading role: He decided what was to be said and often just how to say it.[53]

The national and international challenges he faced as president were much more complex than the ones that were critical when he was growing up in rural New York, and these were more complex than the ones Lincoln faced. However, without successful resolution of the problems of Union and slavery in the 1860s, the nation and the country might not have been able to face the more complex issues of Roosevelt's lifetime.

FDR's intellectual ability was like Lincoln's: Both presidents shared the ability to separate out the important and basic from the trivial and superficial; and to express these in ways that people both in and out of academia could understand. Academicians who certainly would have scored higher than he in conventional intelligence and who served in his administration were at times awestruck by FDR's intelligence. They remarked on his extraordinary memory, his ability to understand problems and relate them to one another, and his understanding of people. In his grasp of fundamentals Roosevelt may have been almost as intelligent as Lincoln, but in his ability to express these fundamentals, he was not in the same class with Shakespeare and Lincoln—or even of Churchill. However, he comprehended as well as Lincoln and much better than Churchill. Roosevelt's performance as a student at Harvard College and the two courses he flunked at Columbia University Law School are less worthy of note.

Roosevelt moved well beyond Lincoln toward the realization of equality: The circumstances were different, and to do his job well, he had to deal not with the problems of the mid-nineteenth century but the early twentieth. By the 1930s, not many people were advocating slavery and those who were practicing it did not usually assert that they believed in it as a moral principle. In his first term, from 1933 to 1937, Roosevelt's task was reducing panic and despair and restoring hope. In the process, he began to increase the still-rudimentary power and dignity of ordinary citizens and to diminish the power of great wealth. As his first term ended, he began to move beyond these problems and he more directly articulated the basic problem of greed as it stood in the way of moving further toward equality.

Shortly after he began campaigning for his second term, FDR in his Jefferson Day speech in April 1936 said:

> America a century ago was regarded as an economic unity. But as time went on the country was cut up, bit by bit, into segments. We heard about the problems of particular localities, the problems of particular groups. More and more people put on blinders; they could see only their own individual interests or the single community in which their business was located.... Economists are still trying to find out what it was that hit us back in 1929. I am not a professional economist, but I think I know. What hit us was a decade of debauch, of group selfishness—the sole objective expressed in the thought: "Every man for himself and the devil take the hindmost."

In the last year of his first term, Roosevelt saw greed as a big problem. Nine years later, on the day before he died, FDR was preparing a draft of another Jefferson Day address. He said:

> The once powerful, malignant Nazi state is crumbling. The Japanese war lords are receiving, in their own homeland, the retribution for which they asked when they attacked Pearl Harbor. But the mere conquest of

our enemies is not enough. We must go on to do all in our power to conquer the doubts and the fears, the ignorance and the greed, which made this horror possible.[54]

Near the end of his last term, FDR said greed was still a big problem, and he implied that it continued to impede the process of achieving equality. Eleanor Roosevelt, like Mary Lincoln, did not seem to have the intellectual ability of her husband. Her public writings, notably in her daily news column, *My Day*, were filtered through her secretary and supposedly cleaned up in subsequent editing by the editors. Her private writings, in letters to her family, vary all over the map: some are clearly and logically written, while others were rather breathlessly incoherent: emotionally very communicative but hardly literary masterpieces.[55] She felt that both she and her husband were of ordinary intelligence, on criteria by which she judged her brother Hall (a Phi Beta Kappa at Harvard) to be extraordinary.

But in her sensitivity, her empathy, Eleanor was at least the equal of her husband—at least before polio increased his sensitivity—and at least the equal of her husband in wanting to realize the values they shared: dignity and equality. She got this way in large part because of being rejected and depreciated by her elegant mother, and she did not dissociate her values from her actions. It is rather uproarious to imagine Eleanor Roosevelt working as hard to have an elegant ball as Mary organized in early 1862. Eleanor didn't even care much what she ate and in the White House insisted on keeping as the cook in charge a woman who mandated much of the very nutritious cuisine.

Perhaps the most striking feature of her mind was her ability to face herself and to face others for what they were, as she did her father and her husband—and at last, in autobiographical writing, herself. She has been described as being tough, but perhaps a better phrase is to say that she had enormous mental and moral courage. This was so much stronger than her "intellect" that the latter suffers by comparison. In an ordinary person of average fortitude, her mind would not have seemed so average as it was in this giant among post-Victorian women, so intensely and energetically involved in social and political life. She moved from initial opposition to women's suffrage to being a pioneer in much of women's liberation that came decades after her death.

Both Eleanor and Franklin also comprehended privately. When her redoubtable mother-in-law died at age eighty-six in September 1942, she was touchingly and magnanimously sensitive to her husband. She acted thus despite her continuous rivalry with Sara over her Franklin. Three weeks later Eleanor's dearly beloved brother Hall died at age fifty-one, his liver destroyed by alcohol.[56] When she came to tell her husband, their eldest son James was present and related the scene thus:

> Father struggled to her side and put his arm around her. 'Sit down,' he said, so tenderly I can still hear it. And he sank down beside her and hugged her and kissed her and held her head on his chest.... [Hall's] life had been a disappointment to her and to him, too.... I think it was the waste that hurt her. And she spent her hurt in Father's embrace. It is too bad they were together like that so seldom.[57]

In many manifestations, one fundamental problem has remained the same, before, during, and after the presidencies of both Lincoln and Roosevelt: greed. Forcibly ending slavery helped diminish the greed of the Southern plantationers but it facilitated the greed of post-Civil War entrepreneurs. While condemning the patriarchal, baronial plantation system and the institution of slavery that supported it, some of them saw themselves as successors to plantationers as the nationally dominant political force. Reforms carried out or at least announced in the late nineteenth century and continued into the 1940s helped diminish the greed of not all but many entrepreneurs from the late-nineteenth to the late-twentieth century. But these reforms did not end greed. It still inhibits the inability of citizens and politicians to see that the welfare of particular groups is not the same as the general welfare.

(Meanness and) Magnanimity

Abraham Lincoln without much question has a lower score for small-minded acts than FDR, but both presidents I think were larger-minded than their spouses. It was not characteristic of Lincoln to turn the other cheek but it was very characteristic of him to keep open communication with opponents, even opponents who got angry or condescending. After being pushed aside by Edwin Stanton in the big McCormick case, the deeply depressed Lincoln stayed to learn from watching the case as it moved toward its end without his participation. He dealt successfully with a former governor of New York, William Seward, who as secretary of state mentally appointed himself the effective ruler over Lincoln as a figurehead.[58]

Lincoln generally dealt with generals who were persuaded of their competence and of his incompetence, without alienating them. Most of them had graduated from West Point and some had served in the Mexican War of 1848-49. Even being charitable, they seemed to be saying: how could generals and colonels be less competent for war than an uneducated man whose worst wounds were from mosquito bites in a war against Indians, during which Lincoln had kept his men from savaging a helpless Indian who had wandered into their encampment? One of these generals, a Democrat who began to think of bringing the war to a compromised and successful conclusion as president, was very popular with his troops and the public: General McClellan, in his thirties, was positively brilliant and also very sensitive to the health and welfare of soldiers. Lincoln eventually got rid of him, because he was evidently more concerned with his popularity and with avoiding harm to the troops than with winning. When Congressman Vallandigham from Ohio got more than feistily subversive in his criticism of Lincoln and the war, Lincoln endorsed the army's silencing of Vallandigham but endured his efforts to subvert the war from Canada and when Vallandigham returned to the United States, "freed" him to go beyond enemy lines into the Confederacy. However, Lincoln did let stand the imprisonment of thousands of "subversives" who were imprisoned without trial.[59]

Mary Todd Lincoln had a much less perfect record for magnanimity. On the positive side, she was not put off by his breach of the agreement to marry. Raised in luxury, when she was first married she lived in rooming houses that she could have disdained. She did much of her own housework in their early years. And as noted in her interactions with her black housekeeper, she could be almost simultaneously demanding, capricious, and generous. But when she got really angry, she chased her husband with household weapons (brooms, etc.) Both before marriage and with professional and political colleagues from the 1840s through the mid-1860s, she was a frequent flirt. But she got furious with the wives of his colleagues who flirted with him. She never seemed to understand that the other wives' motives were similar to her own: not simply a desire to get confirmation of her attractiveness but also a desire to associate with power.

Mary's circumstances were indeed extenuating. She had a miserable childhood after her mother died and her father remarried, quite the opposite of Lincoln in his strong support by two successive mothers. Her mother was perhaps jealous of her husband's daughter and was perhaps as self-centered as Eleanor's mother. Mary was left alone for weeks on end, while her husband was making the circuit of the circuit courts in Illinois and making a living as a lawyer. Like Eleanor with her dissolute father and brother, Mary came from a family in which at least some of the members had serious mental disorders, none passing the boundary to insanity. However, she lacked Eleanor's enormous strength and ability to introspect.

She handled the problems of being First Lady quite well: she was a gracious and charming hostess, most of the time. But deeper problems she handled less well. She went to pieces after their very beloved son Willie died in 1862. Understandably, she felt abandoned after her husband's death, when a not very understanding public snorted at her haughty importuning for pity and a pension. When her eldest son and a close legal associate of her husband got her committed to an insane asylum, she was strong enough to get herself out. Her mental resources were just barely adequate to sustain her after her husband's death. She could not freely say, as Jackie Kennedy did after also losing her promiscuous husband as they sat side by side, that she had maintained her sanity through the challenges of her chaste husband's assassination.

Roosevelt was usually but not always so large-minded as Lincoln. Perhaps the little boy who almost always had his way got mad when he didn't in the White House. He had to win, most of the time, in poker, even if he had to cheat.[60] He had to catch the biggest or the only fish. He had to monopolize the conversation, or at least control it. But in all dealings and on all occasions, he had, like his cousin Teddy,[61] to be the center of attention. Only at the Yalta conference, a few weeks before he died, did his associates feel they had to keep the conversation going.

He got vindictive with some—though by no means all—of his critics. He got angry with the sometimes haughty, even patronizing criticism from Henry Luce and his *Time* magazine. He handled that particular newsman worse than Lincoln had handled Horace Greeley. Roosevelt refused Luce permission to visit the Pacific theater during the war. His differences with Sewell Avery, the president of Montgomery Ward, the giant mail order house, also became small. Avery refused to obey laws relating to union elections in the big mail order house. During the war, the physical plant was taken for the war effort; Avery was physically removed from his office—dramatically sitting in his chair as soldiers carried him out. On the other hand, FDR avoided clashing with Henry Ford, who disliked not only unions but also the president. The clash being avoided, Ford established an aircraft plant that did a speedy and superb job of producing B-24s. These big bombers came off the assembly line faster than one per hour, and the quality was generally better than on the same aircraft made by Convair, its original designer. I doubt that Luce and Avery could get any higher marks for magnanimity than FDR on their differences over principle and over presidential executive power, but for the nonce, FDR did not heed his larger responsibility to help the country win the war.

Far more significant of his limited vision: Roosevelt seemed to have lost his cool when it came to dealing with people of Japanese birth and ancestry who lived in the Western states. By executive order, he put them all in detention camps, without any formal charge for anything more felonious than being ethnically Japanese. He did not put Japanese in Hawaii in camps, even though the single major strike by Japan against the United States was in Hawaii. Japanese in the Western states numbered about 100,000 (mainly in California, Oregon, and Washington) out of a population of a bit less than 10 million in these three states. While the portion of the population detained without trial in the Civil War and in the Second World War was roughly the same, the threat to the war effort was far greater among the detains in the former than in the latter war. No ocean separated the Unionists from the Confederates. Aside from anger, the justification for this contradiction is a rather strange one: A very small fraction of the population could be accommodated in camps, but it was not practical to imprison, conservatively estimated, more than 100,000—a fourth of Hawaii's population of 423,000. Not only was FDR angry: Perhaps most citizens on the West Coast exploded into anger against Japanese.[62]

At war's end, hostility persisted in the West, even toward Japanese Americans who had served in combat for the United States. Roosevelt seemed to show more hostility to Japanese in the Pacific war than did MacArthur, the general in charge of fighting that half of the war.[63] Eleanor began to demand that her husband do something to alleviate the conditions of Japanese in the camps.

Eleanor Roosevelt by legend at least seems to have been as free of malice as Lincoln. Not quite so. When American flyers were shot down over Saudi Arabia and sometimes allowed to die by neglect or made to die by butchery, Eleanor suggested that Saudi Arabia be carpet bombed. This would have been a bit like carpet bombing the Australian outback, because Saudi Arabia was mostly desert. Perhaps she could have pleaded geographical ignorance. FDR explained the situation.

On another matter, she couldn't plead ignorance. Theodore Roosevelt, her uncle and his remote cousin, was FDR's model from before their relationship began. During the war, it was evidently already becoming clear to Eleanor that her husband had risen in stature above her uncle. Even before the war, Eleanor made comparisons with TR's character that teased and angered her husband.[64] This was Eleanor at her worst and her infrequent needlesomeness. After her husband's death, which Lucy and not she had attended in Warm Springs, Eleanor sent to Lucy the portrait of FDR that was painted by Elizabeth Shoumatoff, a friend of Lucy's. The somber and quite humorless partner was much less inclined to pettiness than her husband occasionally was. In this she was more like Lincoln than her husband was.

How Lincoln and Roosevelt managed their mix of intelligence and empathy was an important factor in their ability to endure the incessant demands of high office in their respective times. Neither Lincoln nor Roosevelt ever fundamentally violated their belief that the publics that had put them in office were higher authority than their two elected presidents.

Both Lincoln and Roosevelt respected both the public and the democratic process. Both had opportunities to seize power, to override the conflicts within the country by issuing decrees and orders that would have destroyed the process of governing constitutionally. But Lincoln got his cabinet members to sign a document he would not let them read, promising to resign if he lost the 1864 election. Lincoln was frequently charged with being a tyrant; so was FDR. Lincoln deprived thousands of slaveowners in the South of billions of dollars' worth of property—slaves—without due process of law. But, aside from the thirteen thousand people detained without being charged with sedition, Lincoln abided generally by constitutional restrictions.

Roosevelt's strong actions were similarly limited. In 1942, farm prices were rising rapidly and wages were generally frozen. Fearing reactions at home in an election year, Congress refused to act to contain the rapid rise of prices that affected everyone: food. FDR sent a message to Congress, saying that if Congress didn't act, he would act by executive order. Congress promptly passed the requested legislation. That is probably as close as FDR came to acting in a manner that was questionably constitutional—except for the detention of about a hundred thousand people, whose crime was having Japanese ancestors. He showed more sympathy later in the war, when Eleanor brought the question of detention to his attention.

When he lost the fight to pack the Supreme Court at the start of his second term and after the massive support he had won in the 1936 election, he abided by the decision. There would have been a big fight if he had not, but if he hadn't accepted the decision of Congress, he might have won. His contemporary Huey Long, nominally a Senator from Louisiana in Washington but actually dictator of the state of Louisiana, repeatedly violated constitutional practices, and he generally succeeded until he was assassinated. FDR could have taken more liberties with unconstitutional or unlawful acts than he did. He probably adhered more closely to constitution and laws than did Lincoln.

The Unconscious Minds of the Two Presidents

When he was thirty-three and beginning his rise as a politician and a lawyer, in 1842 Lincoln addressed the Washington Temperance Society. Himself really abstemious, he expressed his abhorrence of heavy drinking but said that "if we take habitual drunkards as a class, their heads and their hearts will bear an advantageous comparison with those of any other class." He advocated "the temperance revolution," saying that it is a noble ally. . . to the cause of political freedom [when] every son of earth shall drink in rich fruition the sorrow quenching draughts of perfect liberty. Happy day, when, all appetites controlled, all passions subdued, all matters subjected, mind, all conquering mind, shall live and move the monarch of the world. Glorious consummation! Reign of Reason, all hail![65] Two decades later, after he had matured as the war president, Lincoln might have put it more succinctly: When people's minds get control of their appetites, they will be free. They will have freed themselves.

His optimistic view of the power of mind diminished as Lincoln saw more of the frail efficacy of human endeavor, notably after he and his fellow citizens entered and immersed themselves in civil war. In March 1865, in his second inaugural, when the war had almost ended and he was a month away from assassination, he expressed a more seasoned, less optimistic view of the power of mind and of people: "Fondly do we hope—fervently do we pray—that this mighty scourge of war may speedily pass away. Yet, if God wills that it continue, until all the wealth piled by the bond-man's two hundred and fifty years of unrequited toil shall be sunk, and until every drop of blood drawn by the lash, shall be paid by another drawn with the sword, so still it must be said 'the judgments of the Lord are true and righteous altogether."

Lincoln established in his mind a dynamic equilibrium between fatalism and refusal to accept fate. He evidently reconciled these two opposing forces by believing that there was no arbitrary fate, no arbitrary determination that human beings must live, suffer, and die without purpose, without goals. In the Temperance Union speech he was—to put it in more contemporary academic usage—saying that the universe and people are governed by natural law, which, if discovered, can improve the ability of human beings to control events and control themselves. They can free themselves if they discover their own nature.

Twenty-three years later, he was less optimistic but still believed that if mind discovered natural law or divine will, progress could be made, not just in diminishing evil and suffering but in relieving pain and realizing "perfect liberty." That is, Lincoln's belief in acting—in doing something—was founded on the belief that acting could make a difference. Life was not simply or ever just a matter of engaging in action that inevitably is futile: not a Sisyphus perpetually moving the huge rock up the hill, only to have it roll down again. Acting was not all and it did not always accomplish its intended goals, but it was the means of improving human circumstances, of gradually realizing human fulfillment.

Franklin Roosevelt's basic orientation was similar but became established when he was a little older—thirty-nine in comparison with Lincoln's age thirty-three when he spoke to the Temperance Society. The influences that shaped Roosevelt's unconscious mind took very different form from those that shaped Lincoln's. FDR's parents both indulged and disciplined him. His affair with Lucy and Eleanor's reaction to it and the terrible trauma of polio strengthened him greatly. So did the continuous association with intimate friends, associates, and an affectionate, enthusiastic public. He reciprocated this affection and highly valued its contribution to his personal and political success. In his mind, as in Lincoln's, a way of living and acting got established: he accepted "fate" but acted vigorously within its limits. Like Lincoln, Roosevelt was not sure he had discovered what his own fate and mankind's were but he was determined to do what was possible. As he said, early in his presidency: "The country needs and, unless I mistake its temper, the country demands bold, persistent experimentation. It is common sense to take a method and try it. If it fails, admit it frankly and try another. But above all, try something."

As events turned out his proposal was not really Sisyphian: some of the rocks he pushed up the hill did not roll back down.

Melancholy and Euphoria

In one aspect of their temperament Lincoln and Roosevelt were as different as black and white. Lincoln was deeply melancholy. People who saw him when he was not aware of being observed said there was a deep sadness in his face that disappeared as soon as he put on the mask he wore in public. Roosevelt on the other hand, even as a child, was perpetually optimistic. As an adult, he was terribly depressed in the few excruciating and uncertain days after polio struck him, but he quickly recovered his optimism, and he retained it, up to the day he was preparing his Jefferson Day speech, the day before he died. These differences make it evident that there is a broad range of behavior that we can consider normal, before judging that a person has lost touch with reality. Lincoln was not far from being a fatefully inert failure, yet in reality he was a splendid triumph. Roosevelt was not far from being hysterically out of touch, when he supposed that badly crippling polio need not end his political career—less than a year after he was the vice presidential candidate of the Democratic party when it was defeated in the 1920 election. Yet Roosevelt, too, was a splendid triumph.

The challenges facing Lincoln and the nation in 1861 are perhaps well enough known in the perspective of close to 140 years and need not be further reviewed. However, it is well to stress that it was a most critical challenge. It could have been a lost cause and if it had, the history of the whole world would have to live with the reality of a president and a nation that proved popularly responsible, democratic government was not possible in any large and diverse nation. Lincoln said as much, majestically, in the Gettysburg Address. Nations—peoples—in the century following the American Civil War would not have had the proof that progress toward democracy can indeed be made.

Roosevelt had the success of Lincoln and his fellow citizens to build on, and things had got out of whack in the 1920s as they had in the 1850s. The economy was in collapse and the national community was splintering. Greed was widespread. Prestigeful groups demanded that they continue controlling the economy and the polity. And views of right and wrong were increasingly strident and inflexible. FDR felt confident enough of his basic values, derived from his conventional Protestant Christianity, and of his means, the Democratic party, not to be bothered by ideologues who could point out the exact route from here to Utopia. As James MacGregor Burns precociously put it, just eleven years after Roosevelt's death: "So sure was he of the rightness of his aims that he was willing to use Machiavellian means; and his moral certainties made him all the more effective in the struggle. To the idealists who cautioned him he responded again and again that gaining power—winning elections—was the first, indispensable task."[66]

Because a strong and for a time unified nation had resulted from the Civil War, FDR could face the awesomely frightening threat from huge and powerful economies under the control of demagogic dictatorship in Germany and military dictatorship in Japan. He had to get his fellow citizens to face up to this world crisis, right after making substantial but only limited progress in helping the nation knit itself together after the pell-mell and greedy pursuit of wealth and power.

FDR was not unique by any criteria in seeing the threat of fascism in Europe and militarism in the Orient. He was sympathetic to the liberal and radical Loyalist government in Spain when the Spanish army under Franco began its successful revolt. But he resisted the demands of people who saw the connection between fascism in Spain and Nazism in Germany: He said he could not risk losing the Catholic vote by publicly opposing the Franco rebellion, which had a devout, conventionally Catholic base in a nation split between the Catholic majority and the atheistic anarchist minority that supported the elected government.[67]

What was so striking in Roosevelt's government was like Lincoln's: the ability to keep in mind both the rather small things (like lending old destroyers to England, in order to beat the submarine blockade) and the very large things (like keeping his own focus on the threat of war and the threat of loss of New Deal domestic reforms if the United States were to enter the war—and, above all, the danger of losing touch with what the public would support). At the same time that he was keeping such big and small things under control and showing his ability to distinguish between them, he kept assessing the ability of the public to come to an understanding of the big things. He lied, he bamboozled with his verbal skills (saying England would pay for the old destroyers after the war!), and he sometimes deviously negotiated (calling amendment of the neutrality act an increase in neutrality). But he led the nation toward facing its commitments, miraculously without losing the basic confidence of most of the public. It was a brilliant case of comprehension.

The Accomplishments of the Two Pairs

What both presidents and their administrations accomplished was to extend the public sense that problems of equalizing opportunity can be successfully addressed. Their wives helped indispensably, Mary Todd Lincoln mostly by her close personal support of her husband, and Eleanor Roosevelt mostly by direct action on her own and pressure on her husband to effect policies to help establish greater equality. Lincoln's administration kept the American society from regressing to feudalized hierarchy; Roosevelt's empowered people to the point where they no longer had to rely on the largesse of those who get the most of what there is to get.

In short, like Lincoln, Roosevelt dignified people. In the South he reversed the trend of the landed aristocracy of slaveowners to disguise slavery in the system of sharecropping, to tolerate violence against blacks through lynchings, and to degrade them through segregation. He reversed the trend in the South toward moneyed aristocracy and reversed the trend in the North of big entrepreneurs to monopolize dignity and power. In the North he recognized and welcomed the demands of poor people for dignity and power in many ways: social security and the right of employees to organize and bargain collectively with employers being only two.

Both presidents saw the limits to which they could push or pull people. Lincoln told a senator who warned him not to move too fast: "I shall go just as fast and only as fast as I think I am right and the people are ready for the step".[68] In 1862 without collapsing he absorbed criticisms of abolitionists that he could not make up his mind to emancipate and of generals that he was too stupid to let them win the war and stupid enough to try to run it himself. He had the self-confidence to trust his own reading of what the public would do and when it would do so.

Liberals in the 1930s wanted more rapid progress; conservatives wanted much slower progress. To the frustration and vexation of both, FDR saw the limits to which he could push the public toward domestic reform and toward realizing its world responsibilities. In the 1930s, public reluctance to get internationally involved was hidden under the thin veneer of having failed to make the world safe for democracy once and not being fooled into trying to do it again. In 1937 FDR proposed quarantining the aggressor. The speech drew much very hostile reaction but it did direct public attention to what was developing in Europe. In 1940, on the day Italy entered the war against France, just after it had undergone its Blitzkrieg defeat by Germany, FDR declared that "the hand that held the dagger has struck it into the back of its neighbor."[69] The speech got a mixed reaction in the United States, and Roosevelt avoided moving as fast toward war preparation as he wanted to. He remembered that Wilson failed to get the American public to face its international responsibilities after the 1918 armistice. He remembered that one reason Wilson failed was that he lectured the American public, as though they were in one of his college classes. And he remembered that another reason was that Wilson was too far ahead. Stimson, a Republican who became FDR's secretary of war in 1940, got impatient at the slow pace with which Roosevelt was facing up to Nazi, Fascist, and Japanese aggression. FDR, like Lincoln, had the courage to rely on his own judgment as to what was politically possible. In the middle of the war, Roosevelt announced the policy of unconditional surrender of both Germany and Japan, without agreement on that policy with Churchill. He remembered the failure of a mere armistice—a weapons still-stand—in 1918.

Citizenries

One of the major deficiencies in writing about great political figures is a lack of both consideration and appreciation of the role of the citizens who have taken part in the sometimes superhuman efforts to accomplish political ends. When leaders and publics are resonant, there is wider latitude for leaders to act, whether or not the leaders are inclined to obey institutions making them responsible for their actions. This resonance is something deeper than democratic institutions, which make it easier for leaders to find resonance and made it harder for them to become dictators. We need neither damn nor praise the actions of France during the period when Napoleon rode astride the white horse of liberal revolution and made it imperialist. The French public, by and large, followed him not only in his wars with Western and Central European nations but also when the nation backed his attempt to conquer Russia. The German public similarly welcomed Hitler's successful efforts to increase economic and social opportunities of people degraded by a heavily hierarchized social system and an ossified economic system. And the German public followed, with passive or active enthusiasm, the invasion of Russia—until the more than decisive defeat at Stalingrad.

People in the Soviet Union were both coerced and at times didn't need coercion to support or at least to obey Stalin. During the war he said the people were not fighting for the system but for the land. They followed Stalin, nonetheless, and thereby not only thrust back the German invasion, as French people followed Napoleon in the French invasion a century earlier. They also thereby willy-nilly kept him in power until his death—and the system in power—for another generation, another three decades, after his death.

Perhaps most of their identification with ordinary people came naturally to both Lincoln and Roosevelt. In Lincoln's case nurturance of his nature was easy: he was raised among ordinary pioneering farmers, perhaps most of them illiterate in his parent's generation. These people rather intimately shared with one another life and death, triumph and tragedy. In Roosevelt's case it was not so easy. He had acted on his unavoidably rather abstract sympathy with the Boers in South Africa while he was a student at Groton and then Harvard,[70] as they were brutally suppressed in South Africa—and as Winston Churchill was participating in the suppression. But it took Eleanor to elicit his natural empathy to ordinary people by unavoidably exposing him to slum poverty in New York, and his polio to put him in contact with inescapable suffering.

These experiences would have gone for naught, in both presidencies, but for the resonance of what Lincoln and Roosevelt wanted to do and what the publics wanted to do. What in normal times would have been superhuman efforts ultimately were made by the publics in both eras.

It is not hard to see why Lincoln and Roosevelt merit their positions as leaders far above Napoleon, Hitler, and Stalin. These two American presidents identified with American citizens as human beings and not just as Americans.[71] People sensed this identification and responded to it, with superhuman efforts that were categorically indispensable to the great achievements in their times.

The public that supported Lincoln generally believed very strongly that he and they were created equal. The public was in that time willing to go to the point where slavery was ended and the Union preserved. They also welcomed the improvement in equalizing their opportunities for enrichment and self-fulfillment that were a product of a defeat of the threatened permanent establishment of a neofeudal class of landowners whose ownership of human beings was necessary to their endurance.

Roosevelt and the public that supported his domestic and international actions did so because of his genuine identification of people denied opportunity and nations denied self-rule as victims of German and Japanese imperialism. They were willing to go to the point of helping establish institutions that diminished some, though hardly all, of the abuses of a free-enterprise economic system. And—in contrast to the public consensus at the end of the First World War, which had not at all made the world safe for democracy—the American public supported commitment of their country and to some degree of themselves to share responsibility with people in other nations, in the never-ending pursuit of universal dignity, of recognition of the inherent worth of each individual human being. Without the collaboration of ordinary citizens in Lincoln's time and Roosevelt's, the United States and the world would not have made the progress they have toward further realization of universal ideals. Leaders and followers are as necessary to each other as are spouses to fruitful marriages. And progress toward equality makes greater leaps forward in both kinds of pairings when those involved comprehend.

Politicizing Dignity and Equality

As I noted at the outset, the simple moral principle of human dignity and equality goes back to the teachings of religious leaders who were active a thousand or two thousand years ago. This is not to say that they or their followers always practiced it or politicized it. Only in the modern era, starting with the widespread exchange of goods and with the sixteenth-century Protestant Reformation did the principle get associated with political life. It got more overtly politicized in the eighteenth century, during the American and French revolutions.

Two of the biggest trials of political equality occurred during the administrations of Lincoln and Roosevelt. These two presidents did more to advance the never-ending process of realizing dignity and equality than did any others since the Founding Fathers. They did their work in an age when advancement toward equality required political assistance. Eventually the achievement of equal dignity may be so universal that it no longer requires any action by governments, but that time is not yet here. In accepting the nomination of the Democratic party convention for his reelection in 1936, Roosevelt told his view of the basic power problem in the country:

> It was natural and perhaps human that the privileged princes of these new economic dynasties, thirsting for power, reached out for control over government itself. They created a new despotism and wrapped it in the robes of legal sanction. . . . Private enterprise became too private. It became privileged enterprise, not free enterprise. . . . Liberty requires opportunity to make a living—a living decent according to the standard of the time, a living which gives man not only enough to live by, but something to live for.

In his 1942 State of the Union message, FDR voiced his belief in what is here called equal moral dignity: "We are fighting, as our forefathers have fought, to uphold the doctrine that all men are equal in the sight of God."[72] At the end of the 1936 speech in which he accepted the Democratic Party's nomination for a second term, FDR referred back to half a millennium, to the fourteenth-century author of the Divine Comedy. He said: "Governments can err—Presidents do make mistakes, but the immortal Dante tells us that divine justice weighs the sins of the cold-blooded and the sins of the warm-hearted on different scales."

Claiming no special competence to invoke divine authority, I can't say whether Dante is right. But it does seem clear that human beings generally do judge differently the faults of the warm-hearted and the cold-hearted. They do this on impulse, without a second thought, when their friends and family err[73]; they also, usually after more thought, judge public figures the same way. Lincoln and Roosevelt both acted on their values, at whose core was their real affection for and identification, not with the abstract masses but with real ordinary people. Perhaps it is sensing this that fuels our continued efforts to understand these two very gigantic, very human beings.

ENDNOTES

1. In evaluating political leaders, criteria for ranking are harder to come by than in ranking great baseball players. Even in the latter exercise, too often it seems a matter of taste, about which there can be no dispute. (Was Babe Ruth greater than Henry Aaron?) Nevertheless, starting with James David Barber's typology of U.S. presidents, William D. Pederson has made real progress in establishing criteria that can be quantified and applied to leaders (e.g., William D. Pederson and Kenneth G. Kuriger, Jr., "A Test of Jimmy Carter's Character," in *The Presidency and Domestic Policies of Jimmy Carter*, ed. Herbert D. Rosenbaum and Alexej Ugrinsky (Westport, CT: Greenwood, 1994), 243-57). Neither being angelic nor believing any other human beings (including chiefs of state) are angels, in this chapter I happily venture a comparison of two very great political leaders and leave further evaluation open.

2. Aristotle, *Politics* (London, 1932), 570-71. Aristotle evidently did not mean a polity in which there were people of distinct and different status—alike in having equal value but not equal property, etc. He did not have to wrestle with the problem of equality in modern politics in which there are firmly established differences in status, like that between employers and employees, skilled and unskilled workers, and thousands of different occupations.

3. William Herndon and Jesse Weik, *Herndon's Life of Lincoln* (Greenwich, CT: Fawcett, 1961), 95.

4. Lincoln thought his mother Nancy Hanks was illegitimate; if so, Nancy's father deserted her mother. Whether or not Thomas Lincoln thought his first wife Nancy was illegitimate, he accepted into his crowded household Dennis Hanks, his nephew and congenial friend of cousin Abraham. Dennis was an acknowledged illegitimate and was raised by Lincoln's father and stepmother after Nancy Hanks Lincoln died.

5. One of Lincoln's biographers, Benjamin Pratt Thomas, *Abraham Lincoln* (New York: Knopf, 1952), 12, says that Lincoln called his stepmother, Sarah Bush Johnston Lincoln, his "angel mother." A new biography, David Herbert Donald, *Lincoln* (New York: Simon and Schuster, 1995), 23, says he called his natural mother, Nancy Hanks Lincoln, his "angel mother." It seems more likely that both authors are right than that one or the other is wrong.

6. He was acting like Senator Wayne Morse, who in 1964 was one of two senators who opposed the Gulf of Tonkin Resolution, which ratified the hasty, highly charged and popular American commitment to fight Communism halfway around the world in Vietnam. Morse was defeated when he ran for reelection four years later.

7. In this position Mary Todd Lincoln was acting not like the First Lady, whom so many people then and later condemned as an arriviste and spendthrift snob. She was acting like Sumner and a few million other citizens: she saw slaves as human beings even though they were not frequent or distinguished guests at the White House.

8. Stephen B. Oates, *With Malice Toward None. The Life of Abraham Lincoln*. (New York: New American Library, 1977), 17-21.

9. Carl Sandburg, 113.

10. Franklin Roosevelt's lover, Lucy Mercer Rutherfurd, destroyed the letters he wrote her, without this causing biographers to suppose that nothing much was there because there are no corroborating letters. Lyndon Johnson's lover, Alice Glass, destroyed her letters from him, even though it would be hard to suggest that they didn't have a long affair because there were no corroborating letters. FDR was deeply in love with Lucy and Lyndon with Alice (Robert A. Caro, *The Path to Power*, chapter 25 (New York: Knopf, 1982). It seems likely that the two presidents revealed much about themselves to their beloved lovers; it is a great loss because, except in LBJ's interviews with Doris Kearns Goodwin's biography of Lyndon Johnson, *Lyndon Johnson and the American Dream* (New York: Harper, 1976), neither president was very open about his inner self.

11. Stephen B. Oates, *With Malice Toward None* (New York: New American Library, 1977), 24-25.

12. Justin G. Turner and Linda L. Turner, *Mary Todd Lincoln* (New York: Knopf, 1972), 4-5.

13. Ibid., 35.

14. Stuart had been elected to Congress in a contest with Stephen A. Douglas in 1838, Oates, *With Malice Toward None* (New York: New American Library, 1977), 53.

15. Roy P. Basler, *Abraham Lincoln* (Cleveland: World Publishing, 1946), 115.

16. It wasn't until much after the event that historians found documentary evidence of who wrote which letters.

17. Eight months after Lincoln was shot, Mary wrote a friend: "My husband was always so ashamed of it that months before our marriage we mutually agreed never to speak of it ourselves." Later she wrote of its coming up in a White House reception, "A general visiting the White House said playfully to my husband," 'Mr. President, is it true . . . that you once went out to fight a duel and all for the sake of the lady by your side?'" Mr. Lincoln with a flushed face replied, 'I do not deny it, but if you desire my friendship, you will never mention it again.'" Justin G. Turner and Linda L. Turner, *Mary Todd Lincoln* (New York: Knopf, 1972), 295 and 299.

18. Ibid., 40.

19. Lloyd Ostendorf and Walter Olesky, eds., *Lincoln Unknown Private Life* (Mamaronek: Hastings House, 1995).

20. Much of the depreciation of Mary's role in the life of Lincoln traces back to the dislike of William Herndon, Lincoln's law partner for more than a decade, for Mary Todd Lincoln. It was a reciprocal dislike; she would not ever let Herndon set foot in their house–she said because he was slovenly and drank. But she may also have been a bit offended at Herndon's statement that Ann Rutledge was the only true and the perpetual love of Lincoln.

21. Justin G. Turner and Linda L. Turner, *Mary Todd Lincoln* (New York: Knopf, 1972), 122.

22. This sequence of Mary's mental breakdown, threat of confinement, and then recovery was repeated after Lincoln's death. After their eldest son Robert pursued in a law court the declaration of insanity that was necessary to put her away, she was confined. And she did then go out and did keep herself sufficiently under control to avoid later confinement.

23. Long after her husband was killed as he sat beside her in November 1963, Jackie Kennedy said of herself that she was very proud that she had retained her dignity. Mary almost did not. Ibid., 124.

24. Geoffrey C. Ward, *Before the Trumpet* (New York: Smithmark, 1985), 128.

25. Ibid., 141.

26. Ibid., 239.

27. Frances Perkins, *The Roosevelt I Knew* (New York: Harper, 1964), 29.

28. During his third term, during the war, a White House visitor and doubtless a charlatan, told FDR how he could walk again. He gave the visitor's recipe a try. It didn't work, but Roosevelt with characteristic optimism, said he'd wiggled one toe.

29. Ted Morgan, *FDR: A Biography* (New York: Simon and Schuster, 1985), 259.

30. Geoffrey C. Ward, *Before the Trumpet* (New York: Smithmark, 1985), 128.

31. Ibid., 253.

32. He had got a scoop when on the Crimson staff from conversation with TR, and he talked his way out of TR's angry reaction at the political confidence FDR had violated.

33. Ibid., 319.

34. Ibid., 319n.

35. Gore Vidal, "Love on the Hudson," *New York Review of Books* (May 11, 1995).

36. At the cocktail hour, after a hard's days work, FDR's practice was not to discuss business. One afternoon in early 1944, Eleanor handed Franklin a pile of papers and said she wanted to talk them over. FDR blew up, grabbed the stack and tossed it to Anna, saying: "Sis, you handle these tomorrow morning." Doris Kearns Goodwin, *No Ordinary Time* (New York: Simon and Schuster, 1984), 504.

37. She never got back to work in the White House and died in July 1944, Ibid., 534-35.

38. Raymond Moley, an early close adviser to the president, believed the FDR-LeHand relationship was not sexual, Geoffrey C. Ward, *A First-Class Temperament* (New York: Harper and Row, 1984), 713-714.

39. Catherine the Great in Russia was notoriously energetic in bed. She would wear out one sex partner after another, rewarding them in some cases with enormous tracts of land and the serfs who were attached to it. One of her favorites, for his twenty-two months of service, was rewarded inter alia with a palace, 100,000 rubles, various gifts, and 7,000 "souls" (serfs). Voltaire called her "a benefactress of the human race" and a "saint." Nonetheless, she was a great ruler. Thomas G. Masaryk, *The Spirit of Russia* (London: Allen and Unwin, 1919), 71; 79n.

40. In December 1942, a big dinner was set in honor of George Norris, the Republican senator from Nebraska who had worked courageously for much liberal legislation and for establishment of the Tennessee Valley Authority. He was defeated in 1942 in his campaign for reelection. Douglas was already on the Court and planned to attend the dinner. A call came through, indirectly from the White House, that a poker game was called for the same evening as the Norris dinner. Douglas canceled his appearance at the Norris dinner. Otis L. Graham, Jr., and M. G. Wander,

eds., *Franklin Roosevelt* (Boston: G. K. Hall, 1985), 295-97; William O. Douglas, *Go East Young Man* (New York: Random House, 1974), 330.

41. Similarly, there was evidently a closer bond between the Kennedy children and their promiscuous father, Joe, than there was between them and their mother Rose. Goodwin reported that when Joe Kennedy was on a trip, he would sometimes ask that he be supplied with a woman when he landed at a particular city and one or another of his children would arrange it.

42. Eleanor Roosevelt, *The Autobiography* (Boston: G. K. Hall, 1984), 56.

43. Newton did have success in politics as it related to his scientific activities. He served for twenty years as head of the most influential scientific organization in England, the Royal Academy. That job was intensely involved in politics of the academic sort. But no one that I know of has suggested that he would have been good at solving some of the major political problems of the late seventeenth- and early eighteenth- century England. Some of these were relationships between the Church of England, Protestants and Catholics; relationships between England and Scotland; territorial rivalries between England, France, Spain, and the Netherlands; dynastic rivalries for the English crown that ended when the Stuarts were succeeded by the Hanoverians; and the chronic party rivalries between Whigs and Tories. All of these problems were intertwined with each other.

44. Two categories of philosophical intellectuals are Realists, of whom Plato is the best known, and Nominalists, of whom Aristotle is perhaps the best known. Realists believe that characteristics of various objects that they share in common are the real characteristics; Nominalists believe that these common characteristics exist only in the mind and therefore are items in the abstract world. In this essay, I regard both as abstractors. Without abstraction, no phenomena may be analyzed or interpreted in any general way. Intellectuals tend to think they are better at seeing reality than are politicians, without adequate proof that they are. So in suggesting that intellectuals be more modest, I am suggesting that they have common problems in interpreting phenomena outside their own minds. There is no point, at least in this footnote, to say that Platonists or Realists are better at making realistic abstractions—i.e., ones that more truly represent reality outside their minds—than are Aristotelians or Nominalists. The fabled tree may or may not have actually fallen in the forest when no one heard or saw it. The forces in the universe may or may not have been operating before nuclear scientists made theories about these forces. In any event, we can reasonably conclude that Realists, Nominalists, and every other person on earth cannot be definitively right and holistic, in any mental representation of phenomena outside the mind.

45. Some recent writers—notably Howard Gardner (1985) and Daniel Goleman (1995)—have reminded us that individuals who can memorize lists of stock market

quotations or utter page-long passages of immortal poetry or prose, or understand abstractions of a logical, mathematical or philosophical sort may be highly intelligent. But they may be emotionally obtuse or insensitive. Howard Gardner, a psychologist who is himself intelligent and sensitive, has explored the relationship between intelligence as measured by tests that come up with an intelligence quotient and measures involving individuals' "access to [their] own feeling life" and their "ability to notice and make distinctions among other individuals." He does not depreciate what is conventionally called intelligence, as it is manifest among intellectuals and ordinary mortals. But he emphasizes that what he calls "the personal intelligences" are distinct and that they are enormously important. Deriving much of his work from Gardner, Goleman in 1995 said much the same thing, Howard Gardner, *Frame of Mind* (New York: Basic Books, 1985), 239; Daniel Goleman, *Emotional Intelligence* (New York: Bantam, 1985).

The extraordinarily sensitive French writer of the 1940s and 1950s, Albert Camus, in his novel *The Plague*, a metaphor of Nazism and the Holocaust, said that his moral code was "comprehension." Rather enigmatically but succinctly, he was pointing to the cast of mind that Gardner and Goleman have later explicated. It seems almost as evident and as elusive to locate comprehension in our own actions and interactions with others as it is to judge the same mental cast in political leaders. Less enigmatically, Robert Burns, one of Lincoln's favorite authors, bespoke the need to understand others, including poor people, saying: "Oh wad some power the giftie gie us, to see ourselves as others see us." More enigmatically, the ancient Oracles of Delphi admonished: "Know thyself."

46. After losing an election he came up with one of his most frequently mentioned anecdotes. Somebody asked him how he felt. He said: "it hurts too much to laugh and I'm too old to cry." Such a response saved a lot of time and gave an accurate report. A psychiatrist might have appraised Lincoln's twelve-word report as "the frustration of deep-seated power drives that very possibly were unconscious and had to be anecdotalized, to conceal from the listener and the speaker that the latter had such drives" (thirty words).

47. Stephen Oates, *With Malice Toward None*, (New York: New American Library, 1977), 112.

48. John J. Duff, *A. Lincoln* (New York: Rinehart, 1960), 322-24; 333-45 for a report on *McCormick v. Manny*, U.S. District Court, Cincinnati, 1855; on *Hurd v. the Rock Island Bridge Co.* (The "Effie Afton" case), U.S. District Court, Chicago, 1857.

49. As Herndon reported Lincoln's self-appraisal, he said: "I may not emit ideas as rapidly as others because I am compelled by nature to speak slowly, but when I do throw off a thought it seems to me, though it comes out with some effort, it has force

enough to cut its own way and travel a greater distance," William Herndon and Jesse Weik, *Herndon's Life on Lincoln* (Greenwich, CT: Fawcett, 1961), 278-79.

50. See the quotation from the Temperance Society speech below, in the section on "The Underminds of Lincoln and Roosevelt," excerpted from Roy P. Basler, *Abraham Lincoln* (Cleveland: World, 1946), 131-41, at 140.

51. James G. Randall, *Lincoln the President* (Urbana: University of Illinois Press, 1992), vol. 2, 313-14.

52. Early in her work for Mary Lincoln, Mariah Vance told of her resentment of the inperious demands Mary Lincoln made on her: "Some way, I didn't feel so good towards that woman. I prayed the Good Lord to take that awful sin of hate out of my heart." Mrs. Vance ("Aunt Mariah") went up to see what the sick Mrs. Lincoln wanted. Mary ("De Missy") said, as "Aunt Mariah" reported it: "De Missy say: "Mariah, I owe you an apology. I know I have hurt you deeply and so unjustly. I am sorry for what I said to you on the Fourth of July and I sense you haven't got over it. Can't you find it in your heart to forgive me?" . . . I declare I wilted plumb down like the little snow man Mastah Robert have made. I almost thought I was the sinna 'stead of de Missy, for the sin of hate in my heart. Maybe it was not hate, maybe I was just proud. I don't know what of the two are the worse." Lloyd Ostendorf and Walter Olesky, eds., *Lincoln's Unknown Private Life* (Mamaronek: Hastings House, 1995), 129-30.

53. In his annual message to Congress on January 6, 1941, Roosevelt announced the goals of the war that the United States, eleven months before Pearl Harbor, had not yet fully entered: freedom of speech and expression, freedom of religion, freedom from want, and freedom from fear. In the session preparing this annual message with his speech writers, FDR gazed at the ceiling for an uncomfortably long pause. Then he slowly and orally uttered the Four Freedoms almost exactly as they were finally spoken to Congress and the world, Samuel I. Rosenman, *Working with Roosevelt* (New York: Harper, 1952), 263.

54. These and other excerpts from FDR's draft on April 11, 1945 are taken from James MacGregor Burns, *Roosevelt: The Soldier of Freedom* (New York: Harcourt, 1970), 596.

55. See, for example, her letter to her longtime friend Lorena Hickok and to her daughter, Anna, and to Joe Lash (427-28), Joseph P. Lash, *Love, Eleanor* (New York: McGraw-Hill, 1982), 176-77, 246-47; 427-28.

56. Doris Kearns Goodwin, *No Ordinary Time* (New York: Simon and Schuster, 1994, 143).

57. James Roosevelt, *My Parents* (New York: Playboy, 1976), 113.

58. David Donald's 1995 biography of Lincoln does a remarkably specific job of showing Lincoln's penchant for disarming opposition by absorbing opponents into his

cabinet and the Union army. See David Donald *Lincoln* (New York: Simon and Schuster, 1995), 261-62, 328-42, 359-62, and 408-12.

59. In the famous habeas corpus proceeding that was appealed to the Supreme Court, Lincoln's old friend in court in Illinois, Judge David Davis, whom Lincoln had appointed in 1862 to the Supreme Court, wrote the majority opinion for the Court in 1866, a year after Lincoln's death, invalidating the detention of Milligan without trial.

60. Once when he was playing a game with his mother, he demanded that she give him the token with which she won. She gave it to him, and then she won again. Franklin sulked. Sara related that then "quietly I picked up the boys and told him in as firm a tone as I could muster that, until he learned to take a beating gracefully, he could not play any games again." Geoffrey C. Ward, *Before the Trumpet* (New York: Smithmark, 1985), 127.

61. Theodore Roosevelt's daughter Alice Roosevelt Longworth said that at weddings he had to be the bridegroom and at funerals the corpse, Carol Felsenthal, *Alice Roosevelt Longworth* (New York: G. P. Putnam, 1988), 105.

62. George Wade, and J. C. Davis (1957) report on postwar interviews conducted among internees in Manzanar, one of the relocation centers, on their reactions to their internment in 1942. Many of those interviewed reported being very angry at the time of internment but at the time of being interviewed a decade later, felt that they might have suffered more at the hands of hateful whites if they had not been removed from their homes. If they had not been removed, they would have been an easy target for people unable to do anything immediately effectively in their violent anger at Japan's attack on Pearl Harbor. I think Japanese Americans were a scapegoat not only for people on the West Coast but also for Roosevelt.

63. About thirteen thousand people were detained in the North without trial during the Civil War. The population of the northern states was about nineteen million. The ratio of detainees to total northern population: 1:1500. About 100 thousand people of Japanese birth or ancestry were detained during World War II. The population of the United States was about 132 million. The ratio of detainees to total national population in 1940: 1:1300 and to population in California, Oregon, and Washington: almost 1:100. Population data for the three states come from U.S. Bureau of the Census, *Historical Statistics of the United States: Colonial Times to 1970* (Washington, D.C.: Government Printing Office, 1975).

64. Joseph K. Lash, 664-65.

65. Roy P. Basler (Cleveland: World, 1946), 131-41.

66. James MacGregor Burns, *Roosevelt: The Lion and the Fox* (New York: Harcourt, Brace, 1956), 477.

67. Ted Morgan, *FDR* (New York: Simon and Schuster, 1985), 438-39.

68. William William, and Jesse Weik, *Herndon's Life of Lincoln* (Greenwich: CT: Fawcett, 1961), 397.

69. Samuel I. Rosenman, *Working with Roosevelt* (New York: Harper, 1952), 198.

70. Geoffrey C. Ward, *Before the Trumpet* (New York: Smithmark, 1985), 231-32.

71. The substantial accomplishments of Richard Nixon as president tend to be neglected because of his evident inability to really identify with people as human beings–or even as Americans sharing common problems and expecting to receive evidence of affection and trust from their leaders. As he put it in his parting words on the day of his resignation on August 8, 1974, "others may hate you, but those who hate you don't win unless you hate them, and then you destroy yourself!"

72. James MacGregor Burns, *Roosevelt: The Solder of Freedom* (New York: Harcourt, Brace, 1970), 192. During his first inauguration in 1933, FDR put his hand on the Bible opened to the thirteenth chapter of First Corinthians, in which the Apostle Paul said faith, hope, and love are the great three, and the greatest of them is love.

73. Scott Simon, a journalist with National Public Radio, visited Cannes, France in early 1994. Cannes had been heavily bombed, in error, by English air forces during the war. Simon reported that French people in Cannes did not blame England. He said, "we don't look at the mistakes of friends in the same way as the misdeeds of enemies" (Simon, April 16, 1994).

4

FDR and Lincoln in Stone (and Bronze)

C. Todd Stephenson

On October 24, 1994, *Time* magazine announced an important "milestone" for preserving the memory of Franklin Delano Roosevelt. Along with reports on newsmakers recovering, divorcing, suing, wounded, and recently deceased, the thirty-second president of the United States was listed as "memorialized" by "a monument in his honor; in Washington."[1] After trying for several decades, the FDR Memorial Commission gained a foothold on the Mall to create a memorial in the company of national heroes George Washington, Abraham Lincoln, and Thomas Jefferson. Symbolically, securing a position on the Mall is paramount. It is likely that Theodore Roosevelt would be better known had he, as Congress had intended during the early 1920s, received the spot now occupied by the Jefferson Memorial. However, TR is probably better known or elevated in the minds of many Americans by his placement on that other major presidential pantheon, Mount Rushmore.

The quest by the FDR Memorial Commission brings into focus the question: How relevant are presidential memorials in the 1990s? Some scholars argue that the United States is in a "postnational" phase of commemoration. That in a highly factionalized and pluralistic country, race, gender, family, and local identifications have eclipsed the importance of a "cult of the presidency." To examine which perspectives have changed and which have endured over the course of this century, this chapter compares FDR memorial plans and debates over the past thirty years with those surrounding the creation in the early twentieth century of a Mall-based marble temple erected to the man who most often tops the list of great American presidents: Abraham Lincoln. Memorials are wonderfully useful to historians as windows into the politics and culture of the times during which they were created. They reveal at least as much—probably more—about commemorators and their societies as they do about the people or events ostensibly being honored. This chapter, then, is as much about Americans *ca.* 1900-1925 and 1960-95 as it is about Abraham Lincoln and Franklin Roosevelt.

Before relating the stories of the FDR and Lincoln memorials, a few words are needed about the study of memorials and commemoration in general. Since 1990, scholarly interest in memorialization has exploded.[2] Once it was believed that memorials were solid, permanent reflections of a unified, official culture. It is now widely understood that the memorial process is contested and multivocal.[3] It is clear that many national traditions in industrial countries have been invented during the past 150 years.[4] The past is mutable: It is made and remade for present use.[5] Memorials do not have an immutable meaning. Over time, different people take away and add different messages. Pierre Nora speaks of layers of meaning. An example is the association of the Lincoln Memorial with civil rights for African Americans.[6] In no way did the creators of the memorial intend this meaning. They did everything in their power to play down the image of Lincoln as emancipator, instead celebrating the role of Lincoln as preserver of the Union and healer of sectional division. Yet, Marian Anderson's Easter concert in 1939 and Martin Luther King's "I have a dream" speech in 1963 have linked the Lincoln Memorial with the cause of civil rights in contemporary minds.[7]

Much continuity is found in many of the major issues surrounding presidential commemoration in the early and late twentieth century. Certainly, however, some things have changed. There clearly was a period of heroic or imperial commemoration which began sometime after the Civil War and ended sometime in the mid-twentieth century. Nationalism and heroism have been questioned more often and reconfigured in the post–World War II period. Some assert and some reject the idea that the United States has entered a postnational phase of commemoration, that "the reality is that the nation is no longer the site or frame of memory for most people and therefore national history is no longer a proper measure of what people really know about their pasts."[8] The Mall in Washington, D.C., became a central site of national memory and remains so today, as attested to by controversies over the Vietnam Veterans Memorial and the Holocaust Memorial Museum. Debates regarding the proper forms of commemoration shifting constellation of national heroes still finds room for multiple interpretations of traditional figures of national prominence such as Franklin Roosevelt and Abraham Lincoln.

The Origins

Lincoln's commemorators first organized in the late 1860s, hoping to create a significant memorial to their martyr. Sculptor Clark Mills designed an elaborate memorial structure crowded with statues of generals and statesmen, horses and allegorical figures. But the project remained unfinished, and the Lincoln Memorial Commission appears to have been in disarray when Mills died in 1883. On a lesser scale, a group of African Americans met with success in their efforts to develop a memorial to the "Emancipator." The result, in 1876, was a statue of Lincoln standing over a bondsman dedicated in Lincoln Park, the central section of the relatively unknown East Mall, which stretches from the Capitol to the Anacostia River. The next significant effort undertaken was by the Lincoln Farm Association—a group of "progressive" reformers and business people—to save the logs of the Lincoln birthplace cabin from exhibition at Coney Island and return them to their original site in Kentucky to be enshrined in a neoclassical mausoleum. While their effort was successful, his birthplace has never been an indelible point in the national memory of Lincoln. Other commemorators recognized that Washington, D.C., was to become the focus of the national memory and used the events of 1909—the centennial of Lincoln's birth—to kick off the campaign to create a national memorial in Washington, D.C.[9]

Similarly, efforts to establish a national memorial to Franklin Roosevelt began soon after this death. By 1945 commemorators were much better organized than had been their "amateur" predecessors in 1865. Groups such as the [Theodore] Roosevelt Memorial Association and the Thomas Jefferson Memorial Foundation had advanced publicity and fund-raising techniques greatly during the 1920s. Indeed, FDR began the process of his own commemoration before his death with the development of the first presidential library. After FDR's death, commemorators discussed a variety of potential memorial forms, including statues, various living memorials, and an institute at Warm Springs, Georgia. Cities and towns named streets and schools for FDR. A recently built aircraft carrier, intended to become the USS Coral Sea was christened instead the USS Franklin Roosevelt. By

1955, however, most attention had settled on a memorial to FDR in Washington, D.C. An architectural competition in 1960 produced a winning modernist design which was hotly debated. A series of revisions and new designs came and went through the 1960s and 1970s. Finally, a landscape solution by Lawrence Halprin survived the official approval process. It is a modified version of this design—featuring a series of open rooms defined by granite walls containing water, sculpture, and engraved quotations which ultimately triumphed in West Potomac Park. A detailed examination of the first unsuccessful 1960 design by Pedersen, Tilney, Hoberman, Wasserman, and Young (hereafter Pedersen and Tilney), and the present Halprin conception is included in this chapter.[10]

The Lincoln Memorial: Searching for a Form

Criticism of the Lincoln Memorial—Henry Bacon's neoclassical temple that anchors the western end of the Mall—came in several forms in the first decades of the twentieth century. Some complained about its borrowed classicism and called instead for the development of an American aesthetic. Gutzon Borglum—the brash, outspoken sculptor best known for his work on Mount Rushmore–asked: "Is it possible this can beget nothing in a nation of ninety millions of the stoutest hearted world builders ever known but a colonnade, torn from the pages of little Greece. I can't believe it!"[11] Borglum called out for Americans "to stop this vulgar, unfelt, boughten taste that is steering the likeness or symbol of a great nation's tenderest of memories into a cold, meaningless pile of imported garments from the past." He pleaded, "In heaven's name, in Abraham Lincoln's name, don't ask the American people to associate a Greek Temple with the first great American." The *Independent* called for an indigenous architecture "adapted to our purposes, expressive of our ideals." But it is much easier to criticize a lack of originality than to create new forms.[12]

Negative opinions divided along other fault lines as well. Some did not approve of the site selected for the Lincoln Memorial. While the present location of the Lincoln Memorial seems "natural," central, and prominent to us today, it is important to note that it took a certain amount of vision to select this site in the early 1900s. At the time, Potomac Park was an unimproved addition to the city formed by recent landfill. Inspired by the City Beautiful Movement and Chicago's White City of 1893, the McMillan Senate Commission of 1901 first proposed this site for a Lincoln memorial as a prominent point in its reconfigured and extended plan for the Mall. While a variety of critics and journals endorsed the plan, many had a hard time seeing Potomac Park as anything other than an out-of-the-way swamp. House Republican Joseph Cannon of Illinois objected to locating the memorial to Lincoln so far from any important center of the city. He stated that he would oppose any measure "that will not place the monument where all the people will and must see it when they come to Washington." Put by the river, according to Cannon, "The monument itself would take fever and ague, let alone a living man." He said to Elihu Root, "I'll never let a memorial to Abraham Lincoln be erected in that God damned swamp."[13]

Others pictured different locations in the city. Some wanted a colonnade near Union Station or on Meridian Hill or a triumphant arch on Capitol Hill. These people sought elevation. George Keller, a Hartford architect, proposed building a second obelisk near the Washington Monument. The Washington Monument, which was supposed to be built at the intersection of the main axes of the Mall, is actually several hundred feet to the east of the north-south axis which runs from the White House to the Tidal Basin. Keller suggested correcting the perspective by building a second obelisk—Egyptians always built them in pairs anyway, according to Keller—an equal distance to the west of the axis. "In fact, he wrote, "the obelisk would be a more characteristic form for a memorial to Lincoln than it is to Washington. One was a courtly gentleman and the other was one of nature's noblemen, plain and upright."[14]

Some critics sought more functional memorials. While early nineteenth century concerns about imperial monuments in a republic were muted by the beginning of the twentieth century, some Americans found large, functionless memorials of any type ill conceived. One person suggested erecting in Washington a Peace Palace, "a building where labor disputes and all subjects, national, local, and international, could be arbitrated."[15] Another proposed a national school in the capital.[16] An African American named William H. Davis suggested that the Lincoln memorial be a "Temple of Justice" to house the Supreme Court, located halfway between Union Station and the Capitol. Davis called for the building to include "a finely sculpture statue, representing *EMANCIPATION*, the cost of which to be defrayed by voluntary contributions from all members of the emancipated race, included school children all over the land, who would count it a privilege to thus present a *SPECIAL* concrete token of the respect, affection, and gratitude felt by them toward FREEDOM'S FOREMOST FRIEND."[17]

As unthreatening and traditional as the elements of this proposal appear, there is no evidence that anyone considered it seriously. Lincoln's role as emancipator was conspicuously absent from most of the dialogue surrounding the proper form of a Lincoln memorial.

The most significant challenge from a "functional" conception came from a group that proposed a seventy-two-mile memorial road from Washington, D.C., to Gettysburg, Pennsylvania. According to Representative James McCleary, the memorial should not be a shaft, an equestrian statue, an arch, or a building. To use such a form "would be to overlook the vital fact about Abraham Lincoln's fame—namely, that his is a growing fame, not a fading fame." A seventy-two mile long memorial road provided seemingly endless opportunities for commemoration. It would "be of such a character that each generation [could] contribute something to its improvement and embellishment." Each state could ornament a specific section and so, too, could various organizations and associations. A Lincoln highway also provided symbolic reconciliation between national sections. "The road would cross the famous Mason and Dixon line, formerly the dividing line between the North and the South [and], therefore, serve as a wedding ring for the sections once temporarily disserved—as a symbol of the Union to which Lincoln dedicated his life." McCleary envisioned rich spiritual and inspirational benefits for those who could finally take an easy day trip from Washington to Gettysburg. "What a never-to-be-forgotten day that would be! Imagine such a trip being taken by hundreds of thousands of Americans every year! Can any one measure the mental and moral uplift, the exultation of the spirit, the deepening and strengthening of patriotic sentiment and devotion to public duty that would result?"[18]

McCleary's Gettysburg highway provoked a series of negative editorials in the *New York Times*. According to the *Times*, a road could not be a suitable national memorial, and the federal government had no business building a road which benefited only two states. "Good Roads are needed in every State, of course, and it is the duty of the State to build them. It would be morally bad to build a road for Maryland at the expense of the Nation or with the money subscribed in every State for a National memorial. A good road is better, even when it leads to nowhere in particular, than a bad group of statuary. But a highway is not stirring to the popular imagination."[19] The need for good roads should not be confused with the need for a Lincoln memorial. The *Times* asserted that "the place for the memorial is the National capital."[20]

Though derived from a visit to the Roman Appian Way, the idea of a memorial road did pose one answer to the search for an American form. It is clear in the late twentieth century that such a celebration of mobility, space, and the automobile would indeed be a fitting form. In the early 1900s, however, the universal benefits of goods roads were not clear to everyone. Automobiles were still the playthings of the rich, and, to make matters worse, journalists soon revealed that a group of real estate speculators had bought up land along the route and stood to make huge profits. Nonetheless, Congress nearly adopted the idea of the road memorial in 1913 before finally giving approval for Bacon's temple.

The FDR Memorial: Searching for a Format

Criticism of Pedersen and Tilney's 1960 design of the FDR Memorial—a modern, sculptural composition of five "tablets" (stellae), each engraved with well-known speeches by FDR, to be located at a point between the Potomac River and the Tidal Basin and between the Lincoln and Jefferson memorials—resembled that voiced about the Lincoln Memorial: aesthetic criticism, questions regarding location, and calls for functional, "living" memorials to FDR. Aesthetic debates, moreover, had shifted significantly since the early 1900s. Faint rumblings against classically inspired designed turned into large-scale battles during the construction of the Jefferson Memorial throughout the 1930s and 1940s. By the early 1960s, modernism had the upper hand among professional architects and artists, but large numbers of Americans were far from won over. Much of the public preferred something more along the lines of the Lincoln Memorial, or at least a design with a realistic, identifiable statue. Criticism of Pedersen and Tilney's 1960 design of the FDR Memorial—a modern, sculptural composition of five "tablets" (stellae), each engraved with well-known speeches by FDR, to be located at a point between the Potomac River and the Tidal Basin and between the Lincoln and Jefferson memorials resembled that voiced about the Lincoln Memorial: aesthetic criticism, questions regarding location, and calls for functional, "living" memorials to FDR. Aesthetic debates, moreover, had shifted significantly.

Publication of the Pedersen and Tilney plan ignited instant criticism in the press and in letters to the editors of various newspapers around the country. The *Washington Post* labeled it "Instant Stonehenge."[21] Others called it a group of "gigantic concrete book ends" and "left-over parenthesis." Noting the resemblance of the stellae to tombstones, still others referred to the "tired gravestones from a cemetery of broken dreams" and "a necropolis on the Potomac." [22] One person suggested that "the Republicans did it for revenge."[23] Peter Tapke, a professor of philosophy at the College of William and Mary, asked "What could more perfectly shatter the serenity of our classic Mall and river front than this group of monoliths clawing at the sky?"[24] To many Americans, modern art was inaccessible and threatening. Protesting against the "revolting design" of the FDR memorial, one woman wrote the *New York Herald Tribune* that contemporary architecture and design were dehumanizing and based on a Central European Achill disregard of the values of ordinary human beings."[25] Art historian Karal Ann Marling has suggested that many Americans during the 1950s saw modernism as stark, sterile, authoritarian, and foreign. That visual austerity implied social regimentation and un-American tendencies. In short, that modern art was the weapon of a Communist conspiracy.[26] (Soviets, on the other hand, criticized modernism as a symbol of bourgeois decadence.[27])

While the Pedersen and Tilney design was a radical departure from the Lincoln Memorial in many ways, it did borrow one significant feature: the engraving of important speeches into the stone of the memorial. The two side chambers of the Lincoln Memorial contain the full texts of the Gettysburg Address and the second inaugural speech, and are among the most successful features of the memorial. Critics such as Borglum claimed that no one would stop to read the lonely speeches surrounded by nothing but expanses of marble and Jules Guerin's rather unobtrusive murals.[28] Architect Bacon, however, claimed, "I believe these two great speeches made by Lincoln will always have a far greater meaning to the citizens of the United States and visitors from other countries than a portrayal of periods or events by means of decoration."[29] He was probably right: It is amazing to visit the Lincoln Memorial today and watch people read the lengthy text of the second inaugural speech.

The Thomas Jefferson Memorial Commission borrowed this same device, as did Pedersen and Tilney. The problem, as several critics pointed out, was that Lincoln and Jefferson wrote many more of their own words than did FDR. The *New York Mirror* asked whether the tablet bearing the quote: "The only thing we have to fear is fear itself," would contain "an asterisk and a note crediting Henry David Thoreau with, 'Nothing is so much to be feared as fear.'" And how much stone would be required if all of FDR's ghostwriters were listed?[30] The tension between nineteenth century devotion to the written word and twentieth century ghostwriters and devotion to the audio and visual record was addressed by Marcel Breuer in his 1965 design, one of those almost-accepted plans between the first Pedersen and Tilney and the final Halprin. Breuer called for hidden speakers broadcasting FDR's speeches—the act of speaking thus became at least as important as the act of writing. The ghostwriting criticism persisted in the early 1980s, as a writer to the *Washington Post* reminded, "Not since the days of Woodrow Wilson have our presidents had time to write their own speeches, and the famous sayings attributed to President Roosevelt would only be a memorial to his ghost writers in the sky."[31] And, yet, the final Halprin version features words in their now traditional form—carved on walls.

Appeals for a functional memorial to FDR also figured prominently at the time. Support for functional memorials had made great strides since the early 1900s. During the 1930s and 1940s, many artists and critics with modern sensibilities readily proclaimed that one could not have a "modern" monument. In 1938, critic Lewis Mumford wrote, "The notion of a modern monument is a contradiction in terms: If it is a monument, it is not modern, and if it is modern, it cannot be a monument."[32] During the later 1940s and 1950s, modern architects began to admit the possibility of a modern monument. Indeed, Lewis Mumford participated in the selection of a site for the FDR memorial though he declined to participate on the jury charged to select a design. He declared, "My prescription, rather, would be to formulate the program, to choose the site and to wait for a decade or a generation—or even longer if necessary—for the right design to emerge."[33]

Suggestions for a living, functional memorial have appeared from many quarters. In 1961, one woman wrote, "In our capital city where poverty, strife, juvenile crime, poor race relations and slums are all too prevalent, would it not be more fitting to endow a settlement center or recreation or housing plan to commemorate a life interested in human welfare?"[34] Representative Charles Bennett proposed a graduate school of political science on the Tidal Basin spot as a living memorial. In response, the *Washington Post* asked, "We wonder what FDR would prefer. Five massive slabs—or a living memorial in the form of a school and scholarships dedicated to the strengthening of democratic government."[35] A man suggested naming the "new $20 million D.C. stadium"—now named RFK—for FDR.[36] A woman wanted something people could use, like "An aquarium, with exhibits, meeting rooms for fishing clubs, lectures and movies for the public. Or a wild life library. Or a stamp library."[37] Another called for a "Franklin Delano Roosevelt Children's Hospital" with a heroic statue of FDR on the grounds.[38] In response to the persistent demands for functional memorials, Representative Eugene Keogh, chair of the FDR Memorial Commission, declared "We want people to think about FDR when they enter the memorial and not whether they survive their operation, pass their exam or win the football game."[39]

Some memorial advocates proposed other locations for an FDR shrine. Those suggesting another D.C. site often had the goal of using the memorial to help develop other parts of Washington. In 1964, Delbert Fowler, citing the example of the space needle in Seattle, suggested building a rotating spherical restaurant atop a tall column as a memorial to Roosevelt. He suggested locating this tribute at Lincoln Park, the midpoint between the Capitol and the D.C. stadium, in an effort to make the East Mall more visible.[40] Indeed, as the Jefferson Memorial Commission worked during the mid 1930s to find a spot for their memorial, they, too, considered contributing to the development of the East Mall by locating the Jefferson Memorial on the banks of the Anacostia River.[41] In 1983, Eleanor R. Seagraves (FDR's granddaughter) and Mary Anglemyer proposed moving the memorial to Hains Point at the end of East Potomac Park—that spit of land that extends southwest from the Jefferson Memorial to a point opposite National Airport. Too removed? Add a Tourmobile stop, they suggested sensibly.[42]

Others, centering on FDR's homes, pushed for a memorial outside of Washington. Echoing the concerns of John Adams and other leaders of the early republic, one man wrote, "The lovely estate on the Hudson enshrines his memory; what more or better, except in the hearts of his countrymen?"[43] A Warm Springs, Georgia memorial received serious consideration right from the beginning in 1945. In 1982, shortly before launching into a balance-the-budget argument against funding the FDR Memorial, Representative Newt Gingrich of Georgia declared that he liked the idea of "a memorial at Warm Springs."[44] In 1964, George D. Watrous Jr., proposed erecting the Pedersen and Tilney memorial at Campobello—FDR's summer retreat in New Brunswick, Canada, just across the Maine border. According to Watrous, the design would fit well with the rugged setting and act as a tourist attraction.[45] And in a bizarre composite scheme, several people suggested moving FDR's hilltop cottage, the retreat overlooking the Hudson which FDR helped design and to which he had hoped to retire, from Hyde Park to West Potomac Park.[46]

Enduring Questions

While the meaning of Lincoln's legacy was perhaps more sharply contested—emancipator versus preserver of Union—than that of FDR, fewer voices in the 1900s and 1910s protested that Lincoln did not deserve a memorial compared with the number who labeled FDR unworthy during the 1960s. Some unreconstructed southerners complained, though many subscribed to the myth of reconciliation which held that under Lincoln, "radical" reconstruction would never have taken place. Many more, however, believed—or at least found voices in print—that FDR did not deserve a memorial. Norma C. Williams wrote that she could not believe there will be a memorial for a president "who sold this country down the river" and did his "utmost to fundamentally change our form of free government."[47] Stanley Shaw wrote sarcastically that "The proposed Franklin D. Roosevelt memorial is so brilliantly conceived and so perfectly designed that it should by all means be constructed." To him, it was a symbol of the unfulfilled promises of the Roosevelt years and FDR's gales of useless words. He suggested that "The entire structure should be erected on swampy ground so that it may finally sink out of mortal sight," which, of course, is what would happen on the reclaimed land of West Potomac Park without significant underpinnings.[48]

Some opponents to commemorating FDR focused on the inscriptions of the Pedersen and Tilney design. One writer recommended adding this FDR quote to the list: "I promise every American mother that her boys will not be sent to fight in foreign wars."[49] Another suggested marking the headstones of this New Deal burial ground with the appropriate epitaphs. For the National Recovery Act they proposed:

> Here lies beneath this pillar gray
> The late-lamented NRA.
> It lived and breathed and had its day
> But thank the Lord, it went away.

And in honor of the change of the official date of Thanksgiving from the last to the fourth Thursday in November:

> I was a child of commerce purely
> To get folks Christmas shopping early
> But, sad to say, my mournful pater
> Found out folks were thankful later.[50\]

Timing—as well as any difference in "greatness" between the two presidents—is an important issue here. As Washington, D.C., has become cluttered with monuments and Congress is inundated with memorial petitions, requests, and suggestions, many have proposed a fifty-year waiting period following a person's death before a memorial could be built. The idea, as several of FDR's supporters noted in the early 1960s, is to let a more balanced assessment of a person's legacy develop. By the 1900s and 1910s, Lincoln was close enough to meeting the fifty-year test. In fact, most people talked about "neglecting" his memory. We see now with Roosevelt, as with Lincoln, that partisan and personal animosity diminishes with time. While Republicans attack the New Deal, the most creative among them—such as Ronald Reagan and Newt Gingrich—have added FDR to their personal pantheons of heroes. In 1982, for example, Gingrich said, "I think Franklin Delano Roosevelt deserves a memorial because I think he was the greatest president of the twentieth century."[51] Significant milestone anniversaries have helped, too. In the aftermath of 1876—the nation's centennial—Congress voted to fund the completion of the Washington Monument. Likewise, Lincoln's birth centennial in 1909 spurred the creation of the Lincoln Memorial. The centennial of FDR's birth in 1982 opened again, unsuccessfully, the push for funding the FDR Memorial and the fiftieth anniversary of FDR's death certainly had sometime to do with the timing of construction in Washington, D.C.

Assessing the impact of both Lincoln's and Roosevelt's legacies, an essential element of their inspiration is that each overcame adversity. The Lincoln story is well known: born in a log cabin, learned to read by firelight, picked himself up by his boot straps, an inspiration to the poor and dispossessed. For FDR, born and reared in privilege, polio served as his adversity. Historian Paul Conkin wrote: "Polio made an aristocratic Roosevelt into an underdog. For him it replaced the log cabin."[52] Questions of how to depict the adversity—whether to focus on it as the source of strength or to emphasize adversity overcome has created important rifts among those attempting to celebrate Lincoln in the 1910s and FDR in the 1990s.

In 1917, a heated debate arose regarding a statue of Lincoln to be erected in London. The conflict pitted images of Lincoln the dignified statesman against a more vernacular Lincoln—Lincoln the rough frontiersman and product of American soil. Several years earlier, British and American committees had decided to erect a copy of Augustus Saint Gaudens's standing Chicago Lincoln in London in celebration of one hundred years of Anglo-American peace. The British government pledged a prime site for the statue in an enclosure in the shadow of Westminster Abbey. A last minute substitution of a copy of a far more controversial statue of Lincoln by George Grey Barnard provoked an intense examination of the meaning of Abraham Lincoln and of American democracy.

Barnard's Lincoln created a powerful effect then as it still does today—the original stands in Lyttle Park in Cincinnati. One is immediately impressed with the large, coarse hands, solid feet, and furrows on the face of the figure. Lincoln's clothes and hair are rumpled, and he sports no beard. This is the Lincoln of the prairie. It is Lincoln the debater. Barnard explained, "He must have stood as the Republic should stand, strong, simple, carrying its weight unconsciously without pride in rank or culture. He is clothed with cloth worn, the history of labor." After a two-year search, Barnard located a model for the project in Kentucky. He chose a 6'4" rail splitter who had been born fifteen miles from Lincoln's birthplace. Here, he felt, was the shape of the American frontiersman. "The Greeks had nothing like that. [Barnard's model] was a genuine product of American soil, as typical in its way as the Indians. . . . I have seen the models of Europe—men of Greece and Italy—symmetrical and beautiful in a classic way; but nothing ever appealed to me like the form of this Kentuckian."[53]

Reaction to the statue was sharply divided. Theodore Roosevelt declared upon seeing it, "I have always wished that I might see him; now I do." The *Outlook* emphasized the inspirational qualities of the work. "The most ignorant alien before Barnard's Lincoln may understand something of the American spirit and perhaps go away with some measure of the inspiration that lies in Lincoln's name."[54] An old man from Springfield, who had seen Lincoln as a youth, viewed the statue and said: "That's him. That's the nearest to his living self I've ever seen."[55] Lincoln's biographer, Ida Tarbell explained, "There is not a line of the figure that does not express a great spiritual quality. . . . How any mortal man can look into this face that the sculptor has wrought by years of loving and reverential toil and not be stirred to the depths, I confess I cannot understand."[56]

However, when the offer was made to send a copy to London, Robert

Todd Lincoln, son of the president, and Frederick Ruckstuhl, editor of a staunchly antimodern art journal, launched a series of vehement attacks on the statue. Ruckstuhl wrote, "The figure stands there with hands pressing the stomach, with a lugubrious expression on the face with only half-opened eyes, a mournful mouth giving the impression of a man saying, 'Friends, for pity's sake, relieve me of my pain–I have the colic.'"[57] Ruckstuhl feared that erecting a copy of Barnard's Lincoln abroad would "suggest that even in its great hero democracy breeds nothing but a stoop-shouldered, consumptive-chested, chimpanzee-handed, lumpy-footed, giraffe-necked, grimy-fingered clod-hopper, wearing his clothes in a way to disgust a ragman."[58] Robert Todd Lincoln wrote to William Howard Taft, "That my father should be represented . . . by such a work . . . would be a cause of sorrow to me personally, the greatness of which I will not attempt to describe."[59] Lincoln worked tirelessly behind the scenes to effect the substitution of the Saint Gaudens statue for the Barnard, putting up $25,000 to make a copy on the condition that his name not be used. In the end, London received the more ceremonial Saint Gaudens statue while Barnard's man of the people ended up in working-class Manchester.

A similar argument arose during 1995 regarding the adversity which challenged FDR. A vocal set of interests contended that the Roosevelt memorial under construction should include a depiction of FDR in a wheelchair or using braces and crutches to stand. An equally vocal set of Americans believe, for a variety of reasons, that FDR's handicap should be neither emphasized nor celebrated. This mini-debate represented the most press attention garnered by the FDR memorial in thirty years.[60]

Those opposing the depiction of FDR with a handicap emphasize several factors. Some argue that to reveal his handicap in a public image is revisionist. They cite that of the tens of thousands of pictures of Roosevelt at the FDR library, only two or three show him in his wheelchair. Roosevelt and the press took great pains to hide his paralysis. In a letter to the *Washington Post*, Stewart Sutton wrote that depicting FDR as handicapped was "a ludicrous attempt at historical revisionism." He stated that "FDR should be memorialized in the manner that he was primarily perceived by the public during his lifetime."[61] Dorann H. Gunderson, executive director of the FDR Memorial Commission supported the statues which conceal FDR's handicap: "This is historically accurate. We know that President Roosevelt himself chose to present this kind of image to the public. To do otherwise would be revisionist history."[62] David Roosevelt added bluntly that he did not want his grandfather turned into "a modern-day poster child."[63] Historical accuracy and filial piety aside, several Americans wrote that a handicapped FDR was just plain uninspiring. Judith Patterson declared "I would hope that he might be memorialized as I and others of my generation throughout the world remember him: not as a helpless cripple—in the light of what is politically correct in 1995—but as a strong, courageous and vibrant leader, one who would never admit defeat in the face of daunting physical odds."[64]

Those who favor depiction of the paralysis range from the near militant to the moderate. Speed Davis, acting executive director of the National Council on Disability, stated, "It was so much a part of who he was, and for them to continue to hide it kind of undermines everything we're trying to do . . . . It reinforces the idea of shame, the negative value of having a disability, which is less and less true every day. If they want to show the whole person, they have to show all aspects." Declared Alan Reich, president of the National Organization on Disability—a lobbying group for the disabled: "To push his disability aside, to hide it, is not only an injustice to FDR but an historical aberration and misinterpretation. We should not. . . hide it, we should portray it. It doesn't need to be the paramount feature of the memorial, but it's a fact, an important fact."[65] Michael Marino, a consultant for Americans with Disabilities Act compliance and barrier-free living asked, "How much further along the road to full equality for people with disabilities would we be had FDR been more willing to reveal how he was affected by the disabled experience?"[66] Ray Teichman, supervisory archivist at Hyde Park, concluded that FDR's attitude would be different today: "He might very well support something that would indicate that he had this kind of problem. He was a product of his age . . . but he had an optimistic view of life and an inclination toward helping people."[67] A writer for the *Omaha World-Herald* offered a balanced suggestion which the FDR Memorial Commission might do well to consider: "Perhaps the memorial could show a cane leaning in a corner, a discreet hint of leg braces, an unobtrusive wheelchair off to the side. His irrelevant physical limitations shouldn't be the center of attention. But neither should history be rewritten by ignoring their existence."[68]

Debates regarding revisionism and wishes of the family beg the question, does it matter what the person wanted? And more broadly, who are memorials for? For the past forty years, each time the subject of an FDR memorial in Washington, D.C., has come up, someone has raised the story of a conversation that Roosevelt had with Felix Frankfurter one day in 1941. As Frankfurter reported it, FDR said

> if any memorial is to be erected to me, I know exactly what I should like it to be. . . . About halfway between here and the Capitol is the Archives Building. . . . And right in front of the Archives Building is a little green triangle. If, as they say, they are to put up any memorial to me, I should like it to consist of a block about the size of this (putting his hand on his desk). I don't care what it is made of, whether it is limestone or granite or whatnot, but I want it to be plain, without any ornamentation, with the simple carving, 'in memory of.' That is all, and please remember that, if the time should come.[69]

In addition, FDR consciously created another memorial to himself through the development of the first presidential library. Many have argued over the years that to build anything else is to go against the explicit wishes of Roosevelt.

But again, do the wishes of the public figure or his family matter? The answer is both yes and no. Families have a great deal of sentimental and political clout. Robert Todd Lincoln's opposition was instrumental in derailing the effort to place Barnard's statue in London. Lincoln's son occupied a place of honor at the dedication of the Lincoln Memorial in 1922, a carefully orchestrated event with heavy symbolic importance. FDR's children played a critical role in the design wars of the 1960s. On the appearance of the Pedersen and Tilney conception, son James Roosevelt commented, "It's a good deal more modernistic than my father would have approved of."[70] And, "I'm afraid I'd have to live with this a long time before I could enjoy it."[71] Daughter Anna Roosevelt Halsted said, upon hearing a description of the memorial, "Good Lord" and "We'll just have to hope for the best."[72] Eleanor Roosevelt withheld comment.

But does family opinion matter? In an editorial, the *Washington Star* wrote "It is too bad that the Roosevelt offspring disapprove. In all due respect, however, their feelings, whether pro or con, could hardly be decisive."[73] True enough. James Roosevelt issued the same response to the hundreds of people who wrote to him in 1961 and 1964: "As you may know, we—the children of FDR—have no official authority in the selection of the memorial, nor do we have any veto privileges."[74] Yet, the children of FDR did exercise a veto. When the Commission of Fine Arts approved a modified version of the Pedersen and Tilney design in 1964, Roosevelt's five children met at Hyde Park and issued a proclamation that "We are unalterably opposed" to the original or modifications.[75] When James Roosevelt threatened television and radio speeches denouncing the design and a Congressional resolution to dissolve the FDR Memorial Commission, fundraisers rightly noted that the memorial would be impossible to fund. The Commission then withdrew its support.[76]

The intervention of children and those who knew the subject well argue for the fifty-year rule. In 1964, one FDR grandchild wrote her Uncle Jimmy that the family had been approaching the whole issue too personally. In her opinion, it didn't matter whether FDR or his family favored traditional or modern designs. "Basically, the question is not whether Papa would have liked it, or whether it is the kind of design any of us would have ever conceived. I believe we have to try to view it as an artistic entity in which the extraordinary personality of a great leader and some near-revolutionary ideas of his time are symbolically combined in a dignified, fluid, modern structure."[77] There is something to be said for the broader perspectives of later generations.

Conclusion

In the end, there are many similarities between the attempts to memorialize Franklin Roosevelt and Abraham Lincoln. During the main periods of debate, the years around 1910 and the early 1960s, Americans questioned locations, styles, and functions of national memorials. In the creation of both memorials, the development and maintenance of Washington, D.C., as a national ceremonial center weighed heavily in the debates. Certainly the Mall changed greatly between 1900 and 1995. Before the McMillan Plan, it was unorganized, remote, and crisscrossed by railroad tracks. The placement of the Lincoln Memorial was critical in creating the space which exists today. Clearly, the function of organizing and beautifying the city was every bit as important to many urban planners at the turn of the century as was the function of commemorating Abraham Lincoln. And to some extent, a major memorial, like any major building, remains an opportunity for architects, planners, and designers to make an aesthetic and cultural statement about their times. The never built Pedersen and Tilney memorial was considered by many as an attractive expression of the mid-twentieth century.[78]

From the 1920s forward, the Mall in Washington, D.C., has conferred legitimacy and power on the people and events memorialized there. Witness the struggle between supporters of Theodore Roosevelt and Thomas Jefferson for the last major point of the Mall at the Tidal Basin. Space for memorials on the Mall has been even more sharply contested since the early 1960s. Every memorial threatens softball fields and dwindling recreational space. That the Vietnam Veterans Memorial was built on the Mall was a significant victory for its supporters. Its location relative to the Lincoln Memorial and Washington Monument gave it early importance and made the memorial "national." Critics and commentators refer repeatedly to the proximity of the Holocaust Memorial Museum to the Mall—to many people, a position on or right next to the Mall is recognition of significance. Many Americans who look at those memorials may imagine that they must have been selected judiciously, even omnisciently. Dispelling this concept, Borglum claimed that the figures on Mount Rushmore were chosen not for their general "greatness" as presidents, but rather for their importance in the territorial expansion of the United States. Many visitors must assume that, as of the 1930s, these four were picked by some "impartial" group to have been America's "best" presidents.

Over the course of the twentieth century, the debate over the form of memorial should take evolved; yet many of the central issues that arose in the early 1900s remained important in the late 1900s. The FDR Memorial Commission did a remarkable job of avoiding controversy from 1980 to 1985. Many Americans might be stunned to learn that the federal government borrowed some $40 million to pay for most of the memorial. Critics from the 1900s through the 1960s argued vigorously that large, functionless memorials represent a huge waste of money. The push for functional living memorials seems to have peaked during the 1940s and 1950s, but people argued strongly for Lincoln schools and FDR hospitals in the decades before and after. While aesthetic debates have shifted they retain some constant elements. Over the course of the twentieth century, modernism has become less threatening to artists in general though large numbers of Americans fear too much abstraction and seem to feel most comfortable if a realistic statue is included in an ensemble. Revisions of the Pedersen and Tilney design featured a statue of FDR and Frederick Hart's statue of Vietnam veterans at the Vietnam Veterans Memorial seem to have quieted certain critic segments. And from the Lincoln Memorial to each version of the FDR Memorial, the written word has remained an essential component.

How do memorials function, and who are they for? Perhaps they principally inspire and give pause for reflection. They are created for the living not for the dead. It makes a great deal of sense to wait fifty years before passing judgment on the national contributions of an individual. The generation that knew the hero, as well as the hero's children, need to pass from the scene so that the decision is dispassionate. Memorial debates also reveal a great deal about the concerns of the present generation. In the discussions of FDR's handicap, one senses a considerable frustration with "political correctness" in the 1990s over whether difference is something to be concealed or overcome or, conversely, is something to be celebrated. Likewise, the generation of the early 1900s debated whether Lincoln's background was something admirably overcome or if it were an intrinsic source of strength for him.

Will the FDR memorial ever be as important as the Lincoln Memorial? No. This conclusion is based in part on its location. Thomas Jefferson truly was accorded the last good spot. But design is also an element. The Lincoln Memorial is actually very abstract—a statue, some words, two allegorical murals, and balanced, classical forms. The Pedersen and Tilney design, too, was abstract. In the revised version, visitors would do the same things there as at the Lincoln Memorial: walk through an attractive space, gaze up at a statue, read inspiring words. The Vietnam Veterans Memorial, likewise, is a powerful, abstract, and thought-provoking place. The Halprin design, by comparison, is many-sided and compartmentalized. It imparts no sense of unity, which is not a commentary on the interpretation derived. The image of Theodore Roosevelt is perhaps less effective than those of Lincoln, Washington, and Jefferson because the commemorators of TR chose to celebrate a multifaceted person, good at many things but not great at one or wo. Finally, memorials can do only so much for a reputation. For example, based upon Abraham Lincoln's domination of the lists of presidential greats, there is reason to believe that Lincoln's legacy will continue to be more resonant with the public than the legacy of Franklin D. Roosevelt.

ENDNOTES

1. "Milestones," *Time* (October 24, 1994): 26.

2. Charles Todd Stephenson, "Celebrating American Heroes: The Commemoration of George Washington, Abraham Lincoln, Theodore Roosevelt, and Thomas Jefferson, 1832-1943," (Ph.D. diss., Brown University, 1993). On commemoration, in addition to the books listed below, I have been most influenced by Michael Kammen, *Mystic Chords of Memory: The Transformation of Tradition in American Culture* (New York: Alfred A. Knopf, 1991); Edward Tabor Linenthal, *Sacred Ground: Americans and Their Battlefields* (Urbana: University of Illinois Press, 1991); Michele H. Bogart, *Public Sculpture and the Civic Ideal in New York City, 1890-1930* (Chicago: University of Chicago Press, 1989); James E. Young, *The Texture of Memory: Holocaust Memorials and Meaning* (New Haven, CT: Yale University Press, 1993); Casey Nelson Blake, "Richard Serra, Tilted Arc, and the Crisis of Public Art," in Richard Wightman Fox and T. Jackson Lears, eds., *The Power of Culture: Critical Essays in American History* (Chicago: University of Chicago Press, 1993); all essays in John R. Gillis, *Commemorations: The Politics of National Identity* (Princeton, NJ: Princeton University Press, 1994); G. Kurt Piehler, *Remembering War the American Way* (Washington, DC: Smithsonian Institution Press, 1995); Karal Ann Marling and John Wetenhall, *Iwo Jima: Monuments, Memories, and the American Hero* (Cambridge, MA: Harvard University Press, 1991).

3. John Bodnar, *Remaking America: Public Memory, Commemoration, and Patriotism in the Twentieth Century* (Princeton, NJ: Princeton University Press, 1992).

4. Eric Hobsbawm and Terence Range, eds., *The Invention of Tradition* (Cambridge, MA: Cambridge University Press, 1983).

5. Maurice Halbwachs, *The Collective Memory*; trans. F. J. Ditter (New York: Harper and Row, 1980); David Lowenthal, *The Past is a Foreign Country* (Cambridge, UK: University Press, 1985).

6. Pierre Nora, "Between Memory and History: Les Lieux de Memoire," *Representations* 26 (Spring 1989): 7-25.

7. On the connections between the Lincoln Memorial and civil rights, see Scott A. Sandage, "A Marble House Divided: The Lincoln Memorial, the Civil Rights Movement, and the Politics of Memory, 1939-1963," *Journal of American History* 80 (June 1993): 135-67.

8. John R. Gillis, "Memory and Identity: The History of a Relationship," in Gillis, ed., *Commemorations*, 17.

9. On the creation of the Lincoln Memorial in Washington and the birthplace memorial in Kentucky, see Stephenson, "Celebrating American Heroes," 84-169. On the Lincoln Memorial, see also Christopher A. Thomas, "The Lincoln Memorial and Its Architect, Henry Bacon (1866-1924) (Ph.D. diss., Yale University, 1990) and Kirk E. Savage, "Race, Memory and Identity: The National Monuments of the Union and the Confederacy," (Ph.D. diss., University of California, Berkeley, 1990). On the Lincoln image more broadly, see Merrill D. Peterson, *Lincoln in American Memory* (New York: Oxford University Press, 1994).

10. The FDR Memorial has received considerably less attention than the Lincoln Memorial. Significant clippings files on the various memorial debates exist at the FDR Library in Hyde Park, New York, and in the Division of Washingtonians at the Martin Luther King, Jr., Library in Washington, D.C. On the Pedersen and Tilney

design and the 1960s competition, see Thomas H. Creighton, *The Architecture of Monuments: The Franklin Delano Roosevelt Memorial Competition* (New York: Reinhold Publishing Corporation, 1962) and Helene Lipstadt, "Transforming the Tradition: American Architecture Competitions, 1960 to the Present," 95-99, in Lipstadt, ed., *The Experimental Tradition: Essays on Competitions in Architecture* (Princeton, NJ: Princeton Architectural Press, 1989). The story is taken through the early 1970s by Barry Macintosh in National Park Service report "The Making of a Monument: The Franklin Delano Roosevelt Memorial, 1955-1972." On the Halprin design, see Malcolm N. Carter, "The FDR Memorial: A Monument to Politics, Bureaucracy and the Art of Accommodation," *Art News* (October 1978): 51-57. The official listing of the names of the creators of the 1960 design produced significant controversy. It appears that Norman Hoberman, a junior member of the Pedersen and Tilney firm, played the largest creative role in the process. See Papers of the FDR Memorial Commission, FDR Library.

11. Borglum to George P. Wetmore, January 13, 1912, Records of the Lincoln Memorial Commission (LMC), Record Group 42, Entry 32, Box 2, National Archives, Washington, D.C.

12. Borglum to the editor, New York *Sun,* January 15, 1912, Ibid; "Lincoln As a Greek God," *Independent* 72 (February 8, 1912): 320-22. Borglum's eventual response was the creation of Mount Rushmore–though the use of colossal sculpture certainly had precedent in antiquity.

13. Cannon quoted in Thomas, "Lincoln Memorial," 369-71.

14. Letter to the editor, George Keller, *New York Times,* November 8, 1908 (hereafter cited as *NYT*).

15. William T. Smedley to editor, Ibid., January 17, 1909.

16. Raymond Riordon, "Lincoln Memorial School: A New Idea in Industrial Education," *The Craftsman* 22 (September 1912): 614-18.

17. William H. Davis to Lincoln Memorial Commission, March 23, 1911, Records of the LMC, Entry 362, Box 1.

18. James T. McCleary, "What Shall the Lincoln Memorial Be?" *Review of Reviews* 38 (September 1908): 337-41.

19. "The Lincoln Memorial," *NYT,* July 3, 1908.

20. "The Lincoln Memorial," Ibid, July 20, 1908.

21. "Instant Stonehenge," *Washington Post* (January 13, 1961), 60.

22. "Poor FDR," *Washington Post* (December 31, 1961); "Sermons in Stones," *Washington Post* [date illegible] (October 1962), MLK Library.

23. Peter Edson, "New Deal Graveyard," *Washington Daily News* (January 5, 1961), vertical files, FDR Library.

24. Peter Tapke to the editor, *Washington Star* (January 22, 1961), MLK Library.

25. Majorie O'Shaughnessy to the editor, *New York Herald Tribune* (January 8, 1961), vertical files, FDR Library.

26. Karal Ann Marlin, *As Seen on TV: The Visual Culture of Everyday Life in the 1950s* (Cambridge: Harvard University Press, 1994), 269.

27. Piehler, 164.

28. Borglum to Wetmore.

29. Henry Bacon, "The Lincoln Memorial," *Art and Archaeology* 23 (June 1922): 253-55.

30. "Fine Arts Victory," *New York Mirror* (February 23, 1962), clipping in Pedersen papers. See also Walter Briehl to the editor, *New York Herald Tribune* (January 8, 1961), vertical files, FDR Library.

31. K.D. Vass to the editor, *Washington Post* (September 12, 1981), vertical files, MLK Library.

32. Lewis Mumford, *The Culture of Cities* (1938).

33. Mumford to the editor, *NYT* [date illegible] August 1961, vertical files, MLK Library.

34. Mrs. E. William Hall to the editor of the *Washington Post* (January 8, 1961), vertical files, MLK Library.

35. Erwin Knoll, "Riverside Political Science School Urged as Living Memorial to FDR," *Washington Post* (March 1, 1961); *Washington Post* asked "A Memorial School?" *Washington Post* (March 5, 1961), vertical files, MLK Library.

36. Tony Nerl to the editor of the *Washington Post* (January 8, 1961), vertical files, MLK Library.

37. Fern Whiteside to the editor, *Washington Star* (January 22, 1961), vertical files, MLK Library.

38. Gino J. Simi to the editor, *Washington Star* (June 30, 1964), vertical files, MLK Library.

39. Wolf Von Eckerdt, "Fine Arts Unit Rejects FDR Memorial Design," *Washington Post* (January 28, 1967), vertical files, MLK Library.

40. Delbert M. Fowler to the editor, *Washington Post* (August 28, 1964), vertical files, MLK Library.

41. Stephenson, "Celebrating American Heroes," 248-49.

42. Eleanor R. Seagraves and Mary Anglemyer to the editor, *Washington Post* (September 13, 1983), vertical files, MLK Library.

43. James M. Groves to the editor of the *New York Herald Tribune* (January 8, 1961). In a 1982 appeal for funding for the FDR Memorial, Representative Claude Pepper used similar "in the hearts of his countrymen," neorepublican language: "It is not necessary, Mr. Chairman, of course, that we build a memorial here in the national capital for Franklin Roosevelt to be honored for generations to come—for his face and his spirit are to be seen all over America: in the fertile fields where once was the Dust Bowl; in the harnessed rivers which once were the source of devastating floods; in the roar of the water pouring over dams that he made possible to provide energy for America's peace and even for the preparation of our defense. The waterways, the rivers and harbors, the highways all over America, is the hand of Franklin D. Roosevelt. I see him in educational institutions of many forms. I see his handiwork in the improved art of painters and musicians and dramatists that he did not forget in those terrible disastrous days of the Depression. I see him in the lights of rural homes lighted by the REA; in the rural homes connected with the world by rural telephones; in rural and city libraries." *Congressional Record*, House, July 14, 1982, H4053.

44. Ibid., H4057.

45. George D. Watrous, Jr., to the editor, *Washington Star* (June 30, 1964), vertical

files, MLK Library.

46. Maxine Cheshire, "FDR's Self-Designed 'Dream Cottage' Proposed as Memorial to Him Here," *Washington Post* (April 29, 1961), vertical files, MLK Library.

47. Norma C. Williams to the editor, *Washington Star* (January 22, 1961), vertical files, MLK Library.

48. Stanley N. Shaw to the editor, Ibid.

49. Peter Edson, "A New Deal Graveyard," *Washington Daily News* (January 5, 1961), vertical files, MLK Library.

50. "Still Stonehenge," *Washington Post* (January 15, 1962), vertical files, MLK Library. And the Post continued: "We might suggest a slight amendment to the design–an heroic reproduction of that famous cigarette holder and cigarette, at customary jaunty angle, giving forth continuously clouds of derisory smoke rising symbolically and triumphantly over the failings and mischances immortalized on the cluttered collection of up-ended cobblestones below it." FDR's cigarette holder, universally paired with the word "jaunty," figures prominently in almost all caricatures of the man both by those who liked and disliked him. Recently the town of Hyde Park which uses a "jaunty" profile of FDR, "cigarette holder clenched between his teeth" as its unofficial symbol, has come under fire for advocating smoking. ("FDR's Cigarette Ignites Flap," [Cokeville, Tenn.] *Herald-Citizen*) (July 26, 1995).

51. And yet he argued against funding the FDR Memorial from taxpayers' money–or from money borrowed in their name, suggesting "that if this Congress cannot delay its gratification long enough to balance the budget on an item as simple and small as a memorial made out of granite, then there is probably no hope for us ever balancing the budget." After all, "Granite is going to be in Minnesota when we finally balance the budget. It may be older granite by that point, but it is going to be there." *Congressional Record*, House, July 14, 1982, H4057, 4060.

52. Paul Conkin, *The New Deal* (NY: Thomas Y. Crowell, 1967), 7.

53. Ibid., 26-28. See also with Barnard in Milton Bronner, "A Sculptor of Democracy," *Independent* 89 (February 26, 1917): 355.

54. "George Grey Barnard's Statue of Lincoln," *Outlook* 114 (December 27, 1916): 891.

55. Bronner, "A Sculptor of Democracy," 355.

56. Ida Tarbell, "Those Who Loved Lincoln: A Word for Barnard's Lincoln," *Touchstone* 2 (December 1917): 224-28.

57. "A Mistake in Bronze," *Art World* 2 (June 1917): 224-28.

58. "Lincoln: Was He a Slouch?" *Art World* 2 (August 1917): 416-18. In August 1917, Rucksuhl published a photo of George H. Storey's portrait of Lincoln. In preparation for this work, Storey observed Lincoln for extended periods in 1861 and wrote down his impressions in a notebook. The *Art World* published excerpts from these notes in an attempt to discredit Barnard's work. An example: "Hands and feet appear rather small for a man of his size, his feet are in fine, close-fitting calf-skin boots, his clothes of the finest broadcloth and well-fitting." See "A New Portrait of Lincoln," *Art World* 2 (August 1917): 422.

59. Lincoln to William H. Taft, March 22, 1917, Huntington Library, San Marino, California.

60. Heather Bruce, "FDR Memorial Has New Critics," *Boston Globe* (December 27, 1994) [front page]; Heather Bruce article in *Boston Globe* picked up by several papers around the country including *Detroit News* and *Free Press* (January 2, 1995) and *San Jose Mercury News* (December 28, 1994); "Remembering FDR," *Indianapolis Star* (January 21, 1995), vertical files, FDR Library; Hugh Sidey, "Where's His Wheelchair?" *Time* (March 6, 1995): 105.

61. Stewart Sutton to the editor, *Washington Post* (April 22, 1995).

62. Heather Bruce, "FDR Memorial Has New Critics," *Boston Globe* (December 27, 1994), 1. *The Santa Cruz County Sentinel* noted that the FDRMC has taken a more "politically correct" view on another issue of representation. They report that *The Animal Times* magazine of People for the Ethical Treatment of Animals, has bestowed as "Purr" (a word of praise) on designers of the FDR Memorial "for scrapping plans to exhibit a bronze statue of Eleanor Roosevelt wearing her trademark fox boa." She will instead be shown in a cloth coat from UN delegate period. ("Memorial for FDR Tries Hard to be PC," *Santa Cruz Sentinel* (April 27, 1995), vertical files, FDR Library.

63. "FDR's Handicap Didn't Matter Then, Now," *Omaha World-Herald* (April 8, 1995), vertical files, FDR Library.

64. Letters to the editor, *Washington Post* (April 22, 1995). Carlton Brownell, Little Compton, Rhode Island, added "President Roosevelt never allowed himself to be seen as an invalid, and there is no reason to show him that way 50 years after his death." From letters section of *Time* (March 27, 1995): 11.

65. Bruce, "FDR Memorial."

66. Michael Marino, consultant for ADA compliance and barrier-free living, "FDR Could've Done More for Disabled," *Poughkeepsie Journal* (April 18, 1995), vertical files, FDR Library.

67. Bruce, "FDR Memorial."

68. "FDR's Handicap Didn't Matter Then, Now," *Omaha World-Herald* (April 8, 1995). Though if the FDR Memorial Commission followed my advice here, they would further add to the eclectic "many-sided" approach which, as I explain below, contributes to the weakness of the Halprin design.

69. Justice Felix Frankfurter, "The Memorial to FDR: What the President Wanted," *Atlantic* (March 1961): 39-40.

70. "Son Questions Design of Memorial to FDR," *Washington Star* (December 31,1960), vertical files, MLK Library.

71. "Instant Stonehenge," *Time* (January 13, 1961), 60.

72. "The Roosevelt Memorial: A Set of Bookends?" *Newsweek* (January 16, 1961): 26, 28.

73. "Change of Heart," *Washington Star* (June 27, 1964), vertical files, MLK Library.

74. James Roosevelt to Virginia Hunt, August 5, 1964, James Roosevelt Papers.

75. James Roosevelt to Francis Biddle, June 23, 1964, Ibid.

76. "Try Again," *Newsweek* (July 5, 1965): 20.

77. Mrs. Van H. Seagraves (Sisty) to James Roosevelt, June 28, 1964), James Roosevelt Papers.

78. Ada Louise Huxtable, architectural critic for the *NYT*, defending Marcel Breuer's modernistic design in 1967, wrote: "Washington is in no desperate need of memorials, but it is monumentally short of the architectural and esthetic contributions of this extraordinarily creative century." (Ada Louise Hustable, "If at First You Don't Succeed," *NYT* (January 3, 1967), vertical files, FDR Library.) While the above comment refers to the Breuer design, Huxtable had been a supporter of the Pedersen and Tilney plan, especially in its scaled-down revision. She called it "full of promise" and reported "It has the possibility of the kind of architectural grandeur that can be more moving and evocative than the most realistic representation of the man memorialized." (Huxtable, "Monumental Troubles," *NYT* (June 26, 1964).

II

COMPARATIVE POLITICAL LEADERSHIP

5

Warrior, Communitarian, and Echo: The Leadership of Abraham Lincoln, Winston Churchill, and Franklin Roosevelt

Frank J. Williams

Abraham Lincoln, Winston Churchill, and Franklin Roosevelt are the three political giants of the nineteenth and twentieth centuries. Each was a successful wartime leader of a democratic nation and each articulated for both their constituency and for posterity the underlying principles for which their nations fought. Apart from these factors, are there other common threads running through their leadership? One way possible to approach a comparative view of these modern leaders is to explore them in terms of how premodern societies viewed leadership. For example, the highland Mayans of Guatemala used three categories of progressive ascendency for adult males: the warrior, the community man, and "the echo man."[1] Though the step from boy to warrior was fundamental and celebrated, the young warrior was not yet considered mature. At the next stage was the communitarian, who lived for the community—caring for widows and orphans, using his earlier-developed warrior disciplines to protect them; protecting the group with rituals, decisions and prayers; acting here, intervening there. The ultimate stage of personal development was that of "the echo"—an individual who transcended a culturally defined role and learned to truly hear his people. This person became a leader embodying compassion and intuition. The focus of the echo man was less on action than on a philosophical understanding of the community's role in the world and the responsibility of the living to both their ancestral past and future generations.

In a sense, Lincoln, Roosevelt, and Churchill represent modern versions of this Mayan ideal. Each became "the echo" of his era, earning a place in modern history. Perhaps the greatest difference between these three leaders and those in premodern societies is that modern leadership requires a greater degree of action than contemplation. Yet action alone is not enough.

This study examines these three phases (warrior, community leader, and echo man) in the leadership development of Lincoln, Churchill, and Roosevelt. In many ways, it shows that the Mayan evolution of leadership defines their political legacies and suggests links between the distant past, the present, and the future.

The Warrior

As a warrior, Lincoln had the least practical military experience of the three. But he was a fast learner and demonstrated astute appreciation of the role of the warrior in modern warfare. In much the same way, Roosevelt learned the importance of military policy and planning on his job during the Woodrow Wilson administration. As president, he assembled a competent staff on which to rely during World War II. Both Lincoln and FDR grew beyond their warrior stage, whereas Winston Churchill, who had far greater practical experience in military matters, was ultimately restricted by his inflated view of himself as strategist.

Lincoln's early military leadership was minimal. The Black Hawk Indian War offered as an opportunity to meet Lincoln's need for public acceptance. He was elected captain by his men and he made political contacts. He later deadpanned that his principal enemies on campaign were the "mosquitoes."[2] Ironically, his military service worked against his first political campaign as it left him too little time to campaign for office. He had announced his candidacy for the state legislature before his enlistment, which he extended.[3] His opponents enjoyed ample time to campaign against him and Lincoln lost. But his military service worked to encourage him to reenter politics and begin the practice of law.

Once in national politics, Lincoln adopted the unpopular stance of opposing the role of the warrior-presidency of James Polk.[4] Abraham Lincoln believed in Athenian democracy for the United States rather than a Spartan "military industrial complex" state. In fact, once president, he confounded his critics by coming to understand the political role of the military and the reason wars are fought, and won or lost. He eventually displayed a better understanding of war and politics than military leaders.

Lincoln used his role as commander-in-chief to take charge of the political arena. With Congress out of session, he called for troops, instituted a naval blockade, revoked John C. Fremont's emancipation decree, suspended the writ of habeas corpus, and announced the preliminary emancipation proclamation. He was a determined political leader with a goal.

He intuitively recognized the link between war and politics. Lincoln lacked diplomatic training, but, contrary to the opinion of many, he did not ignore issues of international interest and their effect on the United States. His direct involvement, for example, helped defuse the *Trent* affair which could have led to war with Great Britain.[5]

Circumstances in the war forced Lincoln to contend with the military situation. Rather than passively react to his commander-in-chief role, he studied the situation carefully and then took decisive action in the selection of commanders and in the determination of strategy. In light of the limited military experience, Lincoln became an outstanding commander-in-chief. Though less than a flawless performance, he readily understood the war.

John Hay, one of Lincoln's private secretaries, wrote to colleague John G. Nicolay, on August 7, 1863:

> The Tycoon is in fine whack. I have never seen him more serene & busy. He is managing this war, the draft, foreign relations, and planning a reconstruction of the Union, all at once . . .There is no man in the country, so wise, so gentle and so firm. I believe the hand of God placed him where he is.[6]

Military leadership by the commander-in-chief was even more essential for a global war than for a fratricidal war four score years earlier. Franklin Roosevelt was, in a sense, the political offspring of his famous "warrior" cousin, Theodore Roosevelt, who had inspired FDR's political development and molded his world views. TR's warrior role was shaped largely by his Southern maternal ancestry which led to his eventual publication of the classic naval study of the War of 1812, and apparent guilt over his personal hero's evasion of military service during the Civil War.[7] Given his earlier influences, the Spanish-American War became a necessity in the development of Theodore Roosevelt. Though the popular image of Theodore Roosevelt as a warrior president is overdrawn, he had a sophisticated appreciation of America's place in the world. Like Theodore, Franklin understood the importance of the role of the United States and its navy in world affairs.

In September 1940, Franklin Roosevelt transferred fifty obsolete destroyers to Great Britain in exchange for leases of naval bases. He told the new session of the 77th Congress in January 1941, that the United States must become the "arsenal of democracy," a bold assertion in an inherently isolationist country.[8] A few days after it assembled, the House received a bill, appropriately numbered 1776, that called for supplying material to the enemies of Hitler. Despite the opposition of non-interventionists, this bill was passed in March. The Lend-Lease Act was a virtual declaration of war against the totalitarian powers. The legislation effectively ended American neutrality. Using a Lincoln-like analogy Roosevelt explained, "Suppose my neighbor's home catches fire. . . .if I can take my garden hose and connect it up with his hydrant, I may help him to put out his fire."[9]

As long as the war continued, most of the glimpses Americans caught of their president were Roosevelt as commander-in-chief, a role he relished. As commander-in-chief, Roosevelt's long-term objective was a Lincolnesque world order in keeping with Franklin Roosevelt's Four Freedoms: freedom of speech and expression, freedom of religion, freedom from want, and "freedom from fear. . . ."[10] Eric Larrabee, author of an excellent study of FDR as *Commander-in-Chief,* "the ultimate standard in presidential military performance" was Abraham Lincoln.[11] But he found comparing FDR to Lincoln difficult because their "situations were vastly different."[12] Larrabee asserts that "Lincoln dealt with his commanders seriatim, as one by one he had to recognize their inadequacies and replace them."[13] Larrabee's view ignores Lincoln's trust in his Generals in the West who were left alone and in command.[14] While Larrabee indicates that Lincoln, "possessed no general staff but had to invent it in his own person,"[15] he fails to mention the roles of Henry W. Halleck, who became in actuality the first chief-of-staff of the army and Secretary of War Edwin M. Stanton, who handled many of the details of running the war. Larrabee's image of Lincoln,

> . . . in the War Department telegraph office—looking into space and forming the words with his lips, as he wrote some of the most thoughtful and concise. . .military instructions—is not one in which Roosevelt can be imagined."[16]

Larrabee concludes that "Lincoln was a natural, a born military mind, one of the finest his country has produced."[17]

Roosevelt's foremost concern was securing the speediest possible end of the war at the smallest cost in American lives. But realities forced compromise on FDR, just as they did for Lincoln and Churchill. The extent to which FDR's wartime actions fell short of his long range goals is a measure less of failure than of his skill in achieving a consensus among his own military commanders, the American people, and the allies. In exercising his powers as commander-in-chief, Roosevelt, like Lincoln and Churchill, operated at the apex of the total war making, production, and diplomatic structures of the nation. His was the ultimate power and his were the ultimate decisions.

As war leader, FDR was a superb judge of officers. As Eric Larrabee has shown, Roosevelt's greatest contribution to victory was his appointment of men like George Marshall, Ernest King, Dwight Eisenhower, Chester Nimitz, and even Douglas MacArthur.[18] He gave these men enormous responsibility; he remained informed on campaign details; and he usually, but not always, responded to their advice. Marshall and King ensured that FDR did not neglect the war in the Pacific. They counterbalanced Roosevelt's propensity to be swept up by Churchill's unrealistic and impractical plans. The extraordinary organizational skill and passionate attention to detail of Marshall and Eisenhower complemented FDR's habit of improvisation and taste for sweeping generalizations. Roosevelt's excellent general staff handled the details, whereas Lincoln, lacking such staff, was forced to deal personally with details.

As Larrabee points out:

> Roosevelt was no Lincoln, if one is looking for Lincoln's penetrating grip on what was wrong, say with Meade's failure to pursue Lee after Gettysburg. Roosevelt did not have to concern himself at that level; he did have a general staff, and one he could rely on; he could get some elements wrong and the general propositions right, as he did at Guadalcanal, the campaign he especially cared about, where he wrongly thought that we had overreached ourselves but rightly saw that the point of it was attrition, wearing the enemy down.[19]

Roosevelt did not have to pressure his field commanders to fight, "as Lincoln did."[20] He had military leaders who "would see to it"[21] without having to be presidentially pushed and prodded. "Roosevelt did not have Lincoln's tactical gift,"[22] but he exhibited the ability to identify the key issues and prioritize them. Nonetheless, "measured against Lincoln,

Roosevelt had a mind of similar strategic capacity, and he put it to work with similar effect."[23]

By the time Germany attacked Great Britain in 1940, Winston Churchill had enjoyed ministerial office on and off for almost fifty years. He entered politics under Queen Victoria and retired as Prime Minister under Queen Elizabeth II, fifty-five years later. Churchill was elected to the House of Commons the year before President William McKinley was assassinated in 1901 and was still sitting there in 1964, the year after President John F. Kennedy was assassinated.

His "finest hours" occurred during World War II. He rallied the British against Hitler.[24] In one sense, the highland Mayans offer an insight into Churchill's greatest triumph as well as his most severe limitation. If the warrior is fundamental and still admired, both premodern and modern societies recognize there is still a recognition that there's more to life than the traditional Spartan spirit in democratic states. Churchill's triumphs are fully deserved: victories over political enemies, foreign aggressors, and the childhood parental torments he endured. Fortunately, both Abraham Lincoln in the presence of his "angel" stepmother, and Winston Churchill, in the presence of his nanny, were able to overcome obstacles faced at home. Without those enduring life supports, both democratic leaders may have become instead demonic leaders. Even with the support of the women each suffered recurrent bouts of depression for the remainder of their lives.

In 1940, at the moment of England's and Europe's greatest peril, Churchill at last became prime minister and, in A.J.P. Taylor's simple and eloquent phrase "the saviour of his country,"[25] a phrase often ascribed to Lincoln in 1865.[26]

On May 13, 1940, Churchill delivered his patriotic "blood, toil, tears, and sweat" speech to the House of Commons: "You ask, What is our aim? I can answer in one word: It is victory, victory at all costs in spite of all terror; victory, however long and hard the road may be."[27] Fifteen days later, when threatened with the prospect of losing a large part of the British army, he told his cabinet colleagues, "Of course whatever happens at Dunkirk, we shall fight on."[28] This meant that there would be no compromise with Hitler, rejecting in advance any negotiated peace. For this, Churchill has been universally praised, except by author John Charmley, who faults Churchill for not negotiating with Hitler. Charmley apparently forgets that Hitler had a poor record in keeping his promises.[29]

Churchill was able to overcome Conservative party reservations as events of the war silenced their opposition. Magnanimous like Lincoln, he did not purge his opponents in the Conservative party. Churchill won the support, not only of the Conservatives, but also of the Liberal and Labor parties and the trade unions by including Ernest Bevin in his government. As a result, he established political cohesion and unity and engineered an efficient machine for conducting the war. He directed the war, aided by the chiefs of staff, while the war cabinet concentrated on home and party matters.

Lincoln could *listen* to others as professional equals. For example, as president he crafted a cabinet which contained his primary political competitors who considered themselves far superior to him. Despite their attitude, he selected William H. Seward as secretary of state, Edwin M. Stanton as secretary of war, and Salmon P. Chase as secretary of the treasury. Lincoln easily delegated to the competent and would *listen* to their advice with an open mind before making up his own mind. Yet, Lincoln led his cabinet. "I never knew with what tyrannous authority he rules the Cabinet until (sic) now. The most important things he decides & there is no cavil," private secretary, John Hay wrote approvingly in 1863.[30] Lincoln had both an unusually focused mind and a traditional respect for the role of the Congress. Though he was the primary player in the direction and conduct of the war, he expected Congress to lead in other areas of domestic legislation. As a result, it was Congress which initiated the Homestead Act, the Land Grant College Act, the protective tariff and the national banking laws. He had a Whiggish attitude about the presidency—less is more. This was the root of his assuming executive powers slowly, almost reluctantly, in the Whig party tradition.

The major exception to Lincoln's role in domestic legislation was, of course, on the matter of slavery. However, his activist role in this area grew out of his assumption that the issue of emancipation and union were tied together in the war effort. Because the Constitution failed to give Congress jurisdiction over slavery in the states where it already existed, the commander-in-chief's role could be extended into this area. In his 1861 annual message to Congress, he urged the members to adopt the plan for gradual, compensated emancipation in the border states. In 1862, when Congress passed the Second Confiscation Act, Lincoln threatened to veto it until Congress addressed his objection to the provision that those in rebellion would forfeit their property forever in violation of the constitution's prohibition against bills of attainder. Following his re-election, he used his influence to gain passage of the proposed Thirteenth Amendment abolishing slavery.[31] Seldom before had he assumed such leadership in domestic legislation. But, like Roosevelt and other modern presidents, Lincoln found Congress to be a severe trial. While at times strained, as in his taking the unusual step of giving the Wade-Davis bill a pocket veto, his liaisons with the legislature were never totally terminated. A congressman, frustrated with the president's way of diverting attention from the real issue by telling a joke, admonished him,"I think you would have your joke if you were within one mile of hell! To which Lincoln responded, "Yes . . . that is about the distance to the capitol!"[32]

Ever the consummate politician he knew how to keep his options open. He delayed calling Congress into session for more than two months at the onset of the war. Yet he always clearly understood that eventually Congress would have to pass judgment on his unilateral actions, even if it had little choice in ratifying Lincoln's *faits accompli*.

One of Churchill's private secretaries, John Colville, thought that Churchill "had no conception of the practical difficulties of communication and of administrative arrangements."[33] Yet, Churchill was determined not to follow the example set by former prime ministers H. H. Asquith and Lloyd George who had allowed politics to obfuscate strategy and for generals to do as they chose. He recognized that the system of administering the war should be centralized without emotion and politics. General Sir Hastings Ismay, his chief staff officer, saved Churchill from making the fatal mistake of creating an *ad hoc* staff composed of the prime minister's cronies. As soon as he became prime minister, Churchill, who was already chairman of the Committee of Military Co-ordination, named himself minister of defense.[34]

When the British declared war on September 3, 1939, Neville Chamberlain responded to popular demand by appointing Churchill to his old post at the admiralty. Churchill's energy was soon felt, not only within the department but also throughout the cabinet. The Norwegian defeats in April and May of 1940 shook public confidence in Chamberlain's leadership and on May 10, when the German armies entered the Low Countries, Chamberlain resigned in favor of the one leader, Churchill, capable of forging a national coalition government. Parliament gave him a unanimous vote of confidence.

This confidence was sustained throughout the four and a half years that followed, stimulated by Churchill's rocklike faith in ultimate allied victory and by his frank, memorable and dynamic oratory.

Churchill also believed that he was a great strategist, but the evidence is to the contrary. Unlike Lincoln and FDR, Churchill was, in truth, the worst kind of amateur general. From beginning to end of both world wars, Churchill was an adventurer who tried shortcuts and back stairs approaches, with sometimes disastrous outcomes. He had earlier been rightly blamed for the Gallipoli fiasco in 1915. Between 1940 and 1945, his schemes included bringing Turkey into the war and invading Norway. His "Mediterranean strategy" mired the British and the Americans in an endless campaign in Italy and delayed the essential invasion of northern Europe by at least a year. His worst decision may have been the "strategic bombing" offense that destroyed the cities of Germany and killed 600,000 civilians without appreciably shortening the war.

As A.J.P. Taylor tried to explain it, "He lived for crisis. He profited from crisis. And when crisis did not exist, he strove to invent it."[35]

Yet, to John Keegan, Winston Churchill as war leader is easily compared to Abraham Lincoln.

> Like Lincoln, Churchill remained throughout the war at the seat of government; like Lincoln, he embroiled himself throughout the conflict in the processes of representative democracy; like Lincoln, he never rested in his search for generals who could deliver victory, peremptorily discarding those who failed him; like Lincoln, he clung to no doctrinaire principles of strategy, preferring to trust in a few broad policies that he believed best served the long-term interests of the people and the alliance of states he represented.[36]

The Communitarian Leader

The highland Mayans recognize that people do not live for arms alone. Once the peace has been won or a relative state of security has been established, the quality of community life assumes primary importance. Abraham Lincoln's genius was recognizing the fundamental nature of America's experiment in self-government, its inherent opportunities through which he was able to fulfill himself, and his willingness to participate in his community to maintain this political heritage for others.

Prior to the presidency, almost all of Lincoln's political life was in state politics where he accepted the values of the Whig party in promoting internal improvements for a growing nation. He believed government should help trigger economic development. As a state legislator he was a "big spender" for those purposes that benefited both the community and entrepreneurs.

Retreating from active politics for a short time, he reentered it when America's fundamental values were threatened. His enduring legacy is one of preserving the Union in order to safeguard the American dream for all its people. He used his sense of community to reconcile the values expressed in the Declaration of Independence with the U.S. Constitution. The ideal of equal opportunity at the community level was nationalized.

Like Lincoln, FDR's political experience began in state politics. He understood that modern political leaders must act—even when they might not have a clear answer to problems. Rather than accept the Great Depression as inevitable, his political steps at least inspired hope.

Roosevelt was known for his legislative management beginning with the ninety-nine day session of the 73rd Congress which began on March 9, 1933. It represented the most daring presidential legislative leadership in American history. Congress dazed, disaffected, and filled with freshmen who owed their victories to Roosevelt's long coattails, found itself subjected to a carefully timed bombardment of bills. Roosevelt sent a rapid succession of presidential messages, sufficiently spaced to avoid confusion. He followed each message with a bill to implement it. FDR thus dealt with the crisis in agriculture, banking, relief, and a dozen other problems with amazing speed. The fact that Congress was passing a presidential menu of laws was never concealed. Never before had the American government so closely replicated the British system of ministerial leadership.

From his inauguration in 1933 until 1939, the president subordinated questions of foreign policy to his battle for the reforms of the New Deal. During the first session of the 76th Congress (January 3 - August 5, 1939) FDR labored with the most recalcitrant Congress of his six years to secure additional appropriations for housing, to liberalize provisions of the Social Security Act of 1935, and to persuade Congress to amend its neutrality legislation. The last initiative would free FDR to deal with foreign aggressors in the time honored way of ad hoc diplomacy.

Though the New Deal may have had many shortcomings, FDR meant it as an experiment to preserve self-government. Even critics today recognize FDR's power to inspire though they desire to dismantle the legacy of New Deal legislation.

In contrast to Lincoln and FDR, Churchill seems never to have truly recognized the needs of ordinary people in ordinary times when the state was not threatened. As James MacGregor Burns has insightfully pointed out, the Labor party had a social package to offer the British people once Churchill had gallantly preserved their safety and security during World War II.[37] Even if much of this legislation proved questionable in the long run in the short run it addressed their immediate lives.

Gratitude in politics fails to endure even if it momentarily endears. This truism is borne out by the 1864 and 1944 elections. FDR's reelection was much like Lincoln's in 1864. In both instances Americans had to choose their leader during wartime. Both incumbents managed only low pluralities.

"The Echo"

Just as there is more to leadership once a society prevails over its predators, there is more to leadership than more transacting bargains among contending factions in society, as James MacGregor Burns has so eloquently described.[38] As the Mayans recognized, leadership must also incorporate the wisdom of those able to discern the true needs of human beings. The "echo" leadership suggests a psychological dimension that leadership theorists James Chowning Davies and James MacGregor Burns both recognize as essential to societal health. The echo leader transcends traditional culture boundaries and sees beyond racial, ethnic and gender stereotypes. Strikingly, the primitive Mayan culture showed as much sophistication in this dimension as some members of the most advanced postindustrial society demonstrate today at the beginning of the twentieth-first century.

Churchill's historical echo, no matter how much we honor his achievements, especially his essential wartime leadership in defending the British against the Nazis, is fainter than the FDR and Lincoln legacies. As Professor Davies pointed out in his comparative view of leadership, Churchill at heart was a traditional conservative primarily interested in defending and preserving England and the British Empire.[39] Even sympathetic admirers acknowledge this. Some even accuse him of being a "racist," but it may be that Churchill was so blinded by the British legacy that he failed to see the needs of colonials. If so, he was not the first English leader with this shortcoming.

Churchill possessed little enthusiasm for women in politics and even for women suffrage unlike Abraham Lincoln who at age twenty-nine already advocated the vote for women. Ironically, it was England's first female prime minister, Margaret Thatcher, who looked to Winston Churchill as her party's foremost doctrinaire over other Conservative prime ministers.[40]

While some may cite Churchill's "Iron Curtain" speech as of "echo" quality, even it seems to be wearing thin for new democracies outgrow their historical chains. Nonetheless, his words suggest the penumbra of the "echo" leader,

>   In War: Resolution
>   In Defeat: Defiance

In Victory: Magnanimity
In Peace: Good Will.[41]

These words signal the abstract principles that Churchill recognized as being important to good leadership.

Churchill's essence in retrospect, is the defiant wartime leader. He said at the time of the Dunkirk evaluation,

> We shall not flag or fail. We shall go on to the end. . . . We shall fight on the seas and oceans, we shall fight . . . in the air, we shall fight in the fields and in the streets, we shall fight in the hills; we shall never surrender . . .[42]

Always the fighter, Churchill, in the end did not quite comprehend—to use Professor Davies' term—the needs of the English *after* World War II nor the non-English speaking peoples of the world.[43] In practice, Churchill patronized people of Third World countries. In a sense, he valued England as a nation-state, the Empire, and the English language more than human beings who were different from him.

In strong contrast, Franklin Roosevelt's imprint continues to strike a resounding echo today—he resonates both in the depths of Americans and those abroad. For example, in the latest rating poll of American scholars, FDR supplanted George Washington in the number two spot.[44] Though the legacy of the New Deal may be mixed and may have tentacles reaching far beyond FDR's intent, his leadership inspiration remains intact even among some Republicans. Roosevelt's "Four Freedoms" remain a national and even international statement of human rights. They are the ideals of an echo leader.

Although his inner reserve, like that of Lincoln's, often baffled even those closest to him, FDR's basic character was in accord with that of many American's: idealism tempered by realism. He seldom talked about his thinking or his plans until he had firmly made up his mind. "John Gunther once asked Mrs. Roosevelt, 'Just how does the President think?' She replied, 'My dear Mr. Gunther, the President never *"thinks"! He decides.'*"[45] On the other hand, Roosevelt would adopt ideas only if he agreed with them. If he disagreed, he simply did nothing."[46] By not sharing his thought processes, FDR fostered an aura of mystery and authority, and he kept power firmly within his domain. These same characteristics also describe Lincoln.

FDR could listen to and hear, the needs of others. Moreover, he had the advantage of a First Lady who perpetually educated him about people from different, less privileged backgrounds. He viewed his wife as his political partner and encouraged her to mold a twentieth-century role for the First Lady. FDR appointed the first woman to a presidential cabinet. He not only could hear the voice of those very different from him, he also could speak their language, as he demonstrated in his fireside chats.

While FDR is highly ranked, Abraham Lincoln consistently polls first among scholars and others who rate American presidents. His warrior career probably was inspired by George Washington, America's quintessential echo leader. Yet Lincoln did not enter the pantheon as a war hero.

Lincoln was the communitarian leader who recognized the needs of his constituents on the frontier. His legislative career was a model of using government to help people achieve economic advancement. Yet even in this traditional Whig view of internal improvements, Lincoln was sensitive toward others, including politically disenfranchised slaves and women. When his principled position on slavery and the Union thrust him into a wartime presidency, his message was compassion, a valid echo for all time:

> We are not enemies but friends. . . . Though passion may have strained, it must not break our bonds of affection. The mystic chords of memory, stretching from every battlefield and patriot grave to every living heart and hearthstone all over this broad land will yet swell the chorus of the union when again touched, as surely they will be, by the better angels of our nature.[47]

Similarly, Lincoln's Gettysburg Address, exemplifies a genuine echo leader. He speaks of the debt to forefathers, to the living and to the soldiers who have just died, while poetically bringing the Declaration of Independence and the U.S. Constitution into sync for the benefit of all.[48]

Seemingly, it was the genius of Lincoln to understand the needs of everyone all the time. He comprehended the values of our founders expressed both in the Declaration of Independence—"our jewel of liberty"—and the inherent restraints required by the U.S. Constitution. Maneuvering between idealistic values while preserving the constitutional restraints imposed on him, Lincoln led the nation during a divisive civil war that ultimately assured greater human dignity for all. Amazingly, Lincoln accomplished his enduring legacy in one-third the time FDR spent in office and half the time of Prime Minister Winston Churchill. Lincoln's leadership is the modern epitome of classical magnanimity.

Conclusion

In a comparative sense, Abraham Lincoln's leadership remains the touchstone echo. As James C. Davies long ago suggested, Lincoln's democratic example and American federalism are the two greatest gifts that our ambitious experiment in self-government have given the world.[49] Though more conservative than Churchill in many ways, Lincoln differed in that he was able to expand democratic values while Churchill fundamentally was tied to preserving the English empire.

Similarly, FDR was able to adjust to an evolving world better than Churchill. FDR was willing to experiment, but retained his ability to listen to others, including Eleanor, his social conscience. Despite their inherent differences, Lincoln, FDR, and Churchill remain fundamentally effective role models for democratic leaders.

Perhaps the reason that Churchill's leadership echo may resonate less vibrantly than Lincoln's or FDR's is that, without question, Churchill endured the most psychologically stressful upbringing of the trio. He was virtually ignored by parents who favored his brother. Fortunately, as Lincoln found warmth from his stepmother, Churchill found support from his nanny. Both however, suffered bouts of depression for the remainder of their lives as a result of their childhood psychological trauma. Churchill's fight for psychological survival may explain his lack of sensitivity toward others. He was the life-long fighter.

In contrast, FDR was afforded the psychological luxury of a secure childhood that allowed him to focus concern on others. Similarly, Lincoln gained psychological security, despite tension with his father, who also had to fight for survival on the frontier.

A comparative study of these three democratic giants of the nineteenth and twentieth centuries helps to clarify—and confirm—the significance of each. It also suggests the difference between the ephemeral and the eternal in political leadership. It also calls to mind F. W. Maitland's rule: that events now long in the past were once in the future and we should interpret these events in terms of how people expected them to turn out, rather than how they did.[50]

Judged by any standard Lincoln, Roosevelt, and Churchill were truly the giants of democratic leadership. Judged by the standards of the highland Mayans in which progressive ascendency characterized personal development, Lincoln, FDR, and—to a lesser extent—Churchill, reached the ancient ideal of "the echo man," who can truly hear people and lead them toward higher democratic goals.

ENDNOTES

1. Robert Bly, "What the Mayans Could Teach the Joint Chiefs," *The New York Times*, July 23, 1993.
2. Roy P. Basler, ed., Marion Delores Pratt and Lloyd A. Dunlap, asst. eds., *The Collected Works of Abraham Lincoln*, 9 vols. (New Brunswick, NJ: Rutgers University Press, 1953-1955) 2:510 (hereinafter cited as *Collected Works*).
3. Ibid., 5-9.
4. Ibid., 420-22. Congressman Lincoln asks President Polk in his "Spot" Resolutions in the United States House of Representatives on December 22, 1847 to show exactly the "spot" where Mexico invaded "our territory."
5. James M. McPherson, *Battle Cry of Freedom: The Civil War Era*. (New York: Oxford University Press, 1988), 391. The president was aware that the action of Captain Charles Wilkes in seizing confederate emissaries Mason and Slidell violated international law, that Great Britain would not stand for the seizure, threatened war with the United States, and embargoed all shipments of saltpeter which the North needed for gun powder. As the president said, "One war at a time."
6. Tyler Dennett, *Lincoln and the Civil War in the Diaries and Letters of John Hay* (New York: Dodd, Mead and Co., 1939), 76.
7. His father.
8. For a full discussion of FDR's machinations see Robert Shogan, *Hard Bargain: How FDR Twisted Churchill's Arm, Evaded the Law, and Changed the Role of the American Presidency* (New York: Scribner, 1995).
9. Frank Friedel, *Franklin D. Roosevelt: A Rendezvous With Destiny* (Boston: Little Brown and Co., 1990), 360.
10. Ibid., 361.
11. Eric Larrabee, *Commander-in-Chief: Franklin Delano Roosevelt, His Lieutenants, and Their War* (New York: Simon & Schuster, Inc., 1987) 643.
12. Ibid.
13. Ibid.
14. Ibid., Historian Richard McMurry believes the war was won by the North in the West. Interview with Carl Zebrowski, "Why The South Lost the Civil War," *American History* (October 1995): 26, 66.
15. Larrabee, *Commander-in-Chief*, 643.
16. Ibid.
17. Ibid.
18. Ibid.
19. Ibid.
20. Ibid.
21. Ibid.

22. Ibid.

23. Ibid.

24. Taken from a speech delivered by Winston Churchill on June 18, 1940, the day after the French capitulated: "Let us therefore brace ourselves to our duties, and so bear ourselves that, if the British Empire and its Commonwealth last for a thousand years, men will still say: 'This was their finest hour.'" Winston S. Churchill, *The Second World War*, 6 vols. (Boston: Houghton Mifflin Co., 1949), 2:198-99.

25. A.J.P. Taylor, *The War Lords* (NY: Atheneum, 1978), 98.

26. See the excellent survey in Merrill Peterson, *Lincoln in American Memory* (NY: Oxford University Press, 1994), particularly "Apotheosis," 26-27.

27. Martin Gilbert, *Finest Hour. Winston S. Churchill 1939-1941* (London: C & T Publications, Ltd., 1983), 333.

28. Ibid., 411-12, 421-22.

29. John Charmley, *Churchill: The End of Glory* (New York: Harcourt Brace & Co., 1993).

30. Dennett, *Lincoln and the Civil War*, 76.

31. Frank J. Williams, "The End of Slavery: Abraham Lincoln and the Thirteenth Amendment—What Did he Know and When Did he Know It?" *Abraham Lincoln and A Nation at War*. Papers from the Ninth Annual Lincoln Colloquium, October 22, 1994 (Lincoln National Historic Site, Springfield, IL, 1995).

32. P. M. Zall, ed., *Abe Lincoln Laughing: Humorous Anecdotes from Original Sources By and About Abraham Lincoln* (Knoxville: The University of Tennessee Press, 1955). Entry Number 48, 35.

33. John Colville, *The Fringes of Power: 10 Downing Street Diaries 1939-1955* (London: W.W. Norton & Co., 1985), 58.

34. John Keegan, "Churchill's Strategy," Robert Blake and William Roger Luis, eds., *Churchill: A Major New Assessment of His Life in Peace and War* (New York: W. W. Norton & Co., 1993), 329.

35. A.J.P. Taylor, "The Statesman," *Churchill Revised: A Critical Assessment* (New York: The Dial Press, 1969), 58.

36. Keegan, "Churchill's Strategy," 330, 331.

37. Interview of James MacGregor Burns by Doris Kearns Goodwin in "True Leadership," William Pederson & Ann McLaurin, eds., *The Rating Game in American Politics* (New York: Irvington Publishers, Inc., 1987), 219.

38. James MacGregor Burns, *Leadership* (New York: Harper & Row Publishers, 1978), 4.

39. James C. Davies, *Human Nature in Politics* (New York: John Wiley & Sons, 1963).

40. John Grigg, "Churchill and Lloyd George," Robert Blake and William Roger

Luis, eds., *Churchill: A Major New Assessment of His Life in Peace and War* (New York: W. W. Norton & Co., 1993), 111.

41. Inscribed on statue of Winston Churchill at Westminster College, Fulton, Missouri, site of the Winston Churchill Memorial Library.

42. Martin Gilbert, *Finest Hour*, 569, 571. Winston Churchill, speech on Dunkirk, House of Commons, June 4, 1940. John Bartlett, *Bartlett's Familiar Quotations. Thirteen and Centennial Edition* (Boston: Little, Brown and Co., 1955), 869.

43. James C. Davies, "Franklin, Eleanor, Abraham and Mary," paper presented at "FDR After 50 Years" conference, Shreveport, Louisiana, September 16, 1995.

44. Robert K. Murray and Tim H. Blessing, "The Presidential Performance Study: A Progress Report," *Journal of American History*, 70 (3) (December, 1983): 535, 555.

45. Larrabee, *Commander-in-Chief*, 644.

46. Edward J. Flynn, *You're The Boss* (Westport, CT: Greenwood Press), 214.

47. *Collected Works*, 4:271.

48. Ibid., 7:17-22.

49. James C. Davies, *Human Nature in Politics* (New York: John Wiley & Sons, 1963), 320.

50. Robert Livingston Schuyler, ed., *Frederic William Maitland. Historical Selections From His Writings* (Berkeley and Los Angeles, CA: University of California Press, 1960), 74-5.

6

An Evaluation of Franklin Delano Roosevelt

Glen Jeansonne

When Franklin D. Roosevelt was five, his father, a wealthy, socially prominent Democrat, took his boy to the White House to meet President Grover Cleveland. Cleveland, the first Democratic president since the Civil War, weary of the turmoil of politics, patted Franklin on the head and said he wished him well, and he hoped fate would spare him the burden of the presidency. Cleveland, who detested political intrigue, did not know that the boy would grow into a man who excelled at political intrigue and would become the greatest American politician of the twentieth century.[1]

Roosevelt's name is etched in history, and in the hearts and minds of Americans who lived during the Great Depression and World War II. Bringing the ship of state safely to port through tempests that included the nation's greatest economic crisis and the gravest foreign threat ensures FDR's place in the pantheon of great presidents. Most polls of historians rank him third among presidents—after Lincoln and Washington—and first among twentieth-century presidents.[2]

Roosevelt's most significant accomplishments were to preserve the nation's morale through perilous times, inspiring confidence with his actions, his oratory, and his personal example, and sustaining fortitude through adversity.[3] Roosevelt's successors—presidents as different as Lyndon Johnson, Ronald Reagan, and Bill Clinton—measured themselves, and were measured by the American people, by standards set by Roosevelt. The first hundred days of a president's term had no special significance until Roosevelt translated his ambitious domestic program into legislation in a special session of Congress lasting 100 days.[4]

As president-elect, Roosevelt was told that if he solved the economic problems ahead, he would be remembered as a great president, yet if he failed to solve them he would be considered one of the greatest failures among American presidents. "If I fail, I will be the last one," Roosevelt said.[5]

When Roosevelt predicted in his 1936 renomination acceptance speech that his generation of Americans had a rendezvous with destiny he was thinking about the Great Depression. He could not have known that a greater rendezvous with destiny would arrive at Pearl Harbor on December 7, 1941.

Roosevelt did not eliminate unemployment and he did not win World War II single-handedly. Yet FDR, like Washington and Lincoln, became a pillar of inspiration, a symbol of American fortitude. After he eased the spiritual crisis of the depression Americans did not panic after Pearl Harbor. There were no contingency plans for a surrender, a withdrawal, or a compromise peace because no one doubted that America would win. With FDR leading, defeat was inconceivable.[6]

In addition to mitigating the Depression and winning the war, FDR wrought a political revolution. After the 1936 election, the Democrats became the majority party. Roosevelt brought minorities, women, and organized labor into the Democratic coalition. Injecting doses of adrenaline, warmth, and vigor, he forged a government that was humane, that served as an employer of last resort, that provided security of the aged in retirement, that supported the arts, and he also designed a political juggernaut that flattened the opposition. His four elections to the White House will stand as a permanent record unless the Twenty-Second Amendment is repealed.[7]

Roosevelt did not seem destined for greatness until relatively late in life. His education was elitist; first, he was tutored at home; then, attended Groton, a private boys' school in Massachusetts; later, graduated from Harvard, and studied law at Columbia. He did not earn a law degree but passed the bar exam. From boyhood to young manhood Roosevelt did not seem highly competitive. A mediocre student, too weak physically to be a first-rate athlete, he did not appear to have unusual talents. Franklin enjoyed the social whirl of Boston and New York, dazzled the young ladies, yet appeared likely to settle into the comfortable lifestyle of a gentleman farmer on his family's estate at Hyde Park, New York. But FDR was not destined to be a gentleman farmer.[8]

While at Harvard, FDR met Eleanor Roosevelt, a distant cousin, and they became engaged. To some, such as Franklin's possessive mother, the marriage seemed a mismatch. Franklin was extroverted and flirtatious;

Eleanor was serious and shy. FDR enjoyed a wide circle of acquaintances but had few close friends while Eleanor enjoyed the intimacy of a small group. Franklin and Eleanor stayed together until his death, but neither could provide what the other needed most. Franklin needed a nurturing woman who flattered his ego and devoted herself exclusively to his needs. Eleanor craved a deep emotional commitment of which her husband was incapable. Roosevelt had empathy with the masses, and Eleanor was more closely engaged with individuals. FDR skimmed books yet was not a serious scholar. Eleanor read serious books intently. More ideologically inclined than her husband, she would defy public opinion to do what she considered right. Eleanor cared more about what *she* thought; Franklin cared more about what *other people* thought. As a political team, they interacted as a synergism, yet there was little passion or romance in their marriage.

Franklin could not satisfy Eleanor's need for an emotional commitment because he could not bring himself to make deep personal commitments. Afraid to reveal his doubts and vulnerabilities, he shared his thoughts with a variety of women—although probably he shared romantic intimacy only with Lucy Mercer Rutherfurd—and revealed his complete personality to no one. A man with special unspoken needs, he filled them with many companions, each of whom fit a niche: Missy LeHand, his personal secretary; Joan Suckley, a neighbor and distant relative; Louis Howe, his political strategist; and Harry Hopkins, the versatile administrator.[9]

Roosevelt's journey to self-understanding did not culminate when he lost use of his legs to paralysis from polio. Inwardly, there were aspects of himself he never came to terms with, feelings and ambiguities he never resolved. Beneath his placid exterior, he had unsettled turmoil. Given his times, his responsibilities, and his tribulations, this should come as no surprise, yet it does; as if we learned that Abraham Lincoln was addicted to pornographic novels. Still, the truth is better than the pose, as truth often is. FDR had a private as well as a public rendezvous with destiny. As he struggled valiantly to define the place of America in the world, he struggled inwardly to understand himself. He did not succeed completely at either difficult task.

Ironically, some of Roosevelt's personal flaws were political assets. Because he did not make emotional commitments to individuals or to ideas he could jettison them when they became political liabilities. Because he was not a serious student of economics, and did not try to understand the complexities of some problems he could proceed with a confidence not justified by the realities of situations. His confidence was based in part on the fact that he did not know how much he did not know. His desire to protect his private thoughts compelled him to design a shield of superficial pleasantness, of charm, of seeming to agree with different people whether he actually agreed or not. Roosevelt had brilliant intuition about politics yet he did not rely on intuition alone. Like the nation he represented, Roosevelt was a mixture of the romantic and the practical. He combined visionary ideals with pragmatic methods.

In a more profound sense, Roosevelt turned personal failures into political assets. He failed at some things that are extremely important to most Americans: He did not have a happy, fulfilling marriage, nor was there any human being he completely trusted and with whom he shared his fears and insecurities. He was not a good, or very successful parent, and some of his children were quite unhappy, especially in their private lives. And one of the things that he most wanted to do, something most young children can do—to walk, to run, he could not do after his paralysis. But FDR realized intuitively, even if he did not realize it intellectually, that not only is it impossible for every person to succeed every time, at every task they undertake—more importantly, it is not necessary that they do so. It takes more character to live with flaws, to recognize them, to concede them, than it would take to lead a spartan and a puritan life. Rather, a person's flaws are parts of that person.

One who has suffered like FDR learns to appreciate the suffering of others. Adolf Hitler, who did not admit his failures, but rather complained that Germany had failed him, died a failure at his own hand. FDR, on the other hand, with many failures on his record, died in dignity and became an icon in world history, and deservedly so.

The generation born after World War II—the baby boomers—have seen the deaths of John Fitzgerald Kennedy, Martin Luther King, Elvis Presley, Malcolm X, and Mickey Mantle—like FDR—flawed heroes. Yet this generation also has seen the collapse of the Berlin Wall, men walk on the moon, and a vaccine for polio.

Nations, too, have flaws. The United States is a powerful, yet young nation, barely an adolescent by the standards of ancient civilizations. We do not have now, and perhaps never had, the material resources to uplift the entire world. It remains to be seen whether we can sustain the moral and spiritual resources for world leadership. We will be tested. A universe in which individuals and nations have the free will to decide to do the right thing is potentially a universe of a higher moral order than one in which history is predestined to unravel in a certain way. American history to this point has been a sprint. But the cycles of history, the evolutions of civilizations, are not sprints, but marathons. FDR's generation was tested and passed. The grade for our generation is now an incomplete. It is only in the long run that the good guys win, if indeed they win at all. We only learn at the finale, not during the initial episodes, the identities of those who wear the white hats.

Thus there is more to FDR's greatness than the man himself. In many respects the man, his times, the trials, and the triumphs of FDR and the nation he led, have affected the course of American history far beyond their own era. American history, for example, is littered with the tattered reputations of presidents who tried to be great when the times did not demand greatness; who strived to emulate the successes of those such as FDR who governed in times of peril. Yet, if it is true that there is no thing so powerful as an idea whose time has come, it might be equally true that there is no thing so futile as an idea that is premature. Ask Woodrow Wilson. After leaving the presidency, Wilson, a devout man, ruminated about the failure of Americans to follow his leadership and join the League of Nations. Wilson came to believe that in the future Americans would join an international organization only when they were ready to accept the responsibilities such leadership demanded. God had been wiser than he had, Wilson observed. Wilson knew he had tried too soon.[10]

John Kennedy to the contrary Americans will not "pay any price, bear any burden," unless compelled to do so by necessity. Lyndon Johnson, Jimmy Carter, and others, became disillusioned to learn that the American people and our congresses and our courts are unwilling to move with speed, with the resolve, and with the willingness to sacrifice what they accept in extraordinary times when times appear normal. Thus, their presidential agendas—ambitious, generous, compassionate, and courageous—were not achievable in the absence of a major, tangible crisis. The challenge of presidents who must surmount challenges on an incremental basis—such as the accumulating national debt—is in some respects more daunting than those of presidents who rule during a time of crisis, when a common, identifiable threat is transparently obvious. More than anything else, the existence of a common enemy or a common threat unites a people and provides the consensus for heroic leadership, for thorough reform, for drastic remedies by unclogging the arteries of the body politic.

It might be true that nations, as well as individuals, must fail before they can succeed. The example of Herbert Hoover's administration can illustrate one of the legacies of the decades of the 1930s and the 1940s. Perhaps Hoover was not miscast for the role that he was destined to play; perhaps he was as necessary for his times as FDR was for his. I do not think it would have been possible for the United States to go directly from the Coolidge administration's policies to the policies of the New Deal without Hoover in between. Hoover's presidency was neither wholly traditional nor entirely modern. A transitional figure, Hoover appears activist and progressive when compared with his predecessors, yet he appears constrained and conservative when compared with some of his successors. Such a figure was needed. The nation would not have accepted a New Deal late in 1929 or in 1930, because Americans would not accept fundamental change until lesser remedies had failed. Although Hoover's role was inadvertent, he provided a blend of continuity and moderate change at a time when the nation needed a settling out period. Even if Hoover had known exactly what to do to terminate the depression, it would have been impossible for him to do it. FDR himself could not, and would not, resort to deficit spending on a scale large enough to end unemployment until America's entry into World War II left the president and his country no choice.

Another lesson we might take from FDR's experience is that timing is as important in politics as it is in delivering the punch line of a joke. It might surprise many people to suggest that Franklin Roosevelt—arguably the most gifted politician in American history—might not be able to win the presidency in the 1990s. First, he would have to stage a two-year campaign in about forty presidential primaries, and he might not have the stamina for that. Secondly, the restraint shown by photographers in the 1930s and 1940s—who rarely photographed FDR in his wheelchair for publication, would not be possible today, especially because of television. No such generosity has been granted, for example, to George Wallace. Roosevelt's handicap would be obvious, particularly if he had to stand or sit for a debate with an opposing candidate. Roosevelt's paralysis was not evident in speeches delivered over radio, but would be on television.

Further, the press is more intrusive. An indiscretion in one's past or present can be magnified, as Gary Hart discovered, as John Kennedy might have learned if he had lived longer and remained in politics. Also, Roosevelt could not today hold together a coalition that included the black masses as well as white Southerners, an alliance that was unstable in the long term.

If Roosevelt somehow had won his party's nomination and gone on to win election in the context of the 1990s, he might have been a one-term or two-term, rather than a four-term president. A candidate's health problems become common knowledge today; refusal to reveal health records arouses suspicions. Paul Tsongas, for example, whose cancer was more serious than he admitted when he campaigned for the Democratic presidential nomination in 1992, would be unable to mount a credible primary campaign again. Investigative reporting and tabloid journalism have changed the dynamics of politics, and the relations between politicians and the press, and between politicians and the people. One might assume, for example, that even a Southern Baptist presidential candidate might be permitted the latitude to lust in his (or her) heart, but Jimmy Carter found out differently. In politics today, there is no such thing as safe sex.

The final difficulty FDR might have in winning reelection after gaining office, however, is the most important one. It is that in the political climate of the 1990s there is much less margin of error for a politician. The relative failures (or incomplete successes) of the National Recovery Administration and the Agricultural Adjustment Administration to resolve definitively the problems of industry and agriculture during an economic crisis might be costly in the politics of the first decade of the twenty-first century. More significantly, fear of failure might be sufficiently intimidating to prevent such bold new departures and to preempt risky experiments in programs and promises. Roosevelt defined the problem somewhat imprecisely when he said in his 1933 inaugural address that "the only thing we have to fear is fear itself."

What we really had to fear was fear of failure. Trying to do even the simplest task is complicated by fear of failure. Many persons, perhaps, could walk a board three inches in diameter if the board were placed on the floor of a room. It would be something else entirely to walk the same board if it were placed between two buildings 200 feet above the ground. The more one fears such as task, the more difficult the task becomes. Fear introduces an element of hesitation, like trying to type a speech for an important conference while thinking of each key one must hit. Roosevelt might not have feared failure as much as most people because he had failed at some things in his life. And he knew that life went on.

Yet Roosevelt's boldness to risk failure by acting decisively was complemented by a boldness to refrain from acting when refusal to act also entailed risks. For example, he did not try to seek declaration of war on Germany while Britain faced the Nazi onslaught alone, even though he would have been morally justified in doing so. As Woodrow Wilson learned, a premature idea is wasted. James MacGregor Burns has utilized apt metaphors in arguing that Roosevelt possessed the courage of the lion as well as the wiles of the fox.[11] There are a few courageous politicians and a few wise ones as well, but not many who combine both courage and wisdom.

However, FDR was not omniscient in his refusal to seek a declaration of war against Hitler's Germany until Admiral Yamamoto's bombs rained on Pearl Harbor, sounding reveille for slumbering Americans. If Hitler had not gambled by invading the Soviet Union without first conquering Britain, it might have been too late for the United States to determine the war's outcome by December 1941. Without luck, Providence, timing, and vulnerable opponents, no nation, no president can work miracles.

The lessons of FDR are simpler and more profound than many might assume. For example, no one, in the present, nor in the future, has or will have definitive solutions for our problems as a nation, collectively, or to our problems as individual Americans. When we ask, as journalists and historians sometimes ask, what FDR would do about the problems of the 1990s, the honest answer is that no one knows. But, more importantly, it does not matter what FDR would do. If our problems are solvable at all, we must solve them ourselves, as creatively as we can. For our generation, like every generation, the buck stops with us.

The worse use we could make of the history of FDR's era would be to use the solutions of the past as excuses not to think for ourselves. Hoover stuck with old solutions after it became evident they would not succeed. Roosevelt's relative success, by comparison, was possible because he tapped creative minds and creative thinkers. We must remember the precedents FDR broke as well as the precedents he set. If Roosevelt had taken the lesson from history that the only, or the best, approaches were the tried and true ones, he would not have succeeded, even in a relative sense. Rather, one of FDR's most important traits was his willingness to break with the past, to ignore the policies that had worked in the past because he knew that the present was different. He was willing to experiment, yet not recklessly, aware that no nation can offer its politicians or its people the promise of success without the risk of failure.

This is no endorsement of Republican panaceas, of Democratic panaceas, nor of third party panaceas. Rather, it is time to recognize that there are no panaceas—no magic bullets. The fact that some of the enemies of the 1990s were subtle and incremental made them all the more insidious. Unlike scientific problems, human problems such as crime, drug addiction, poverty, and lack of learning, begin anew each day, each time a new, unique, human being is born. Human beings, like cold germs, come in infinite varieties. That is why it is easier to land a man on the moon than to cure the common cold.

Simultaneously, each individual, each generation, is born pregnant with infinite promise, hope, and potential. If, in our attempts to solve our problems, we copy FDR's solutions, we delude ourselves. Imitation is flattering only to the person being imitated, not to the person or the nation doing the imitating. We should not want to be someone else, in some other time. Because if we do, even if we succeed, we fail. We should instead want to be the best version of ourselves, in our times, that we are capable of being. Otherwise, historians in the distant future will examine our record and when they peel away the layers it will seem to them as if someone scraped away the paint on Michelangelo's rendition of creation on the ceiling of the Sistine Chapel and found beneath it numbers.

That is the most significant and the most universal lesson and legacy of Roosevelt and of his generation, of their resolution in the face of an economic crisis within and foreign foes without.

Hindsight is not 20/20, or historians would always agree, and of course we do not.

The comic strip character Pogo's wry observation that "We have met the enemy and he is us," is apt. But there is a caveat to Pogo's observation. If the enemy is us, the solution also is us. It is not the past. We shall have to find it ourselves.

ENDNOTES

1. Frank Freidel, *Franklin D. Roosevelt: A Rendezvous with Destiny* (Boston: Little, Brown and Company, 1990), 16; Robert Dallek, *Franklin D. Roosevelt and American Foreign Policy, 1932-1945* (New York: Oxford University Press, 1979), 5.

2. *Milwaukee Sentinel*, March 29, 1976; Arthur M. Schlesinger, Jr., "Our Presidents: A Rating by 75 Historians," *New York Times* Magazine, July 29, 1962.

3. William E. Leuchtenburg, *Franklin D. Roosevelt and the New Deal, 1932-1940* (New York: HarperCollins, 1963), 42. See, for example, Meg Kissinger, "Milwaukeeans Remember FDR's Impact on Their Lives," *Milwaukee Journal Sentinel*, April 12, 1995.

4. The attempts of FDR's successors to emulate him is the theme of William E. Leuchtenburg, *In the Shadow of FDR: From Harry Truman to Bill Clinton* (Ithaca, NY: Cornell University Press, 1991). On the precedent set by the first hundred days of the New Deal, see James MacGregor Burns, *Roosevelt: The Lion and the Fox* (New

York: Harcourt, Brace & World, Inc), 166-74; Leuchtenburg, *Franklin D. Roosevelt and the New Deal*, 41-61; and Rick Hampson, "FDR's First 100 Days Set Tone for a Legacy Larger Than Life," *Milwaukee Journal Sentinel*, April 12, 1995.

5. Gene Smith, *The Shattered Dream: Herbert Hoover and the Great Depression* (New York: William Morrow and Co., 1970), 232.

6. See Richard Reeves, "The Age of Optimism," review of David Fromkin's *In the Time of the Americans* (New York: Alfred A. Knopf, 1995), 9-10.

7. Glen Jeansonne, *Transformation and Reaction: America, 1921-1945* (New York: HarperCollins, 1994),130-35; 156-59; 164-66; 224.

8. Jeansonne, *Transformation and Reaction*, 122-24.

9. Blanche Wiesen Cook, *Eleanor Roosevelt, Vol. I, 1884-1933* (New York: Viking, 1992), 169-71; 177-84; 247-48; 313; 316.

10. John Milton Cooper, *The Warrior and the Priest: Woodrow Wilson and Theodore Roosevelt* (Cambridge, MA: Harvard University Press, 1983), 342.

11. Burns, *Roosevelt: The Lion and the Fox*.

7

Franklin D. Roosevelt, Huey P. Long, and Political Leadership: Room for Just One at the Top

Glen Jeansonne

If Franklin Delano Roosevelt had a second-rate mind but a first-rate temperament as Justice Oliver Wendell Holmes Jr. observed, just the opposite was true of Huey Pierce Long.[1] Both Long and Roosevelt were competitive, ambitious, and successful, yet their approaches to politics and their lifestyles were antithetical. The conflict between the president and the Louisiana Kingfish in anticipation of the 1936 presidential campaign was a battle of egos and personalities as much as it was a contest of rival programs.

A race pitting the manic, uninhibited Long against the calculating Roosevelt might have resembled the mythical race between the hare and the tortoise described in Aesop's fables. Long and other depression-era demagogues who challenged FDR fed on the disillusionment of the masses still needy after three years of the New Deal. Long's charisma and Father Charles E. Coughlin's beguiling, melodious radio talks intersected with the impoverishment of the masses which facilitated the people's seduction.

Huey's compulsive desires for power and recognition reacted synergistically with the desperate needs of the unemployed and the homeless. There are always poor people and there are always ambitious politicians, but in the era of the Great Depression the stakes were higher: Few politicians are so driven as Long; and in few periods of American history have the people been more in need of a messiah. The needs of the people coupled with the personal needs of Long interacted as if someone had lit a match to a fuse that was burning in the direction of a stick of dynamite. Fate intervened and the burning fuse was doused. I do not know how close the fuse was to the dynamite when it was stopped short, nor do I know the dimensions of the explosion that might have occurred. I think such an explosion might have maimed the country, but not destroyed it. If the United States could survive the Civil War, perhaps it could survive anything. But the outcome was not certain.

Every one of Huey Long's attributes were oversized, exaggerated: his talents, his compulsions, and his opportunities to capitalize upon the suffering of his constituents. One reason Huey was ruthlessly effective is that his own drives were so great they provided the energy and the perseverance to win consistently.[2]

Huey had a love-hate relationship with the masses based on mutual dependence. Each was necessary to the other, but only so long as their interests were consistent. In exchange for favors and benefits from Long, the people gave Huey their votes. The bargain of votes for benefits is not necessarily pathological; to a degree, it is necessary in a democracy. Yet in Huey and in the masses at that point in history, the pressure on both sides reached pathological dimensions.

The bargain was unstable because Huey's program for the masses would last only so long as it was in his interest to provide it. Huey could terminate benefits if it served his interests. On the other hand, the people could deny Huey their votes if their interests diverged from his. Each feared the support of the other was fickle, and indeed it was. This insecure relationship exacerbated Huey's own insecurity. That is why Huey could never rest, because the kind of security his psyche demanded could only be supplied internally. Obtained externally, it was only ephemeral, in need of constant renewal and replenishment. For his part, Long aggravated the underlying instability of the era. In the long run, Huey's drives were so compulsive as to be self-defeating.

It is highly unlikely that Long could have been elected president. His best chance would have been if the Republicans nominated a candidate so formidable as to split the vote between the Republican candidate and FDR roughly equally. But the Republicans did not have such a candidate.

Further, Huey had skeletons in his closet: bribes and kickbacks, income unreported for tax purposes, vote stealing, complicity in a kidnaping, and extramarital sexual relationships. In a national campaign he would be subject to scrutiny by the national press that he could not intimidate as he could Louisiana's journalists and their publishers.

More importantly, Huey did not employ first-rate, independently-minded lieutenants because he refused to delegate authority. One might be able to run a relatively small state as a one-man show, but it would be impossible to run an effective campaign for the presidency that way, much less run the country single-handedly. Huey had nothing like Roosevelt's brain trust, and few minds, however brilliant, are as good as many minds.

Long's Louisiana machine thrived on patronage, yet in a campaign for the presidency against an incumbent, patronage would be used against him. Even in Long's own state, the federal government could outspend the state government. Nationally, Long would be overwhelmed by federal patronage. Additionally, although Long might blitzkrieg Louisiana politicians, he could no more blitzkrieg national figures of the stature of Roosevelt than Hitler could blitzkrieg Russia and America as easily as he defeated Poland and Belgium.

Huey was enough of a realist to realize that his candidacy in 1936 would be a long shot. In his own mind, he believed victory might come in 1940, particularly if a third-party candidate such as himself divided the Democratic vote in 1936 and facilitated the election of a conservative Republican. But Huey's entire appeal was based on domestic policy—ending the Depression and redistributing wealth. As fate had it, the major issue in the 1940 campaign was foreign policy, and Long knew little, cared less, and had virtually no public credibility on the subject of foreign policy.[3]

The question of what would have happened if Long had not been assassinated fascinates historians much as other leaders cut down in their prime interest historians—such as Abraham Lincoln and John Kennedy. Such questions are all the more fascinating because they are unanswerable.

Whatever might have happened to Huey's political career, it is easier to speculate about what might have happened to Long personally. Having been elected a governor and a U. S. senator, the only remaining step on the ladder of political success Huey had to ascend was the presidency. A cabinet position or the vice presidency would be an unrealistic goal for one who was never a team player, such as Huey.

In a personal sense, Huey was running on a treadmill propelled by his own compulsions. The only way he could get off the treadmill was to quit running, but that would have deprived his life of its purpose. The only other way to get off, the only other way to get peace of mind, was to die. For all of his accomplishments, Long never had peace of mind, nor was he a happy individual. One does not have to be a happy person to be a great politician, but it helps. Otherwise, over time, the strain of competition in this most insecure profession wears one down. That is why FDR's temperament was a greater asset than Long's brilliant mind. FDR himself was not calm, nor entirely at peace with himself, although that is the image he projected, and what he wanted people to believe. Still, in a relative sense Huey Long was not simply running for something—he was running away from something—and the something he fled was himself. However fast he ran he could not escape, even if he ran all the way to the White House.[4]

ENDNOTES

1. For Holmes's use of the phrase to describe Roosevelt, see Geoffrey C. Ward, *A First-Class Temperament: The Emergence of Franklin Roosevelt* (New York: Harper and Row, Publishers, 1989), xv.

2. William Ivy Hair writes, "Huey led by compulsion instead of statesmanship because he was internally driven by a force he seemed to control." *The Kingfish and His Realm: The Life and Times of Huey P. Long* (Baton Rouge and London: Louisiana State University Press, 1991), 163.

3. Glen Jeansonne, *Messiah of the Masses: Huey P. Long and the Great Depression* (New York: HarperCollins College Publishers, 1993), 158-68.

4. T. Harry Williams states: "But in striving to do good, he was led on to grasp for more and more power, until finally he could not always distinguish between the method and the goal, the power and the good. His story is a reminder, if we need one, that a great politician may be a figure of tragedy." *Huey Long* (New York: Alfred A. Knopf), x.

8
Jesus, Lincoln, and Beethoven: Three Notes on the Same Grand Chord

James Chowning Davies

Why Put These Three Together?

It's easy to see what these three did not have in common: Jesus was a Jew, born in Palestine two thousand years ago, and he never got a college education. Lincoln was an American of English ancestry, born on the nineteenth-century American frontier, and he was largely self-taught. Beethoven was a Rhinelander German of Flemish extraction who was born in Bonn, across the Rhine river from Cologne, had a private tutor for a decade, and settled in Vienna when he was twenty-two. All three spoke different languages and lived in very different cultures. It seems that there are only two bases for comparison: all three were dark-skinned and none of the three was admitted to Harvard or even the University of Heidelberg.

What's more, none of them was an original. Jesus taught moral values that had been kicking around on our small planet for centuries. What Lincoln put into practice was already expressed very nicely, as an ideal, in the Declaration of Independence fourscore and seven years earlier. Beethoven's musical innovations were mere developments of basic ideas already expressed by Bach, Haydn, and Handel, and Beethoven was neither a moral nor a political leader.

What I am suggesting is that they do have some very basic things in common and that these characteristics provide a major part, though not all, of the explanation of their immortality.

Jesus incited and excited his followers to expect and to ask that they be regarded as equal with all other people. He extended to the poorest, the most humiliated, and degraded people in Judea, the belief that they were morally equal with all other people. Most important of all: He was not only willing to die for this belief, he did so, in the exquisite anguish of one of the cruelest and most unusual means by which societies try to coerce conformity.

Lincoln confirmed among his followers—who during the Civil War came to include a majority of his fellow citizens—the same belief in moral equality. His major contribution was to use the power of government, that is, political power and military force, to realize equality. Government and the equality principle had been so used in the American Revolution against England as a colonial power. But after the United States declared its equal station among the world's nations in 1776, the white Anglo-Saxons who led the successful revolution were less enthusiastic about equality. They acted on the assumption that it applied just to male white Anglo-Saxon Protestants and Catholics whose forbears had left England to establish new colonies. Lincoln acted on a wider applicability.

Beethoven in his music and sometimes in his living expressed his belief in the dignity of human beings. And like Jesus and Lincoln, Beethoven empowered people to realize themselves as human beings. There has been a nonverbal sense among his listeners that he respected people and wanted them to control their own lives and fulfill their own selves. Among people he associated with, his sense of being equally dignified and empowered was not so consistent or unequivocal. After briefly discussing the rather self-evident contributions of Jesus and Lincoln to furthering moral equality, I will take more time to argue the more complicated case for Beethoven.

But before starting, let me say how I am using the terms dignity and equality. Doing so may diminish the ambiguity with which people debate the moral and political issue. Dignity refers to the inherent worth, inherent merit, of individuals. Inherent is a critical modifier. People are self-evidently very unequal in their intelligence, industry, creativity, and many other ways. Dull, lazy, unimaginative people are not admired as much as bright, high-energy, and creative people. But admiration is not dignity. As a moral principle it means that each human being deserves getting the same respect and the same treatment as all other human beings simply because each *is* a human being. Each human being by nature needs and expects to be dignified—to be regarded as worthy—for the same reason that every human being needs and expects to be fed and loved: it is a genetically established, natural characteristic of all human beings. We can say and act toward others without taking these natural desires into account, but when we do, we are denying them their humanity. People cannot fulfill their nature if they are not dignified, just as they cannot if they are not fed or loved.

Jesus and Equality

As I mentioned, Jesus built on moral leaders who had gone before him, very likely without knowing of their teachings. In his disputes with religious conservatives in Judea, he said that he came not to destroy the prophets but to fulfill them. This was indeed the case, with some more than minor changes in emphasis.

In the book of *Leviticus*, written no fewer than six and maybe as many as fourteen centuries before Jesus taught, is the statement: "And the Lord said to Moses . . . . You shall not be partial to the poor or defer to the great. . . . You shall not take vengeance or bear any grudge against the sons of your own people, but you shall love your neighbor as yourself."[1] Even more broadly, in *Exodus*, the Mosaic law reads "You shall not wrong a stranger or oppress him, for you were strangers in the land of Egypt"[2] and, more explicitly "The stranger who sojourns with you shall be to you as the native among you, and you shall love him as yourself."[3]

Quite certainly, one of the major reasons the religious establishment in Judea so bitterly opposed Jesus is that they saw him extending to all human beings moral principles that the establishment regarded as the property, the exclusive proprietary rights, of the Jewish nation. Both the Pentateuch, the first five books of the Bible that are a major segment of basic Judaism, and the Torah, whose written parts are the same as the Pentateuch, proposed equalizing dignity. Jesus merely proposed its extension to the entire human race, regardless of the degree of wealth, moral purity, age, or whatever. As the means to universalize dignity, Jesus proposed returning evil actions of others by good actions toward them.

Six to seven hundred years before Jesus lived and preached in Judea, Gautama Buddha in India taught universal brotherhood. He said that if people spent their lives in compassionate service to all others, they would be more happy and more fulfilled than if they pursued a life seeking satisfaction of the passions for food and sex—and happier than if they demanded superior respect, dignification, deference as an attribute of their status. At about the same time, in Syria there was a moral precept: "As for him who doeth evil to thee, requite him with good."[4]

About the same time that Buddha taught in India, two moral leaders in China were teaching much the same thing: Lao-tzu said that if you return good for not only the good deeds but also the bad deeds of others, relationships between all people will become good. Confucius, a late-contemporary of Lao-tzu, gave this prescription to disciples who asked for the most basic word for the moral life: reciprocity, and "what you do not want done to yourself, do not do unto others."

Four centuries before Jesus, Aristotle in the book of ethics dedicated to his son Nicomachus, said: "When men wish the good of those they love for their own sakes . . . they love their own good. . . . Each party therefore both loves his own good and also makes an equivalent return by wishing the other's good . . . for there is a saying 'amity is equality,' and this is most fully realized in the friendships of the good."[5]

It is not to my knowledge known how closely Jesus or his pharisaical critics read Aristotle, or Buddha, or Lao-tzu—or even whether the teachings of these three were readily available in Judea. But Palestine was a colony of the Roman Empire when Jesus lived. The puppet king of Judea was Herod, and he was imaginative and open in many ways. He encouraged trade in both goods and ideas that caravans brought into this crossroads for trade in goods and ideas from the Orient, including India and China, and from Greece and Rome. Jesus "was born and reared in a land (Galilee) where Jews, Syro-Phoenicians, and Greeks rubbed shoulder to shoulder, and where cosmopolitan influences were stronger than anywhere else in Jewish Palestine."[6]

If the desire for equality is natural to human beings, it is clear why at first poor people in Judea and then poor people elsewhere in the Roman empire were immediately attracted to Jesus and his teachings. They were reacting the way that people in India and China and Athens were attracted to the writings of Buddha, Lao-tzu, Confucius, and Aristotle. Two things help explain this attraction, in parts of the world so far removed from each other in location and in culture. One is that it was natural. The other is that the societies where these equalitarian teachings took hold had advanced beyond the point where everyone had to spend nearly all of his and her time staying alive and well.

The power of Rome had established minimal peace, either directly or through puppet rulers like Herod. Pax Romana did not end insecurity about life itself, but it did diminish that insecurity over the very large part of the civilized earth that was included in the Roman empire. The military technology of the imperial government in Rome served that power and facilitated the process of keeping the peace. Herod was the effector in Judea. As long as people there accorded to Rome the power to protect themselves from armed enemies foreign and domestic, they were left pretty much to take care of themselves. In the relatively stable time when Jesus taught, during the rather benign rule of the emperor Augustus Caesar, Rome was not heavy-handed; it left heavy-handedness to such puppet rulers as Herod. We can note that the Roman proconsul, Pontius Pilate, allowed the local religious and political leaders to choose the man they would crucify: Jesus in preference to a robber, Barabbas. Pilate chose not to interfere in a family dispute.

It is well-nigh impossible to scale such matters as physical security and freedom from fear, modes of analysis generated by modern psychology. But it seems clear that in the era when Jesus taught, conditions were not so totally chaotic as in England and Germany during the sixteenth- and seventeenth-century Wars of the Reformation and in central Africa and the Balkans in the late twentieth century.

However, neither Jesus nor his apostle Paul—the conservative, orthodox believer who converted himself when he was on his way from Judea to Syria—was very political. As Paul got farther out from his Judean base, geographically and doctrinally, in his very long *Letter to the Romans* he admonished followers of Jesus to render unto Caesar the things that are Caesar's and unto God the things that are God's. And he did not specify clearly what matters were within the jurisdiction of Caesar and God. Caesar specified.

Nevertheless, the clear and bold preaching of the moral equality of all people was a tremendous advance. While sections in the Pentateuch admonished Jews to love their neighbors and to be kind to strangers, the orthodox, self-designated custodians of Jewish beliefs hardly treated converts to what is now called Christianity with compassion. And the domination of these custodians was accepted by the public, as later was the domination of the Roman church when Christianity became the established religion. Custodians of orthodoxy, whether Hebrew, Christian, or Marxian, have perhaps always reduced universal principles to parochial practices that perpetuate custodians in power.

The Roman government initially reacted to the stubborn converts to Christianity as the proprietors of Judean orthodoxy had reacted to Jesus. Christians were persecuted, even providing entertainment as prey for lions in Roman circuses. But pressures from the converts became enormous.

At last, three centuries after Jesus started the new religion, the Roman emperor Constantine, at Nicea in 325, established Christianity as the official religion of the empire. The Nicean Council did, however, allow the various sects of Christianity and other religions to continue and continue to compete with each other.[7] By thus granting Christianity official establishment, the government recognized its popularity and by tolerating doctrinal diversity, it possibly avoided the threat of rebellion while it planted the seeds of coerced orthodoxy.

By various means, ranging from force to invocation of magic,[8] both secular and religious leaders attempted to control the popularity of Christianity by appropriating and monopolizing its practice. That is, they used both force and magic to control the souls of ordinary people and in doing so separated themselves out as a ruling class. The leaders' efforts were generally successful, because "the masses" were kept illiterate and neither individually nor as groups could contest such force and magic. The "masses" were encouraged and coerced to agree. The custodians thus overrode the principle of equality with the practice of force and razzle-dazzle.

By monopolizing and controlling the practice of Christianity, its ecclesiastical custodians effectively arrested its realization: They kept the simple teachings of Jesus from dwelling in the minds of ordinary people. And those who rejected the ecclesiastical interpretation of Jesus sometimes were given the same punishment that the established religious leaders in Judea sanctioned against Jesus. The practice of equality moved at a ninety-degree angle from its preaching: That is, equality was not denied; it was simply not practiced. As George Orwell put it in *Animal Farm* sixteen hundred years after Nicea—and Orwell was satirizing not Christian rulers but the Communist elite—some people were more equal than others. The political implications of equality were ignored or suppressed.

Lincoln and Equality

Some fifteen hundred years after Nicea, in the century before George Orwell, Lincoln was faced with the same problem, the same contradiction, emerged between the principle and practice of equality. The Declaration of Independence had stated once again the very ancient belief in equality. Plantationers in the Southern states of America had not only gained political, economic, and social control of their own states but also rather effectively of the national government. The succession of Southern presidents, from Washington to Jefferson, Madison, Monroe, and Jackson was only occasionally interrupted by nonsoutherners. James Buchanan, a Pennsylvania Democrat whose deference to the South and the Southern aristocracy was almost automatic, was elected in 1856. Then came the union-shattering election of 1860, in which the Republican party triumphed; and then the Civil War. The victory of the North passed national power from the Southern slaveocracy to the Northern plutocracy, in the well-nigh universal process whereby those invoking universal principles proceed to parochialize them, once they gain power.

These events reduced the Democratic party to minority status, and thus, in the North, reduced the political power of poor people, who were mostly Democrats. The Republican party, whose leaders valued enterprise and great wealth, came to dominate national politics for more than a full generation after the Civil War.

Lincoln's role in this massive change in the power structure of the country derived from his most elemental beliefs, as he had practiced them in his own life, including his political life. He was born poor and raised poor. But he was raised with the belief that if he worked hard and if he accorded to others what he asserted for himself—equal dignity—he could succeed. And indeed he did. He did not hypocritically embrace the principle of equal dignity while evading its practice. With genuine and honest uncertainty about how far he wanted equality to go, he declared during the 1858 Lincoln-Douglas debates that even though he did not certainly believe that black people were his social or individual equal, he certainly believed that they were entitled to the product of their own labor.

After becoming president, Lincoln resisted the considerable pressure of abolitionists in 1862 to free slaves NOW. But the pressure grew, and in the fall of 1862 he drafted a proclamation of emancipation, got the advice of his cabinet, and at last issued the proclamation on the first of January 1863. Lincoln became more determined on the matter of slavery. In his second inaugural address in 1865, he said that if the savage war must continue "until all the wealth piled by the bond-man's two hundred and fifty years of unrequited toil shall be sunk, and until every drop of blood drawn by the lash, shall be paid by another drawn with the sword," so be it, he said, if it is God's will. He did not imagine that it was God's will to perpetuate slavery but that God's will apparently was that the process of ending slavery would be long and violent. Lincoln made this address a month before the war ended and he was assassinated, but it represented the basic dialog in his mind between inevitability—fate, the will of

God—on one hand and the ability to *do* something about events: to control them a little. He fundamentally believed in the gradual improvement of the human condition and that this improvement occurred in accordance with fundamental, natural laws. But he also accepted, even welcomed, the chance to intervene in such ways as to shorten the time and ease the pain that attends progress. Few leaders have more frankly recognized the inability to achieve ultimate ends immediately; few leaders have done more to speed and ease the process.

The savagery of the conflict went on for four years. Southern plantationers, the people who controlled not only their black slaves but also poor white people, thundered their insistence that they be allowed to continue to control, if not the entire nation and its people, then at least the South and its poor whites and enslaved blacks. "The South," as the plantationers declared themselves to be, fought to the point of total exhaustion of not only themselves but also their human and natural resources.

It is hard to overestimate the desire of people who lack equal dignity to gain it and hard to overestimate the tendency, once people have it, to deny it to others. That is, equality is gained and inequality retained in the name of equality. Lincoln's gigantic stature is as a person who believed in economic equality and practiced political equality to a degree it had never before been practiced. He reasserted those values announced in the Declaration of Independence and helped establish their association with actions. He didn't do too badly for an ungainly, ill-mannered, ill-schooled frontiersman who shared more than his sallow complexion with Jesus.

However, in the decades after the Civil War, gradually the same dissociation between values and actions that had occurred in the Roman empire between the Council of Nicea and the Protestant Reformation now occurred again. Both those who succeeded and those who wanted to succeed in gaining wealth and power began the age-old tendency to dissociate belief from practice. And it was all accomplished without anything more than fine-tuning and minor revision of the practice of political equality. The poor were to be objects of Christian charity of the wealthy, but they were not to have political power. Only an increasingly conservative Republican party and increasingly conservative Supreme Court had the education, the erudition, and the temerity to misunderstand equality.

The most serious problem with the admiration, the awe, that surrounds Lincoln is that for some people the awe becomes a halo. He becomes a symbol, an abstraction who represents an ideal and is therefore as unreachable as infinity. He was indeed human, very human, with a small but real set of imperfections. Ignoring these or regarding them as no more significant than the dust on an old statue detaches him from humanity at large and from each human being as an individual.

The detachment, the separation of ideal and real, may reflect a surrender to our own human imperfections—a redundancy that tends to ignore the fact that there is no such thing as a perfect individual. The detachment diminishes the possibility of improvement. Lincoln becomes an icon, like paintings and statues of Jesus, facilitating the dissociation from judgments of our actions as individuals and as citizens from real-life models whom, if we emulate them, may not get us to infinity but at least can get us a little closer. If people worship them rather than try really to act as they acted, it is easier for democratic individuals and governments responsible to their citizenries to act undemocratically with relation to outsiders, whether in the neighborhood, the nation, or the world community.

Beethoven, Equality, and Inevitability

Lincoln was born in 1809, in the boondocks of Kentucky. His wife was born just nine years later in Lexington. It was a very cultivated city on the American frontier of the early nineteenth century and declared itself to be the Athens of the West. It also claimed to have presented the first performance of a Beethoven symphony in the United States, in 1817, a year before Mary Todd Lincoln was born and nine years before Beethoven died. This loose chronological connection suggests nothing more than that Beethoven had rather considerable impact not just in Vienna but also overseas, in newly developing parts of human society.

The letter V became a rallying point during the Second World War. Winston Churchill and millions of other Europeans gave the two-fingered V sign. The Morse Code "dot-dot-dot-dash" for the letter V became associated with the opening bar of Beethoven's Fifth Symphony. Whether seen or heard, the symbol expressed the belief in victory over the Nazi tyranny and holocaust. Beethoven's Fifth was performed by the Sarajevo symphony orchestra to celebrate the new and hopefully peaceful year of 1996 in the Balkans, after some five years of intense and deadly conflict.

Beethoven's Ninth, the symphony variously called the "Choral" and the "Ode to Joy" symphony, was performed in Berlin shortly after the

Wall came crashing down in 1989. That wall had had both symbolic and real success in protecting people in East Germany from the freedom their rulers declared that they didn't really want—or at least weren't ready for. The performance, directed by Leonard Bernstein, was electric and was greeted with wave after wave of applause: For a day, the symbol and reality of freedom were very closely conjoined.

Beethoven's music has moved people all over the world to cheer or smile or cry and it has given them solace, helping them convert despair to hope and hope to realization. The most important question is not whether his music has been so influential: The big question is why. Before addressing that question with timid temerity, let me say something about Beethoven's origins, both familial and cultural; about the varied ways this rather solitary individual interacted with people he dealt with from day to day; and how these factors conjoined to produce his music.

On his father's side, Beethoven came from a long line of musicians. His grandfather Ludwig sang bass and served as musical administrator for the court of the elector of Cologne, who was the governing head of that major political entity as part of the Holy Roman Empire. Ludwig the elder and his wife had three children; only the son Johann who became Beethoven's father survived. And he sang tenor.

The elder Ludwig was indeed prominent, and he was not only full-faced but also full of himself: He sought to dominate not only his family but everyone else whom he regarded as beneath his station. Most particularly he dominated Beethoven's father, who suffered from being continually bossed and depreciated by the court kapellmeister. Johann sought to succeed his father as kapellmeister, and he graduated from singing soprano as a boy to tenor as a young adult. He didn't make it, to either the gleam of his father's court position or the depth of his father's voice.

His most crucial act of devious rebellion came when he insisted on marrying a nineteen-year-old widow, Maria Magdalena Keverich Leym. Johann van Beethoven's father disapproved of her: He said she was of an inferior social position. Her parents had worked in the court kitchen, several notches below working in the court music rooms, but her family background was at least the equal in status to the Beethovens. Johann was not a very strong person, and his father doubtless undermined what strength of character he may have had. In close succession Maria had lost her first child in infancy and then her first husband: It's possible that Johann felt the best he could do was to become a second spouse. But he attached himself to a strong person.

What's more, Maria Magdalena's family did not approve of the marriage. When Maria's mother was fifty-two, her husband had died, leaving her the breadwinner for the two of her six children who survived. She got a job as cook in court, saved money frugally, and died a year after her daughter had remarried. Her son-in-law speedily appropriated most of her very small fortune, and her daughter started having Johann's children.

To summarize her experience, Beethoven's mother lost her father, four siblings, her first husband and their child, and her first child by her second husband, Johann van Beethoven, and then her mother a year after she and Johann were married. She was a durable woman. All these not-so-minor disasters happened before her husband began to take his drinking very seriously and before their second son was born. Ludwig, named after his grandfather, was baptized a couple of days later, on December 17, 1770. Five years after Ludwig's birth, his father's mother died in a home she was put into because of her alcoholism. In a male-dominated society, with an authoritarian father whose mother was hooked on booze and with a strong wife, it is no great surprise that Johann took to establishing his manhood with the quick assurance he got from alcohol.

Nevertheless, Maria Magdalena bore five more children after the Ludwig who was destined for immortality. She endured a total of eight pregnancies—with only the three sons by her bibulous second husband—Ludwig, Kasper Karl, and Nikolaus Johann—surviving. It is little wonder that she had little enthusiasm for marriage, telling a friend not to do it, recommending instead "the most tranquil, most beautiful, most pleasurable life" of spinsterhood, in preference to marriage, which brings "a little joy, but then a chain of sorrows."

Let me list the critical intervals and events in Beethoven's private life. These periods circumscribed major events critical for his public life and his immortality. They were more than phases: They had crucial and cumulative affect on later events. Most of them involved tragedy that would have destroyed a less gigantic person, as FDR's polio a century later could have destroyed him. Like his mother, Beethoven endured. Like FDR a century later with his polio, Beethoven never reversed course. He developed personally and musically, without ever giving up or ever for more than brief moments reverting to earlier stages in his development. These intervals and events, developing first in Bonn and then Vienna, were: *his preadolescent childhood*, from his birth in December 1770 until 1782; *his adolescence*, from 1782 to 1792; *his move to Vienna in 1792*, which he seldom left until his death in 1827; and *his loss of hearing*, which began about 1798 and worsened relentlessly until his death. *His nephew*, Kasper Karl's son Karl was born in 1806 and remained a strong force for the two decades between Karl's birth and Beethoven's death in 1827. *His loves*, which were noteworthy from the time he got to Vienna but which gradually diminished as his deafness and relationship with his nephew intensified.

In Bonn, 1770-1792

Childhood. Beethoven was rather deeply attached to his strong mother and loyally fond of but distant from his weak father. As an adult he spoke affectionately of his mother and hardly at all of his father. He was evidently unhappy about his father's drinking (as Lincoln had been about his father's) and possibly worsened the critical relationship by turning away from rather than contesting his weak father.

In Ludwig, Johann van Beethoven had a child who was clearly very gifted. Before him dangled the example of Mozart's father Leopold, who had made a sensation with his prodigious son. Wolfgang Amadeus began public performances on the harpsichord at the age of six and made an international tour a year later. Ludwig was not so prodigious: He could not be taught music until he was four or five, but to hasten the process of distinguishing himself as the father of a prodigy, this weak man, himself the victim of a harsh and gifted father, often beat and more often humiliated his son. Sometimes he charged guests to hear him play; when Beethoven was eight, his father took him across the Rhine to give a concert in Cologne.

Ludwig was not Mozart and efforts to push him were abandoned, not so much because Beethoven was not a very gifted keyboardist and violinist as because this precocious boy was neither so young nor so brilliant as Mozart. And doubtless Beethoven's father was not so persistent as Mozart's strong father. Mozart burst into prodigy in 1762. When Beethoven was beginning to show signs of his genius, the year was 1774 or 1775. The situation was in this like that of the second person to explore the new world after Columbus, the second person to fly the Atlantic alone, or the second person to contest Babe Ruth's home run record.

Ludwig was eager to show visitors his ability to improvise on the piano or violin, and his father was usually eager to belittle him. Beethoven's reaction to such humiliation was to withdraw, but not to give up. He and his two brothers were occasionally sent to bars to haul their father home; and he lacked strong confidence in his mother in her deference to her capricious and bibulous husband. But this intensely emotional child, raised in an era when it was more common to beat the goodness into and out of children, avoided overt condemnation of his father and disappointment in his mother. He identified with his illustrious grandfather, whose name he bore. His mother kept mentioning the grandfather's distinction as the most outstanding musician in Bonn, and his father seemed determined not only to punish him because he could not punish Ludwig's grandfather but also to so humiliate him that he would not think he could exceed Ludwig's father. Beethoven withdrew into his own fantasy life, which revolved around playing the piano and violin and improvising his own music. He trained so well that he became one of the most outstanding pianists of his time, and he fantasized his compositions so brilliantly that many of them became immortal. To the everlasting glory of the musical world, he sublimated his frustrations in his music, in his playing and his composing. Beethoven's schooling was also rather normal for about the first decade: He attended a public school, which at the time meant going to a convent-run school. As the son of a musician who was not very distinguished but did sing in the elector's choir, Beethoven probably enjoyed some distinction among his classmates; but as the grandson of the distinguished kapellmeister, who had at least occasional direct contact with the elector (whose brother was the emperor in Vienna) Beethoven must surely have enjoyed distinction in the convent school. But he was not a neat and tidy boy, so lacking in this significant virtue that he once defended himself by saying that when he grew up, nobody would care. Meanwhile, when his mother died when he was not yet seventeen, Beethoven became the virtual head of the family and was given a pension for this purpose and kept it after he left Bonn for Vienna.

Early adolescence. Beethoven was nonetheless so gifted that when he was twelve he was put under the mentorship of a man about twenty-two years older than him: Christian Gottlob Neefe, the court organist. Neefe tutored in two very significant ways. He was a humanistic product of the Enlightenment that had such influence before the French revolution of 1789. He was also a Calvinist moralist who firmly but discreetly maintained and imparted his stern and righteous views about God and religion to an extraordinarily sensitive boy. Neefe was sensitive enough as a mentor and at the same time gifted enough musically to be able to develop Beethoven's music potential. He taught the boy Bach and composition.

To the boy Beethoven, after the training he got from his father and in the convent school, the contrast with Neefe must have been very striking. Beethoven remained gratefully loyal to his thirty-ish teacher, who sensitively elicited Beethoven's musical gifts and developed his confidence at an appropriate pace. At age twelve, he directed an orchestra from the keyboard. And unlike Mozart, whose father squeezed him into a wine bottle and marketed him before his time, Beethoven was not pushed to maturity.

The intimate contact with Neefe had a permanent effect on Beethoven: He himself became an inheritor of the Enlightenment. Like Rousseau and Kant before him, he developed a nonsectarian, humanist orientation that he applied—often abstractly but sometimes very concretely—to his political views and his interactions with the heavily hierarchized society in which an untidy, too dark complexioned, and too lowly born young musician developed. When he was twenty-three and in Vienna, Beethoven wrote to Neefe: "Should I ever become a great man, you too will have a share in my success."[9]

Beethoven developed cumulatively: the helpful and harmful interactions with his mother and father and brothers were absorbed in ways that were mostly but not exclusively constructive. His father's unpredictable and often harsh treatment did not turn him away from growing as a musician: He became an outstanding performing artist and he did not give up, as he graduated from improvising themes to composing coherent, elaborated music.

He seems to have delayed his emotional development. It may have "started" with the way he assumed responsibility not only for his brothers but for his father, who dissolved further into alcohol. Caring for family became almost a substitute for attaching his affection to one or another women of about his own age. As we shall note, his emotionally inadequate attachments to family and to a succession of women who were safely unavailable helped turn his emotional life inward to his music. To compose the works that he did involved intense concentration of not only his intellectual but also his emotional resources. Perhaps he was so put together genetically that he could not have composed otherwise. Unlike Johann Sebastian Bach, who composed so much music and sired so many children, by two wives whom he seems to have worn out, and unlike Mozart, who composed so much music so "effortlessly," for Beethoven the process was a continuous struggle. The results were triumphant, but most of the time it seemed to be a battle that required all of his enormous intellectual and emotional resources.

To Vienna in 1792

We can better understand how Beethoven dealt with equality by looking at the ways he dealt with various people after he left home and Neefe and landed in Vienna when he was twenty-two.

Beethoven and his "betters." Bach died twenty years before Beethoven was born. He had played Bach when he was learning music in Bonn, but much later he considered Handel (who died eleven years before Beethoven was born) to be "the greatest composer who ever lived." Beethoven was a late-contemporary of both Haydn and Mozart. Beethoven's brilliance as a pianist and promise as a composer were already recognized before he left Bonn for Vienna and a musical metropolis that still included two greats: Haydn and Mozart.

For some fourteen months, "Pappa" Haydn taught Beethoven. It's hard to say specifically how much musicianship Beethoven got from the widely beloved Haydn—surely a lot—but fairly easy to deduce that their person-to-person relationship had its rough edges. Haydn was said to have unsuccessfully asked Beethoven to dedicate his first works to Haydn. Indeed, while Beethoven was under Haydn's instruction in counterpoint, he felt he was not getting on well enough and without telling Haydn took another instructor. Beethoven rather maliciously enjoyed the secret. Even more, after his father died, he asked Haydn to help him get an extension of his allowance from the electorate, in order to support his younger brothers. The elector wrote back to Haydn that Beethoven was getting more than he said he was. Soon Haydn left for London and Beethoven took up counterpoint instruction from two other prominent teachers in Vienna.

Beethoven's actions toward his musical "betters" suggests that, even when he first arrived in Vienna, he was not sure that he had any betters. He had an ill-controlled tendency to joust with elder composers as teachers. He seemed to be saying to them: Who are you to think you can teach me anything? But with his social "betters" in a heavily hierarchized society, he shared with other composers a seldom controlled tendency to dedicate many of his creations to noblemen who supported him financially. This distinction in his relationships with two categories of "betters" suggests that Beethoven—if not really modest or humble—recognized his own genius and in more mundane matters recognized that he needed constantly the support of wealthy benefactors.

With publishers, he was even more devious and even more impossible. He would take advances from them and then not deliver the promised composition. He would sell the same work to two or more publishers. In at least one case, a publisher sued Beethoven for mishandling negotiations.

There is the story about how Beethoven and Goethe were together on a street when royalty passed by: Goethe bowed obsequiously and Beethoven needled Goethe, saying that the two of them were naturally superior to these distinguished nobles, who were superior only by social convention. Unfortunately the incident probably never happened and is true only in spirit: Goethe did tend to polish noble apples, not for money, as Beethoven did, but because the apples were noble. Beethoven, however, had genuine fondness for many nobles, and enjoyed their company and recognition.

Beethoven and "subordinates." With people beneath his station, Beethoven was often a cad. Naturally untidy and indifferent to the squalor he allowed to accumulate around him, he found it more than difficult to keep household help. But his interactions seemed more the product of his untidiness and preoccupation with composing than of his regard for them as "subordinates." He got on well with a servant provided during the period he was closest to his nephew, and on the street he encountered people not so much his inferiors as people whom he almost did not see. He constantly ruminated about themes for compositions, writing them down in the notebook he always carried with him.

But he was a particular cad with a copyist. This poor man was probably good at his business of expanding and straightening out themes and variations from composers. It may have been that the poor copyist had written eighth notes where he should have written sixteenths, but in any case, Beethoven's errant instructions caused the copyist to snap. He wrote a dignified letter to Beethoven, saying that if Mozart and Haydn had been his copyists, they would have been treated the same; and he concluded it with a couple of sentences that Beethoven did not appreciate: "I request only not to mix with those common copyists who consider themselves happy to be able to maintain their existence by being treated as slaves. At any rate, be assured that I will never have the least bit of cause to blush in front of you on account of my behavior."[10] Beethoven scratched heavy lines through the letter, wrote angry comments in the margins, and added: "Do you do honor to Mozart and Haydn by never mentioning their names," adding that the man was fired as of the day before the letter arrived, if not earlier.[11] In extenuation, it must be noted that the year was about 1826, when Beethoven was almost totally deaf and was composing music he could hear only in his mind. It must be further noted that Beethoven was still bursting with musical ideas that he was compelled to get out of his mind and on to scores. And we must also note that a reply to the poor copyist was probably never sent.[12]

Beethoven was a bear with virtually everyone, including his closest and most steadfast friends. Toward Schindler, who was a rather docile Boswell to his Dr. Johnson, he was usually amicable but sometimes accused Schindler of cheating him. The same was true of his dealings with his brother Johann, who for a time managed some of Beethoven's financial affairs. In these interactions, he seemed to regard others not so much as inferior or even contemptible as individuals who disappointed his expectations. He was highly judgmental: Those who didn't meet his expectations were stupid or devious rather than members of a lower class.

Beethoven's Loves

Beethoven was normally interested in women, even before he left Bonn. In Vienna he often fell in love and he quite certainly had an affair with one of his loves. The affair lasted over a year, the very prominent and psychologically sensitive Beethoven scholar Maynard Solomon believes, but like his other loves, this very special one was with a married woman.

This most intense relationship with "the immortal beloved" was evidently with Antonie von Birkenstock Brentano, the wife of a good friend and admirer of Beethoven, Franz Brentano. After their wedding in Vienna, the eighteen-year-old Antonie and her thirty-three-year-old husband moved to his place of business, Frankfurt. Within eight years she rather promptly and dutifully produced four children for her busy husband, but she longed for the cultural sophistication of Vienna and her distinguished father, a big-time art collector. Her husband adored her enough to move back to Vienna. She was aware of his affection, without really returning it. Frankfurt was (and is) a bustling entrepreneurial city that could not claim the cultural sophistication or even interest of the Vienna that Antonie glorified.

In 1810, Antonie's sister-in-law Bettina Brentano became an object of Beethoven's particular attention, but when she left Vienna Beethoven became increasingly enamored of Antonie. Solomon has quite well established that Beethoven and Antonie had an affair for a year, starting in the fall of 1811, when Beethoven was approaching the age of forty-one and she was thirty-one.

She was awed by the great and already famous composer. Earlier, she had written to a friend that she would do an errand for him, placing a musical score "in the holy hands of Beethoven, whom I venerate deeply. He walks godlike among the mortals, his lofty attitude toward the lowly world and his sick digestion aggravate him only momentarily, because the Muse embraces him and presses him to her warm heart."

She became more than awed, and she acted the Muse. She evidently offered to leave her husband and family for Beethoven. For a woman raised in the conventions of marital practices which almost totally forbade divorce but allowed for affairs—at least when practiced by men—this was an extraordinary offer. It suggests the depth of her love for this untidy and already quite deaf genius. In any event, Beethoven was so taken aback by the prospect of truly including a beloved—not just ideally but really—in his daily life, that he hemmed and hawed and finally backed away.

Antonie was probably the last woman to attract his serious attention—though he never seemed to lose the ability to respond to young, attractive women. At the age of forty-two, he evidently concluded that he could not both realize himself as a composer and experience the enduring love of one woman. He and perhaps Antonie paid a high price for resisting permanent involvement. Nonetheless, the breakup probably intensified his creativity, and the dozens of compositions that were still embryonic in the last fifteen years of his life were realized for posterity.

Beethoven's Most Enduring Love: Nephew Karl

With a father who was not particularly responsible or provident, Ludwig was a major source of support for his two younger brothers, Kasper Karl and Nikolaus Johann. He fell into this role when his mother died when he was seventeen and was even more involved in their support when his father died soon after Beethoven moved to Vienna. His brothers followed him there.

Kasper Karl met and commenced living with a young woman, Johanna Reiss, with whom he had a child four months after their marriage in May 1806. The child was named Karl. Beethoven, still sternly moral in the manner of Neefe and five years before his affair with Antonie, vigorously protested his brother's marriage to such an immoral person. "My brother's marriage, Beethoven wrote, was as much an indicator of his immorality as of his folly." But, like their father, marrying a woman his father disapproved of, Kasper Karl most of the time ignored his brother's low opinion of Johanna. However, he did once turn his wife into the police for theft; she was sentenced to a month's house arrest.

Beethoven became very fond of the boy Karl, even before Kasper Karl died of tuberculosis. A couple of days before he died and on Beethoven's insistence, Kasper Karl wrote into his will a statement giving joint custody of Karl to his wife and elder brother. Ludwig got his mortally ill brother to alter this statement, giving Beethoven sole custody of Karl, who was then nine years old. But Kasper Karl then wrote a holographic statement saying he did not want to give his brother sole custody. Kasper Karl, like his own father in dealings with the formidable grandfather Ludwig, was not very strong in dealing with his formidable brother Ludwig.

Beethoven decided to resolve the ambiguity in the wishes of his weak brother and sued for sole custody in a court which was available only to the nobility. Johanna's lawyer said the court had no jurisdiction because Beethoven was not of noble family. Beethoven made a tactical and fateful error by asserting that maybe his brother was not of noble blood but that he, Ludwig, was a nobleman because of his distinction as a musician and composer. The case was thrown out of court. Beethoven persisted: Some months later he got the appropriate court to declare him sole custodian and to strictly limit the times Karl's mother could visit her son. He put the boy in a boarding school, moved to be near the school, and when he became dissatisfied with the boy's teachers, took him out of the school, established the semblance of a normal household, and brought him to what Beethoven intended to be a normal family—but for the absence of a wife and mother. He hired a new housekeeper and a special tutor for Karl. Four years later mother Johanna proceeded to get pregnant by her financial counselor, thus confirming Beethoven's self-righteous view that she was immoral. She named the newborn Ludovica, doubtless after her brother-in-law who possessed her son.

Beethoven began to fantasize that the mother had poisoned her husband, was shadowing Beethoven, and besides was working as a prostitute. And he wrote: "I am now the real physical father of my deceased brother's child." Johanna blew up, and Karl at the age of twelve was caught between obedience to his famous and autocratic uncle and his wish to go back to his mother. Beethoven was indulged by the Vienna legal system because of his enormous reputation and maintained nearly total control of his nephew. When he gave up trying to make a musician out of a boy who had no gift for music, he sought other means of education, and Karl tried to commit suicide.

Johanna and Ludwig developed a relationship that was—fortunately for her—at arm's length. It had the intense elements of love and hate that so often characterized Beethoven's attachments to his friends, and to his nephew. She thought he was in love with her. And he may have been, four years after the end of his intense affair with Antonie Brentano. His behavior became so erratic that in 1819, Karl's mother sued to get custody of her son, and she won. But his attachment to Karl was so strong that they were in regular contact for the rest of Beethoven's life. Karl was by then in the army. Shortly before he died, Beethoven provided in his will that, in case Karl died first, the woman whom he treated so cruelly was to inherit the bulk of his estate, and evidently she was the only woman present when he died.[13]

Beethoven's relationships with Antonie and with Johanna Beethoven are only two cases that show how strongly Beethoven needed to find and attach himself to objects of his love. He needed people passionately, almost desperately, but he might have been able to fulfill this need only at the cost of critically ignoring his need to compose. With his frequent tantrums, his perpetual tendency to think that people were cheating him or wanting to spy on him, and with his occasional recognition of his own interpersonal ineptitude, including his frequent habit of selling the same composition to two or more publishers, Beethoven was occasionally very contrite, smothering people with affection and asking their forgiveness. But he never let anything interfere very long with his vocation as a composer. The result was that his intense emotion was concentrated on his music. This is exactly the same deflection of emotion into career that both Abraham Lincoln and Franklin Roosevelt experienced. Lincoln did not feel he was a very good husband. Roosevelt had an intense though intermittent lifelong affair with a woman he became involved with in his mid-thirties. Beethoven sublimated the objects of his emotionality in his music.

His Deafness

Like his unrequited love for people close to him, Beethoven's deafness was a well-disguised blessing. His hearing began to fail a couple of years before he left Bonn; in Vienna he lost steadily more of it; in his early fifties, he was almost stone deaf. When he was with other people, he used conversation books: He would ask people to write down what they wanted to say to him, after which he gave his replies orally. His deafness often agonized him and even more often made him more than just irritable: It made him a bit paranoid. Hearing loss does such things to people who cannot use voice as a means of interaction. But his deafness forced him to concentrate on putting onto blank scores that which he could still hear, doubtless better than anyone else: The music that welled and flowed and burst out of his mind.

It is hard not to sympathize, to empathize with Beethoven for his deafness, but ultimately he and later generations have benefited immeasurably from his curse. For Beethoven, deafness had the same effect of concentrating his efforts toward that for which he was so uniquely suited as infantile paralysis had in making Franklin Roosevelt concentrate on his career as a politician and statesman.

Beethoven's Basic Orientation Toward People

Beethoven once wrote in a diary that "Socrates and Jesus [are] my masters." It helps to understand such a complex individual if we bear this in mind. He was slovenly, he was cantankerous, often suspicious, and at times rather vain. He even did not discourage the story that he was sired by the king of Prussia, Frederick the Great. It serves no purpose for us to judge him for his imperfections, except to remind us that it was out of a very human and imperfect being that such great music flowed. Rather our purpose here is to understand how and why he acquired enormous stature while he lived and has retained it ever since.

It seems to me that the two individuals he said were his masters give a basic clue as to his orientation. The optimism of the Enlightenment helps explain his first feelings about Napoleon. Like Kant, Hegel, Goethe, and Schiller—the same Schiller from whose poem Beethoven derived the Ninth Symphony's Ode to Joy—Beethoven initially admired Napoleon. He was widely regarded as a true revolutionary who would in some doubtlessly magical way suddenly—and by force—liberate at least the

European portion of the whole human race. Beethoven cannot be singled out for scorn or for his naiveté when others presumably more sophisticated philosophically and politically were also bamboozled by Bonaparte. Beethoven shared the prevalent view among idealists and democrats of the nineteenth century that it was the duty of leaders who by nature or tradition were noble to do good to the "masses" without sharing power with them. That is, humanitarian intellectuals had not yet graduated from patronizing ordinary people to recognizing ordinary people as equals. A century later many liberal humanists were taken in by the typically idealistic and typically inhumane revolutionaries, Lenin and Stalin. And many people in Germany who might have known better were taken in by Hitler. In such cases, members of the elite fail to acknowledge the effect of their own needs to control, their need for power, just as people generally sometimes ignore it in their political leaders.

Looking at their leaders' ideologies rather than their actions makes it easy for both intellectuals and more ordinary mortals to misunderstand the intensity of their leaders' need for vast power. It is even harder to evaluate the degree of restraint that power-hungry leaders exercise. Napoleon used little restraint, and in some kind of oxymoron used his dictatorial powers to impose constitutions in nations that he conquered: constitutional, limited government by decree. Lincoln limited his own use of power with much more restraint.

Beethoven was indeed politically innocent but he also lacked the desire for political power. As an innocent, he soon realized what Napoleon was up to. He ended up dedicating the Third to an abstraction, "celebrating the memory of a great man." He had concluded before finishing the Third that the real Napoleon should not be confused with a hypothetical great man. Solomon presents a clear and balanced discussion of Beethoven's evolving attitudes toward Napoleon.[14] Scott Burnham goes further, declaring that the Third, the Eroica Symphony, does not symbolize Napoleon even in memory or even an abstracted heroic great man.[15] Burnham cites Richard Wagner for believing that "the real hero of the *Eroica* is humanity itself."[16] But Burham casts Beethoven in the role of hero: he says that Beethoven's music "appears to engage each of us at a deeply personal level, and yet engages us all in roughly the same way, such that the fundamental experience of the heroic style is always described similarly . . . the necessity of struggle and eventual triumph as an index of man's greatness, his heroic potential."[17]

If Beethoven abandoned the hopes he had for the leader that Napoleon pretended to be, perhaps the basic reason was that his masters were not political but moral. He used royalty and noblemen to gain support for his constant need for material support and to serve his needs for recognition. But he did not either worship them or merge his self in their images, even their kinds of images of greed and grandeur. He truly and deeply loved an aristocratic woman, Antonie Brentano; but with ambivalence and harshness, he may also have loved a rather "common" woman, his brother's widow Johanna. At his core, Beethoven loved Beethoven and loved the human race, like Lincoln and Jesus before him.

Beethoven's Fate and His Triumphs

It is as hard to say just what music is as it is to say what painting and sculpture are. The most exquisite word-portraits of a painting pale beside the experience of seeing one. Visualizing great sculpture verbally is likewise inadequate. And so it is with music. Its particular function seems to be to present emotional states as well if not better than they can be described by psychologists and others who are accustomed to verbal communication. The philosopher Langer called 'music the language of feeling,' and she bespoke the competence of music for that kind of expression thus:

> Because the forms of human feeling are much more congruent with musical forms than with the forms of language, music can *reveal* the nature of feelings with a detail and truth that language cannot approach.[18]

Music's elemental nature is exemplified by Beethoven's relationship to it. He started losing the use of his ears when he was twenty-eight, halfway through his life and long before he had reached his peak as a composer. By the end of his life, he had lost nearly all of it. When he was allowed to pretend that he was actually conducting his last symphony, the Ninth, he was so deaf that he did not hear the deafening roar of applause after the finale. He had to be turned around, so that he could perceive it visually. Music was very real inside Beethoven's mind: one of the most elegant examples possible of conjunction between idea and reality. He could not "really" hear what he really composed.

The Ninth expresses a dialog that was truly a dialectic in Beethoven's mind. He varied between his faith and his skepticism, which were related to but not quite identical to his hope and his despair. In 1802, when he was thirty-two, he changed doctors in hopes of finding a way out of his deafness. The doctor recommended that he get out of the noisy city. Beethoven settled on a town well outside of Vienna. It was indeed a pleasant setting, but in addition to inspiring Beethoven to compose, it also gave him solitude to brood about his fate. On a morning walk with a friend, the friend told him to listen to a shepherd the friend clearly heard. Beethoven couldn't hear the shepherd's flute and soon became quiet and depressed.[19]

Beethoven for a time was profoundly depressed by losing the sense that was closest to his life work, but he was depressed also by the social effect of deafness. In a long letter to his two brothers, later known as the Heiligenstadt Testament, he wrote:

> fortune is doubly painful to me because I am bound to be misunderstood. . . . I must live almost alone like one who has been banished, I can mix with society only as much as true necessity demands. If I approach near to people a hot terror seizes upon me and I fear being exposed to the danger that my condition might be noticed . . . But what a humiliation for me when someone standing next to me heard a flute in the distance and I heard nothing. . . . Such incidents drove me almost to despair, a little more of that and I would have ended my life—it was only my art that held me back. Ah, it seemed to me impossible to leave the world until I had brought forth all that I felt was within me. [20]

Beethoven's creativity, like Mozart's, was enormous, but ultimately he was unable to bring forth all that was within him. Some 138 of his works have opus numbers attached to them. More than 200 works, most of them minor (songs and other short pieces), but including two concertos, a symphony, and a quintet remain either unpublished, unfinished, or otherwise unrevealed. These works are catalogued as Wo—*Werke ohne Opusnummer*—many but not all of them because Beethoven did not feel they were ready.

What he *was* able to bring forth ranges all over the map, or over all the instruments he used in compositions both for groups (orchestral, choral, quartets, etc.) and for individual pianists, violinists, and vocalists. The moods of his music range from melancholy to rapturous, often in the same composition. Langer was right in saying that most, though not all, sensibilities, feelings—not thoughts but feelings—can be expressed only by music. That is, Beethoven was able to establish profound and enduring resonance with an elemental means of communicating individual feeling and group feeling that has been in the human brain since it became human.

In many of Beethoven's works there is a dialog between fate, destiny, predetermination, and whatever is beyond the control of individual human beings on the one side, and hope, self-determination, and whatever is within the control of individual human beings on the other. Beethoven was at least conventionally religious, in addition to noting his primary heroes, Socrates and Jesus. He believed there was a God that controlled human actions, but he did not believe that God was either capricious, ungoverned by natural laws, or omnipotent: He believed that human beings could truly do things to control their own actions.

The most eloquent evidence of this is in his refusal to let his deafness end his life as a composer. The most eloquent expressions of this belief in his music becomes a matter of listener's choice, and no two people on earth have the same preferences. So it's a matter of personal choice and personal resonance between composer and listener. The ones that have most clearly expressed this belief to me are commonly mentioned by others, so my choices are not quite idiosyncratic: the late piano sonatas, the late quartets (notably the Fifteenth, Op. 125 in A flat), the first piano concerto, and the Fifth and Ninth symphonies. Hearing even parts of these and other works of Beethoven is bracing at least; they are restorative, even resurrecting at most.

Usually but not always, Beethoven exhibits his fundamental optimism. He has faith and he *believes*, but he has more than belief. He *knows* that there is a dialog between being determined and being a determinant and insists on acting to the limit of his capacity to determine. Not in words, as here, but in his music he communicates that human beings can triumph over fate. They are not totally controlled by random forces because acting against control that seems at once to be random, arbitrary, and total diminishes the power of random forces.

Like Lincoln, Beethoven believed that he could control little inside himself and could control few events that surrounded him. And like Lincoln, he believed that he must do that which he could. Unlike the mythical Sisyphus, Beethoven believed that there was more purpose in composing than just to do something. Humankind, he believed, are not just the victims of fate: They can control things a little, and in doing so can make the world better and individual human beings more fulfilled, more fully realized. Beethoven would perhaps have been not so disturbed as puzzled at the existentialism of the late twentieth century.

To have faith in his ability to have an effect in civilization, Beethoven was living the confidence he had in himself. In this, he was like Lincoln, like Jesus, and perhaps like most people who are remembered for serving on the frontier of human social, political, and cultural progress.

It is most remarkable that Beethoven, like Lincoln, developed his self-confidence as a young man, in the face of ridicule and deprecation in the first two decades of his life, notably at the hands and with the voice of the man who was naturally the closest and ideally should have been his ideal—his father. Beethoven had the fortunate replacement, as a real and ideal figure, of his irresolute and sometimes cruel father by the resolute and humane Neefe. It is perhaps impossible to know whether the father that Beethoven inherited and the mentor he acquired were random events. At least as to the latter, it seems certain that Beethoven's intense, positive response to Neefe was not random. He began to compose and to perform more brilliantly under Neefe's encouragement than he had under his father's capricious and sometimes harsh cruelty. Neefe elicited his self-confidence as a musician, and Beethoven compensated for his uncouthness as a person by composing and thus reinforcing his self-confidence as an artist.

Early on in Vienna he came to a conclusion that he did not need public approval to do his work. His steadily progressive and inescapable deafness helped him concentrate on his music. If he had been more concerned than he was with public approval, perhaps he would have accomplished less as a composer: He might have been a Shakespeare who wrote *As You Like It* but was afraid to take on *Macbeth*. His profound musical self-confidence has inspired people ranging from victims of the Nazi occupation in the Second World War, to victims of the Russian occupation of Germany in the 1980s, to victims of the Balkan wars of the 1990s. Not only has he inspired such people politically: He has inspired people in all pursuits not to deny or ignore pain and reversals but to find the inner confidence to be efficacious, at times even victorious, in their efforts to live and to make better lives for themselves and those who come after them.

The continuity of his belief, in God and in mankind and in himself, is epitomized in his final act. When he was near death, in the middle of a late winter storm in Vienna in March 1827, he distinctly heard a clap of thunder. He raised his arm, shook his fist, and then died. He need not and should not be worshiped, any more than Lincoln should be worshiped, because some of his misdeeds were more than foibles and certainly not less than human. But he gave clear evidence in his life and in his music that human beings are not trapped by fate, God, chaos, or randomness: they can put their efforts together and find direction as they move toward goals that elementally are shared by all human beings–in as many different ways as there are human beings. Beethoven said that people can overcome.

ENDNOTES

1. *Leviticus*, 19:15-18.
2. *Exodus*, 22:21.
3. *Leviticus*, 19:33.
4. William F. Albright, *From the Stone Age to Christianity: Monotheism and the Historical Process* (Baltimore, 1957), 393.
5. Aristotle, *Nicomachean Ethics* (Cambridge, 1934), 471.
6. Albright, 395; for a lucid discussion of the interaction between the Hellenistic Greek ideas, Judaism, and Christianity, see 345-99.
7. Jacob Burckhardt, *The Age of Constantine the Great* (New York: 1949), 300-07.
8. Ibid., 300-07.
9. Maynard Solomon, *Beethoven* (New York, 1997), 26-27.
10. Elliott Forbes, *Thayer's Life of Beethoven* (Princeton, 1967), 937.
11. Ibid., 937.
12. Ibid., 937n.
13. This is the conclusion of Solomon, 292. George R. Marek believes that the only woman present was a housekeeper, see George R. Marek, *Beethoven* (New York, 1969), 627.
14. Ibid., 134-137.
15. Scott Burnham, *Beethoven Hero* (Princeton, 1995), 26.
16. Ibid., 26.
17. Ibid., xiv.
18. Susanne K. Langer, *Philosophy in a New Key* (New York, 1948), 191.
19. Forbes, 304.
20. Forbes, 304-05.

BIBLIOGRAPHY

Albright, William Foxwell, *From the Stone Age to Christianity: Monotheism and the Historical Process* [1940]. Baltimore: Johns Hopkins Press, rev. ed., 1957.

Aristotle, *The Nicomachean Ethics* [ca. 322 B.C.], H. Rackham, translator, London: Wm. Heinemann and Cambridge, MA: Harvard University Press, 1934 ed., 471.

Burckhardt, Jacob, *The Age of Constantine the Great* [1852]. Translated by Moses Hadas, New York: Pantheon Books, 1949.

Burnham, Scott, *Beethoven Hero*. Princeton, NJ: Princeton University Press, 1995.

Eaglefield-Hull, A., ed., *Beethoven's Letters*. Translated by J.S. Shedlock, New York: Dover Publications, Inc., 1972 [unabridged republication of same book published in 1926].

Forbes, Elliot, Thayer's *Life of Beethoven*. Princeton, NJ: Princeton University Press, 1967. (He was a nineteenth-century New Englander who delved deeply in Bonn and Vienna into Beethoven. The original biography was translated into German and first published in German, in three volumes, 1866-1879. The original biography, with some additions and corrections by the present editor, Elliot Forbes, remains perhaps the primary source.)

Langer, Susanne K., *Philosophy in a New Key*, [1942]. New York: Mentor Books, 1948.

Marek, George R., *Beethoven: Biography of a Genius*. New York: Funk and Wagnalls, 1969.

Solomon, Maynard, *Beethoven*. New York: Schirmer Books, 1977.

Sterba, Edith and Richard. *Beethoven and His Nephew*. Translated by W.R. Trask, New York: Pantheon Books, 1954.

Winter, Robert, ed., *Beethoven, Performers and Critics*. Detroit: Wayne State University Press, 1980. A 1977 symposium of the International Beethoven Congress, sponsored by the Detroit Symphony Orchestra, Antal Dorati, conductor.

III

TEACHING A LEGACY

9

The Depression, Eleanor and World War II: What Do Elementary School Social Studies Tell Us About Franklin Roosevelt?

Sherry L. Field

Franklin D. Roosevelt, one of the most celebrated and controversial of American presidents, has been a focus of social studies and history lessons for school children in various ways since the eras of the depression and World War II. Older Americans often recall Roosevelt from their childhoods as "the only president I had known for my entire life," or "a confident voice on the radio," or "the president who saw us through the depression and the war." They remember learning in school about Franklin Roosevelt as an important figure in history, while they were taught lessons of citizenships, patriotism, and preserving the democratic way of life.[1] The study of great American presidents, a long-held tradition in elementary schools, continues to the present. Content about the presidents is advanced in various ways in schools, and Presidents Day is generally acknowledged in the curriculum and celebrated in classrooms across the country.

There can be no doubt that Franklin Roosevelt enjoys a prominent place in history. Certainly, only a few presidents have been accorded the popular attention in literature and in factual accountings from history that have been accorded Roosevelt. This attention would seem particularly prominent in school history. Still, recent curricular revisions have prompted new attention to subjects and issues previously ignored and less attention to some of the more traditional issues, events, and historical figures. Because of this rewriting and compression of American school history, the following questions are raised: What place does Roosevelt enjoy in contemporary elementary school social studies curriculum? Is Roosevelt still a prominent figure in elementary school social studies textbooks? What types of contemporary children's literature are available to elementary teachers as teaching aids? This paper offers evidence about Roosevelt's current status in school history. The portrayal developed is based on a content analysis of five popular social studies textbooks series and an analysis of resources listed in four widely used children's literature anthologies and curriculum material guides.

Roosevelt as Seen in Elementary School Social Studies Textbooks

For this study, five elementary social studies textbook series adopted for use in the State of Georgia were analyzed for content relating to Franklin D. Roosevelt. Examination of curriculum materials, such as texts, seems to be an appropriate starting point to determine one aspect of readily available material. Social studies textbook series in the United States generally follow an extension of the "expanding environments" construct; that is, they call for the following foci: grade one—home and family; grade two—neighborhoods; grade three—communities; grade four—state or regions; grade five—national (American history); and grade six—world.

Fifth-grade textbooks were targeted for this study because of their traditional focus on American history content. Typically, American school children do not learn about historical figures from the twentieth century in any detail until fifth grade, and the presidents who do merit attention in textbooks at earlier grade levels–usually Washington and Lincoln–receive only the slightest attention.[2] Textbooks from Houghton-Mifflin, Harcourt Brace Jovanovich, Macmillan McGraw Hill, Silver Burdett Ginn, and Heath were read and analyzed.[3]

All direct and indirect references to Franklin Roosevelt were recorded. References included mention in textual passages, photographs, charts, and captions in student textbooks and indications to extend textual study related to Franklin Roosevelt in teacher editions. For example, in some instances Roosevelt was mentioned only superficially in the student text, but was indicated in the teacher edition as an extension of a given lesson. Analysis of the content from these textbooks provides an accurate depiction of social studies curriculum content available and presently in use nationwide. Most textbooks in Georgia are adopted for a ten year cycle of use. Therefore, since the textbooks were adopted in 1991, they likely will continue to be used.

Three major categories emerged from the data collection of references to Franklin Roosevelt. Most frequently, references to him were found in chapters or lessons about the Great Depression and the New Deal. Next, Roosevelt was mentioned in chapters or lessons about World War II. Finally, indirect references to President Roosevelt were found in chapters or lessons about his wife, Eleanor Roosevelt. Of the three major categories, by far the most information was discovered in chapters that dealt with the depression and New Deal. An expanded explanation of these references follows.

Roosevelt, the Great Depression, and the New Deal

Four of the five textbooks surveyed included content about Roosevelt in the context of the depression and the New Deal. Direct references to Roosevelt varied considerably in tone and length. Some attempted to reveal a bit about Franklin Roosevelt the man, while others simply characterized the events of the New Deal through Roosevelt. For example, the Heath textbook promoted a lesson titled "FDR's New Deal." [4] In it, Roosevelt's "early efforts" and "long-term recovery" of the nation are discussed. The authors include several quotations from Roosevelt's speeches, and explained the concept of the "fireside chats" for which he became well known. In an explanation about Roosevelt's New Deal acts to provide support for banks in turmoil, the text posits, that, after Roosevelt

> ... asked Congress to provide support for the banks to reopen ... [he]spoke to the entire nation over the radio–the first of his –fireside chats–to lessen people's fears ... and told Americans: 'I can assure you that it is safer to keep your money in a reopened bank than under the mattress.' [5]

At the beginning of this short lesson, teachers are advised that the first lesson objective is to "Describe Roosevelt's early efforts to restore people's faith in America" and to integrate reading skills by having students: (1) discuss what must have been going through President Roosevelt's mind during the depression, and (2) research Roosevelt's "fireside chats" and stage a portion of one of them. In addition, this Heath textbook lesson offers the quotation from Roosevelt that introduces the New Deal: "I pledge you, I pledge myself, to a new deal for the American people." The only photograph of President Roosevelt sitting in a wheelchair that was discovered in this study shows Roosevelt pictured with an unidentified young girl standing beside his chair. The captain reads, "President Roosevelt, wheelchair bound as a result of polio, worked hard to end the Depression."[6]

At lesson's end, teachers are invited to ask several comprehension and critical thinking questions for a lesson review. Included are questions such as: (1) What did Roosevelt do to protect people's savings and provide food and work for the jobless? (2) What laws helped businesses, workers, and farmers, and (3) Roosevelt once said: "We have nothing to fear but fear itself." What do you think he meant? Do you agree?

The Silver Burdett Ginn series, like Heath, mentions Roosevelt for the first time in a chapter that includes the reform legislation of the New Deal.[7] The president's election in 1932 is the first reference to Roosevelt in a timeline at the beginning of the chapter. On it, six other dates are included, beginning with the 1901 discovery of oil at Spindletop, Texas, and ending with the 1945 end of World War II. Four lessons make up this chapter, and references to Roosevelt occur again in Lessons 2-4.

The Silver Burdett Ginn series, unlike Heath, offers a portrait of Roosevelt as a man who had survived personal hardships. Roosevelt is described as a leader who "could do something about the nation's hardships." Roosevelt's tenacity as a fighter was described in the following way:

> Roosevelt knew about fighting back when life got rough. As a young man a disease called polio had left him without the use of his legs. His struggle with polio had given Roosevelt an understanding of suffering. 'If you had spent two years in bed trying to wiggle your big toe,' he liked to say, 'after that, anything else would seem easy.' [8]

Like the Heath series, Silver Burdett Ginn reveals that the president had promised "a new deal for the American people." His plans for recovery are described in two scant paragraphs on the same page, with cursory information about the efforts of the Civilian Conservation Corps. Roosevelt is pictured on the last page of this lesson, seated on the backseat of an open car, shaking the hand of a coal miner. The caption reads, "President Franklin Roosevelt gained the support of the American people by promising a "new deal." What do you think President Roosevelt meant when he promised Americans a "new deal"? [9]

Macmillian McGraw Hill's fifth-grade text asserts in a lesson about "hard times" that Americans were "not clear" about what Roosevelt meant by the New Deal, but that "they were ready to vote for anyone who promised to do something, do anything." [10] The image of Roosevelt depicted in the three pages of text about him and the New Deal's recovery programs was one of a completely confident leader: "Many were fearful about the country's future. Roosevelt wasn't. He told Americans, "This great nation will endure [the Depression] as it has endured [other hardships]. . . . The only thing we have to fear is fear itself." [11] The text also portrays Roosevelt's bout with crippling polio as an example of someone who did not get discouraged easily.

Macmillan McGraw Hill authors suggested that teachers have their students analyze the photograph of Roosevelt that showed him delivering a radio address, surrounded by various microphones, with the caption, "Franklin Roosevelt was the first President to speak regularly to the American people over the radio." Then, teachers were to ask the following discussion questions: (1) Why did many Americans vote for Franklin

Roosevelt? (2) How did Roosevelt's personal battle with polio affect his outlook on life? (3) What do you think Roosevelt meant by saying "The only thing we have to fear is fear itself"? Additionally, in the summary of the lesson, teachers were to ask, "How did President Roosevelt appear as a hero to many Americans?" Students were encouraged in their text to "List two question you can ask to find out more about Franklin Roosevelt's presidency."[12]

The Harcourt Brace Jovanovich textbook introduced the Roosevelts in this way: "In 1932, the American people rejected Hoover as President and elected Franklin Delano Roosevelt. Roosevelt was a hearty, likeable person. He was married to Eleanor Roosevelt . . ." A small photograph of the pair riding in an inaugural parade, Roosevelt waving a top hat, accompanies the text. It is captioned, "Franklin Roosevelt, with Eleanor at his side, gave new hope to many people." In the ensuing paragraph, students read that Roosevelt, though disabled, "made a decision not to feel sorry for himself . . . . and to do something worthwhile with his life . . . . [He] reentered politics and was elected governor of New York . . . and Presidential candidate." Teachers were advised to provide background information for students that, although Roosevelt's victory over Hoover was overwhelming, he "was cautious about interpreting the margin of victory as a mandate for change" while at the same time "was most serious about the need for change."[13]

Roosevelt's confidence in leading the country was emphasized on the next page of the text: "Ending the depression, Roosevelt decided, needed bold, new actions from government. On inauguration day . . . [his] rich confident voice [reassured] "The only thing we have to fear is fear itself." Roosevelt gave people new hope." A discussion guide exhorting teachers to "discuss Franklin D. Roosevelt's early years in office" is provided for teachers on the same page. It includes questions such as 1) What was the name given to Roosevelt's programs? 2) What do you think Roosevelt meant when he said, "The only things we have to fear is fear itself?" 3) What did Roosevelt think the government should do to help the people of America?[14]

Houghton Mifflin Series fifth-grade text revealed no information about Franklin Roosevelt, the Great Depression, or the New Deal in either the student or teacher's version.[15] Surprised by this finding, in light of information found in the other four textbook series surveyed, this researcher also surveyed the fourth grade Houghton Mifflin text, dedicated to regional studies with some emphasis on history. Again, no references to Franklin Roosevelt were discovered at this grade level, although references to some other historical figures (i.e., George Washington, Abraham Lincoln) were found.[16]

Roosevelt and World War II

As infrequently as references to Roosevelt were found in depression/New Deal sections of fifth-grade textbooks, references to him in chapters or lessons dealing with World War II history were even more sparse.

In a four-page lesson titled "United States at War," Heath authors characterize Roosevelt's stance toward the war in Europe as a neutral one: "When fighting first broke out, the United States tried to remain neutral. President Franklin D. Roosevelt spoke for most Americans when he said, 'I hate war. . . . I shall pass unnumbered hours thinking and planning how war may be kept from this nation.'"[17] On the next page, after briefly describing the attack on Pearl Harbor, there is a reference to Roosevelt in relation to the internment of Japanese American citizens: "Giving in to these fears (that Japanese American citizens would aid a Japanese invasion), the President ordered all Japanese Americans on the West Coast be sent to camps further inland, where they were kept like prisoners."[18]

Roosevelt is mentioned only two more times in the Heath text. First, in a two-paragraph explanation of the fall of Germany and Italy, readers are told that "President Roosevelt and his advisers decided to focus on the German and Italian armies in North Africa" (rather than the Japanese).[19] Later, on the same page, readers learn that "Harry S Truman, who had become President in 1945 when Roosevelt died, now had a terrible decision to make" as to whether or not to drop the atomic bomb.[20]

In Silver Burdett Ginn's lesson about World War II, one of only two references to Roosevelt in the student text comes in a section about the bombing of Pearl Harbor, and it is indirect, at best. Under a photograph of ships burning, the caption reads, "Why, do you think, did President Roosevelt call this day 'a date that will live in infamy'?"[21] The other reference is found in a section about the decision to drop the atomic bomb: "Since President Roosevelt had died in the spring, the new President, Harry Truman, now faced the difficult decision."[22] In the teacher's edition, an activity is suggested that includes excerpts from Roosevelt's "Four Freedoms" speech. After students read the excerpted portion they are to practice writing a speech of their own about a topic of their choice.[23]

A section in the World War II lesson in Macmillan McGraw Hill textbook contains the single reference to Roosevelt related to war. In it, young readers learn that "Franklin Roosevelt died on April 12, 1945, just weeks before the defeat of Germany. The year before, he had been elected to a fourth term as President. No other President had served his country for so long or led it through more difficult times."[24]

World War II merits seven pages of text in the Harcourt Brace Jovanovich series. In it, students read, "Roosevelt was reelected in 1936."²⁵ On the next page, the text reveals that, as the war began in Europe, "in the United States, many people felt that the country should stay out of European conflicts." The authors further posit Roosevelt's position as one of preparedness. "As Roosevelt said, war was a disease that could spread. The United States, said Roosevelt, should prepare itself in case war came."²⁶ On the same page, one paragraph further, the section "America Enters the War" recounts the Japanese attack on Pearl Harbor and quotes Roosevelt's famous condemnation of the attack as a day that would "live in infamy."²⁷ Five pages further, students read, "Roosevelt did not live to see victory in Europe. He died in office on April 12, 1945."²⁸

Roosevelt and Eleanor

Of the four textbook series in which information about Franklin Roosevelt was found, three–Heath, Macmillan McGraw Hill and Harcourt Brace Jovanovich–also included information about his wife, Eleanor. Heath devoted more text space to Eleanor than to the president. In the Macmillan McGraw Hill text, approximately the same amount of text is devoted to both.

Heath Publishers' textbook highlights Mrs. Roosevelt in a two-page "Citizenship in Action" spread that details her early life, her life with Franklin, and her life after his death.²⁹ She is portrayed as a vigilant fighter against discrimination and a human rights champion. Three photographs of Eleanor Roosevelt inspecting Ohio coal mines, 1935, visiting sailors at Pearl Harbor, 1943, and opening the United Nations Commission on Human Rights, 1946, illustrate the text. In the accompanying teacher's edition, suggestions are given to help students "understand the accomplishments of Eleanor Roosevelt . . . learn what [she] believe[d] about discrimination . . . and conduct [their] own fact finding tours" in order to learn about the tours Mrs. Roosevelt conducted "in hospitals, prisons, coal mines, and soup kitchens."³⁰ Students are also encouraged to "create a list of Eleanor Roosevelt's accomplishments and . . . to explain why they think she brought hope to people."³¹

Eleanor Roosevelt appears in the Macmillan McGraw Hill textbook in a section about the New Deal. Here, the president's dependence upon her "to find out what life was like for the people of the country" is noted. As well, the number of miles traveled by Mrs. Roosevelt during her husband's first fifteen months in office and the special interests of the First Lady, including "problems of the young, blacks, and women" are discussed.³² At the chapter's end, Eleanor and Franklin are both listed on the chart as important

"People to Know" along with Dwight Eisenhower, Herbert Hoover, Charles Lindbergh, Harry Truman, and Woodrow Wilson.[33]

The Harcourt Brace Jovanovich series mentions the First Lady only briefly and as amplification of information about Franklin Roosevelt: "He was married to Eleanor Roosevelt, a niece of Theodore Roosevelt."[34] On the same page is a photograph of President and Mrs. Roosevelt riding in an inauguration parade. Mrs. Roosevelt's interest in the underrepresented is mentioned three pages later in a one-page tribute to Mary McLeod Bethune that noted, "Eleanor Roosevelt was a personal friend, and worked to aid Mrs. Bethune's causes."[35] The final entry about Mrs. Roosevelt refers to the internment of Japanese Americans. "Not all Americans agreed with the way the Japanese Americans were treated," according to the text. "One who did not was Eleanor Roosevelt. Free societies do not do such things, she said."[36]

Miscellaneous Roosevelt

One textbook, Silver Burdett Ginn, mentioned Roosevelt in two instances other than those already noted. First, in a lesson about the formation of the United Nations after World War II, the text says, "Even before the war was over, President Franklin Roosevelt proposed an idea that he hoped would prevent wars from happening in the future. President Roosevelt wanted the nations of the world to establish a new organization to keep peace."[37] Teachers are advised to supplement this information with a short explanation of the League of Nations and to guide students to answer the questions: "Who proposed the idea for the United Nations?" and "What has the United Nations accomplished?" Second, in a subsequent lesson about the policies of President Reagan, students are reminded, "The new President believed that, except for defense, the federal government should have far fewer responsibilities than it had taken on in the years after Roosevelt's New Deal."[38]

Heath Publishers' text contradicts the notion that the idea for the United Nations began with Roosevelt. "In 1945, before World War II had ended, President Truman suggested a new peacetime organization–the United Nations."[39] In a later chapter about contemporary United States relations with Mexico, Roosevelt's Good Neighbor policy is mentioned: "In the 1930s President Franklin D. Roosevelt . . . began a Good Neighbor Policy toward Mexico and other countries to the south."[40] Accompanying the text is a photograph of Roosevelt and Mexican president Manuel Comacho.

Three of the textbooks surveyed suggest having students conduct an oral history interview. Two, Harcourt Brace Jovanovich and Heath, indicated that interviews might be conducted about the depression and about remembrances of the time, including speeches made by the president.[41] Heath suggests that students conduct their interviews with grandparents, friends, and neighbors who lived during World War II.[42]

References to Roosevelt in Biographies and Collections of Biographies

How often or how much a historical figure is taught about in schools often depends upon the availability of resources in addition to prescribed curriculum materials, such as biographies or collections of biographies. Sometimes the number of books available on a particular subject is an indication of the perception of that person's importance in American or world history. American presidents typically are popular topics for biographies intended for school-aged audiences.

One would expect to find a wealth of biographies cited in an annotated bibliographic index devoted to *American History for Children and Young Adults*.[43] This index is a common reference book used by teachers and it contains a section, "Presidents and Their Families–Roosevelt, Franklin Delano." Annotations for twenty books about Franklin and Eleanor Roosevelt are listed. Of these only nine focus specifically on the life of Franklin while eleven are devoted to Eleanor. All the books cited in this bibliography were published recently (between 1971 and 1988).

A popular subject index that references children's books in print was examined for content about Franklin and Eleanor Roosevelt.[44] In this reference guide, there were thirteen biographies each about Franklin and Eleanor, and one play about Franklin was listed also. Most of the books listed contain content most appropriate for students at a fourth-grade level and above. Interestingly, three of the thirteen books about Eleanor Roosevelt are written specifically for young children (grades K-3) but none of the books about Franklin Roosevelt was written for that young age group.

Another subject index promotes "best" books for elementary-aged children.[45] In it, only four biographies about the former president are identified for elementary school children, and five biographies are noted about Mrs. Roosevelt. Only one of these nine biographies was written with very young readers in mind.

Collections of biographies written for young learners, elementary through middle school students, often contain selected biographies of United States presidents. Frequency of inclusion in biographical collections provides insight into the availability of information about Franklin Roosevelt to teachers and pupils for research purposes. In the *Index to Collective Biographies for Young Readers,* one section contained extensive references to presidential biographies. For example, biographical information about

Franklin D. Roosevelt was found in forty-three different collective biographies. By contrast, other major presidents were listed more often than Franklin Roosevelt. Not surprisingly, George Washington was listed sixty-five times and Abraham Lincoln appeared forty-eight times. Thomas Jefferson was found sixty-two times in various collections of biographies. Life stories of subsequent presidents—with the exception of John F. Kennedy, listed forty-five times–appear less often than Franklin Roosevelt. References to Harry S. Truman occurred thirty-nine times; Lyndon B. Johnson was cited thirty-two times; and Richard M. Nixon was listed twenty-five times. Curiously, there were fifty-one references to Franklin's distant cousin-president, Theodore.[46]

Analysis: What Do the Textbooks Tell Us?

Analysis of these five elementary social studies textbook series leads to the conclusion that the thirty-second president of the United States is accorded only scant attention. He is not mentioned in Houghton Mifflin textbooks despite author Gary Nash's preface to each teacher edition in the series that states, in part, "No one would think of writing a textbook without Abraham Lincoln or Julius Caesar. So it's not that we're completely changing the old vision in which famous people were carved in marble."[47] Yet, the vision of this textbook series seems narrow when dealing with historical figures. Other textbooks provide sketchy information, usually dealing with Franklin Roosevelt only as a fairly remote figure who spearheaded the New Deal or happened to be president during World War II. When information is provided about Roosevelt the person, he is defined as a spunky, determined individual who overcame a physical handicap. None mentioned that he served more terms of office than any other United States president, or that his attempt to regularly use radio to communicate with the American people was a presidential first, or that he appointed women and minorities as advisers and cabinet members, or that his decisions during World War II were just as monumental to national survival as those he made during the New Deal.

What is to be concluded from these tiny vignettes about Roosevelt in elementary social studies textbooks and the availability of quality reference materials that might be used to teach more about him? Certainly, one conclusion is that elementary social studies does not "tell us" much about Roosevelt. Missed are opportunities to teach critically about Roosevelt's humor, tenacity, and his ability to boost the morale of a nation dogged by depression and later swept into a major war. The point should also be made that in elementary school social studies, critical thinking and problem solving skills are primary foci. President Roosevelt's critical-thinking skills have withstood scrutiny and analysis, and they could serve as a model for young Americans. Yet, apparently in these elementary school textbooks, only the most obvious and superficial snippets of history are considered important.

One must assume that the rationale behind this exclusion is that some historians seem to think that young children are incapable of dealing with such matters in an historically accurate manner. Second, analysis of the elementary social studies series revealed that, in these textbooks, many historical figures are represented and perhaps that has been a de-emphasis of some, including Franklin Roosevelt. In some texts, the strand of history that represents the Great Depression, New Deal, and World War II has been significantly underrepresented. Third, the availability of current, quality literature written about Roosevelt for young readers could inhibit research attempts by them to learn more about this historically important person. Finally, a study of the current status of teaching about Franklin Roosevelt in elementary schools is needed to get a clearer picture of what is being taught about this president, the period of history he influenced, as well as the periods preceding and following his terms of office. Teaching about history must not be considered inappropriate, impractical or unworthy. Franklin D. Roosevelt—the events surrounding his life and his contributions that continue to affect our society—should not be forgotten. Instead, teaching about this American hero should be promoted in elementary classrooms to help bring understanding and appreciation to contemporary issues.

ENDNOTES

1. Sherry L. Field, "Scrap Drives, Stamp Sales, and School Spirit: Example of Elementary School Studies during World War II," *Theory and Research in Social Education*, 22, (4) (1994): 441-60.

2. Sherry L. Field, "The Legacy of Abraham Lincoln in the Elementary Classroom," in *Abraham Lincoln Contemporary: An American Legacy*, Frank J. Williams and William D. Pederson, eds. (Campbell, CA: Savas Woodbury, 1996), 205-15.

3. Beverly J. Armento, Gary B. Nash, Christopher L. Salter, and Karen K. Wixon, *This is My Country* (Boston: Houghton Mifflin Co, 1991); Beverly J. Armento, Gary B. Nash, Christopher L. Salter and Karen K. Wixon, *America Will Be* (Boston: Houghton Mifflin Co, 1991); Phillip Bacon, *The United States: Its History and Neighbors* (Orlando: Harcourt Brace Jovanovich, Inc., 1991); Barry K. Beyer, Jean Craven, Mary A. McFarland, and Walter C. Parker, *United States and Neighbors* (New York: Macmillian McGraw Hill Publishing Co, 1991); Joan G. Atkinson, Marianne Geiger, Mary J. Panielleo, and Mary S. Taylor, *Our Country* (Morristown, NJ: Silver Burdett Ginn, 1991); and Clarence L. VerSteeg, Jeff Passe, Evangeline Nicholas, Carol Skinner,

Charles F. Gritzner, and Bert Bower, *Exploring America's Heritage* (New York: Heath Publishing Co., 1991).
   4. VerSteeg et al., 465-67.
   5. Ibid., 465.
   6. Ibid., 466.
   7. Atkinson et al., (teacher's edition), 465.
   8. Ibid., 538-39.
   9. Ibid.
   10. Beyer et al., 504.
   11. Ibid.
   12. Ibid., 505-06.
   13. Bacon et al., 504.
   14. Bacon et al., (teacher's edition), 532.
   15. Armento et al., *America Will Be.*
   16. Armento et al., *This is My Country.*
   17. VerSteeg et al., 477.
   18. Ibid., 478.
   19. Ibid., 479.
   20. Ibid.
   21. Atkinson et al., 545.
   22. Ibid., 549.
   23. Ibid., 543.
   24. Beyer et al., 512.
   25. Bacon, et al, 536.
   26. Ibid., 537.
   27. Ibid.
   28. Ibid., 542.
   29. VerSteeg et al., 470-71.
   30. Ibid., 470.
   31. Ibid., 471.
   32. Beyer et al., 505.
   33. Ibid., 514.
   34. Bacon et al., 532.
   35. Ibid., 535.
   36. Ibid., 539.
   37. Atkinson et al., 577.
   38. Ibid., 605.
   39. VerSteeg et al., 481.
   40. Ibid., 553.
   41. Bacon et al., 543; VerSteeg et al., (teachers' edition), 506.
   42. VerSteeg et al., 477.

43. Vandelia VanMeter, *American History for Children and Young Adults: An Annotated Bibliographic Index,* (Englewood, CO.: Libraries Unlimited, Inc., 1990).

44. *Subject Guide to Children's Books in Print 1995: A Subject Index for Children and Young Adults*, (New Providence, NJ: R. R. Bowker Co., 1995).

45. John T. Gillespie and Corinne J. Naden, *Best Books for Children Preschool Through Grade 6*, 5th ed., (New Providence, NJ: R. R. Bowker Co., 1994).

46. Karen Breen, *Index to Collective Biographies for Young Readers*, 4th ed., New York: R. R. Bowker Co., 1988).

47. Armento et al., *This is My Country* and *America Will Be.*

10

FDR and American Life: Portrayals and Interpretations in Secondary School American History Textbooks

O. L. Davis Jr. and Matthew D. Davis

Franklin Delano Roosevelt, the longest serving United States president (1933-1945), remains central to both meaning and myth about the American nation in the twentieth century. Elected amidst the despair and debris of the nation's economy, Roosevelt, the individual, rapidly became FDR, the nation's symbol. President Roosevelt, although vigorously opposed, only occasionally suffered serious political loss. Especially during the early years of his presidency and later, during wartime, many Americans understood FDR to be more than just the nation's leader. If he were robust, millions of Americans considered themselves hearty; if he expressed optimism about the future, other Americans rekindled their faith in possibility. His impact on the nation was as immediate as it became persistent. Even now, more than fifty years after his death, his political ideas and some legislation that he championed continue not only to exist, but also to attract virulent attack. As well, the myths of his vigor and of his fidelity to conventional American ideals endure even in the face of recent historical scholarship about his administration and personal life.

The conventional and, likely, the popularly preferred and all but "official" historical wisdom about Franklin D. Roosevelt is revealed in the school textbooks used to teach American youth. Thus, to understand how these textbooks portray him makes available a prominent sense of the American people's continuing understanding of FDR's "place" in American history. This chapter contributes to a dimension of that popular, perhaps even "official" understanding. It reports an analysis of the portrayals and interpretations of Roosevelt in American history textbooks currently used in U.S. high schools. In addition to its continuation of a series of textbook analyses,[1] the chapter notes the emphasis suggested for FDR in the high school American history course by the recently proposed national standards in history.

For this study, six high school American history textbooks were analyzed.[2] All are in widespread use in U.S. high schools. Individual titles constitute the basic text in the course for which they are adopted. For each book, each reference to Franklin D. Roosevelt was recorded. Included in these notations were references in textual passages, photographs and other pictorial representations (e.g., cartoons), charts, captions, and student exercises (e.g., end of chapter questions). This evidence was not quantified but was explored to illuminate the resultant portrayal.

FDR: Person, President, and Symbol; Textbook Portrayals

Franklin D. Roosevelt, the person, is submerged in all these high school American history textbooks. Furthermore, his family and his life prior to his presidency is obscured. As president, he is portrayed mainly as remote, a presence, even as he is described as immensely popular and influential. He is known in most of these books, for example, as "Roosevelt," a formal representation; only one book commonly refers to him as "FDR."[3] Likely significant, most of the books refer to this president mainly as symbolic ... of increased federal actions, of the era of depression and World War II periods in American life, and, certainly, of the individual who led the nation from bankruptcy to world power.

Unfortunately, Roosevelt's portrayal in these books present him one-dimensionally. It lacks the complexity and ambiguities that characterize a real person. In just half of the books, only a few public snippets about his life before 1932 are presented. These are limited, in most respects, to his service as assistant secretary of the Navy during World War I, his unsuccessful candidacy for vice president in the 1920 national election, and his governorship of New York. In addition, he ordinarily is portrayed as somber, even if seen as smiling for cameras. In only one setting, remarkably an incident at a wartime summit conference, Roosevelt jokes, teases, and laughs with Stalin and Churchill.[4] Even his sudden death at Warm Springs, Georgia, noted in each book, is depicted primarily as a public event accompanied by the noted lament and grief of millions of Americans, emblemized by the often reprinted photograph of the sobbing black Navy accordionist.[5]

His crippling bout of polio in 1921, mentioned in all the books, refers to a particularly important element of his pre-presidential life. From this serious physical setback, Roosevelt became "determined to return to active political life."[6] In almost all the books, reference to his polio serves as a metaphor for his general strength of will and his valiant struggles for his presidential actions in especially vexing circumstances. Most photographs of Roosevelt in all the books, even so, portray him with his crippled legs obscured. One book, however, called special attention to Roosevelt's disability through a photograph of a seated FDR and a standing man who held a sign, "Enlist with the President to fight infantile paralysis!"[7]

This one-dimensional portrayal extends to the book's treatment of his family. Only one book notes his extended family through a photograph when FDR was a youth.[8] His mother and his children, all prominent in his life and widely known by the public during his life, are omitted. Furthermore, only one book lifts Eleanor Roosevelt, his wife, into studied attention. It includes a photograph of Franklin and Eleanor as newlyweds, notes that she was his distant cousin, who as a young adult, volunteered in a New York city slum settlement house.[9] Also, it highlights her visit in 1938 to Arthurdale, West Virginia, "the first government sponsored community established by the Resettlement Administration, one of President Roosevelt's New Deal Programs."[10] It also observed that "Eleanor gave people . . . the sense that they had access to the president."[11] As part of Roosevelt' generally warm public image, his wife is also depicted in another photograph listening to a Puerto Rican girl read a schoolbook.[12]

Notably missing from every book is a particular and characteristic image of Roosevelt. Not one photograph depicts him smiling with his long cigarette holder jauntily clasped between his teeth. "Political correctness"incorporates his debilitating polio but fails to acknowledge that FDR smoked cigarettes.

Overall, FDR appears in most of these books as a conflation with the nation during two agonizing eras, economic depression and world war. In these portrayals, Roosevelt both obscures and symbolizes the nation during these times. One book cautions readers that "Roosevelt alone was not the New Deal."[13] In most of the books, however, he is presented as larger *and* smaller than individual life and this unfortunate merger diminishes the agonies and triumphs of both his leadership and of the American people and the nation.

Roosevelt as the New Deal President

Roosevelt became president "by a landslide,"[14] "in a sweeping victory,"[15] in the election of November, 1932. The presidential campaign and its issues, however, are poorly addressed by these textbooks. For example, one book notes FDR's prediction of his campaign victory because of President Hoover's and General MacArthur's treatment of the Bonus Army of World War I veterans the previous May.[16] Another book dismisses any special attributes of Roosevelt the candidate by its assertion, "It is safe to say that in 1932 any Democratic presidential candidate could have defeated the Republican Hoover," although it does admit that FDR, an optimist and full of energy, "turned out to be a most popular political campaigner."[17] The election aside, the textbooks acknowledge the impact of Roosevelt's 1933 inaugural address as his launch of the New Deal. FDR "gave hope to the thousands who shivered... and to the millions who listened on their radio."[18] Still, most of the textbooks' descriptions of the event pale beside one dramatic account: "Dull, gray skies... (the) partially paralyzed... mounted the inaugural platform. He had planned his first words carefully... Then he descended the steps, determined to lead the country out of its prolonged economic depression."[19] Lengthy quotations from his address which pledged "a new deal for the American people" are included in two books[20] and the entire speech is reprinted in one.[21]

Roosevelt's leadership and program initiatives, according to the textbooks, invigorated efforts for national recovery. Indeed, students might get the idea from these books that FDR's first one hundred days in office were the most important period of his presidency. The bank holiday, relief programs for needy farmers and unemployed workers, and a variety of industrial reforms appear to define the New Deal. As one textbook stated, "An experimenter at heart, Roosevelt was open to all ideas."[22] The same book, however, recognizes Roosevelt's promises but failure to act in response to southern tenant farmers and labor unrest.[23] In most books, Roosevelt appears to be the central actor in New Deal programs although, in others, discussions of government reforms ignore his influence.

Throughout his first term, the textbooks portray FDR as overwhelmingly successful although detractors and opposition to New Deal programs are noted.[24] One book comments, "Roosevelt not only faced opposition from people who demanded that government do more for the needy but also from people who demanded it do less."[25] President Roosevelt's masterful use of radio for his "fireside chats" with the American people not only consoled fearful citizens but offered them hope. Controversy over the New Deal continues to the present day. One book illustrates this debate by contrasting recent historians' interpretations of the Roosevelt-era programs.[26]

The depression continued to engulf the nation as FDR's first term wound down. Still, his bid for reelection in 1936 yielded immense and nationwide popular support for him and his policies. In an unelaborated comment about Roosevelt's victory, one textbook credits "the working class" for providing him the stunning sweep over his Republican opponent.[27] In his campaign, one textbook notes that "Roosevelt responded to the criticisms of the mid-1930s by proposing more reforms. We call his new program the Second New Deal."[28]

Roosevelt's unsuccessful effort to pack the Supreme Court "seriously undermined congressional and party support" for the president and his New Deal programs.[29] Even with new opposition, Roosevelt's New Deal continued, but its momentum stalled and it failed to lift the nation from the depression. Most of the textbooks, with the exception of minor attention to

Roosevelt's "Good Neighbor Policy" toward Latin America, accord little attention to his foreign policy, especially to the clouds of war that gathered over Europe and Asia during the mid to late 1930s. One exception is a photograph of Roosevelt's 1941 meeting with Britain's Prime Minister Winston Churchill aboard a cruiser off Nova Scotia on which occasion they issued the Atlantic Charter.[30] Other treatment that provides even minimal informative context to this period omits or accords only minor recognition of President Roosevelt's personal roles in prewar foreign affairs.

By the November election of 1940, most of the world's major nations were at war. Roosevelt broke tradition and ran for an unprecedented third term. In the campaign, FDR "ran on his record. Willkie tried to play up the third-term issue and the failures of the New Deal,"[31] but was unsuccessful; Roosevelt was reelected. In most of the textbooks, however, treatment of issues surrounding FDR's third-term candidacy was slighted. Similarly, they quickly pass over his fourth-term election.

Roosevelt as Wartime President

In the aftermath of the Japanese surprise attack on Pearl Harbor, Roosevelt regains the textbook spotlight only briefly. One book includes an excerpt from his war message to Congress.[32] In their accounts of the United States at war, most of the textbooks accord little mention of the president. Indeed, the little information about Roosevelt's wartime leadership provided might lead students to perceive that FDR played only an insignificant role in the subsequent Allied victory.

The textbooks mention President Roosevelt mainly in two roles. In domestic affairs, he is credited with several actions relating to civil rights. Most of the books regard his authorization of the internment of west coast Japanese aliens and Japanese Americans as a flawed and tragic decision.[33] His wartime decision to ban discrimination in defense industry hiring, on the other hand, is recognized as a positive act. "Roosevelt's action gave black Americans their first important civil rights victory since Reconstruction."[34] The books make more prominent, in text and accompanying photographs, Roosevelt's involvement in wartime diplomacy. Principally, this attention acknowledges his advocacy of the United Nations and highlights his wartime meetings with other Allied leaders. Although they skip most other wartime summit meetings of Allied leaders (e.g., Casablanca, Tehran), most of the books mention the Yalta meeting of Roosevelt, Churchill, and Soviet Premier Stalin and include the often reprinted photograph of the three leaders at this meeting. One book observes that the meeting signaled the beginning of the Cold War. Also, it notes that President Roosevelt thought that he could stop

Stalin's postwar expansionism. "However, any such hopes were dashed when Roosevelt died suddenly on April 12, 1945."[35]

President Roosevelt's death only weeks before the end of the war in Europe is noted in each textbook. Commonly, a single sentence punctuates the conclusion of the Roosevelt presidency. One book observed, for example, "American joy at the ending of the war was restrained, for President Roosevelt was dead."[36] Another comments, "Americans mourned his loss with the greatest public outpouring of grief since the death of Abraham Lincoln."[37]

The FDR Legacy

Overall, these textbooks proceed linearly from Roosevelt's death to his successors and the postwar United States story with almost no reference to the FDR legacy. One book compares the rhetoric of conservative congressmen who accused the Supreme Court of judicial activism with Roosevelt's earlier criticism of the Court.[38] Another observes that Eisenhower's policies "reversed Roosevelt's New Deal policy on Native Americans."[39] More important than their failure to deal with the Roosevelt legacy is the books' general omission of prompts or guides to students,' serious interpretation of the period and of relationships of the Roosevelt legacy to subsequent political rhetoric, policies, and actions.

FDR in Possible Future School History Texts

Representation of Franklin D. Roosevelt in current high school American history textbooks slights much about the man, his vision, and leadership, and most of his prominent actions. This situation obviously may continue or even worsen. Of course, by their nature, school textbooks cannot offer elaborate and robust narratives about all people, events, and situations important to a comprehensive understanding of a nation's history. Subsequently published school history textbooks, if publishers and authors continue efforts mainly "to cover" the lengthening saga of American history, will likely become longer, bulkier, and, unfortunately, more superficial. On both pedagogic and financial grounds, some changes in the nature of American history textbooks surely can be anticipated. A single adopted textbook simply is an inadequate format into which a robust history may be compressed. This concern about possible future textbooks, however, only marginally relates to the nature of possible portrayals of President Roosevelt. Even the potential of interactive computer programs does not attend to criteria for selection of substantive history course content.

One development, on the other hand, offers the prospect of substantial improvement in American history offerings in schools. Regrettably currently engulfed in tortured controversy,[40] a set of national standards for courses in United States history recently was issued.[41] These standards were advanced as guidelines for the choice and emphasis of topics for historical understanding and of processes for historical thinking. Their use could signal added attention to a number of topics, including Franklin Roosevelt and his administration, and reduced attention, to be sure, to other matters. This prospect is evidenced by the identified historical eras and examples of student achievement in the standards report.

Of the ten chronological eras identified in the standards report, Era 8 is entitled "The Great Depression and World War II (1929-1945)." That era's Standard 2 specifies that students should demonstrate understanding "of the presidency of Franklin D. Roosevelt and the New Deal,"[42] "the impact of the New Deal on workers and the labor movement,"[43] and "opposition to the New Deal, the alternative programs of its detractors, and the legacy of the "Roosevelt Revolution."[44] Additionally, Standard 3 calls for students to demonstrate understanding "of the international background of World War II,"[45] "of World War II and how the Allies prevailed"[46] and "the effects of World War II at home."[47] Subsequent eras and their standards include additional attention, primarily for historical interpretation, to the Roosevelt era. Were high school students to engage in the suggested sample study activities listed under these standards, they would encounter more attention to President Roosevelt and his work than available in current textbook portrayals. Moreover, students likely would engage history more viably and intimately than most high school students currently find in their American history courses.[48]

Contemporary "official knowledge" about FDR in current American history textbooks seems inadequate for meaningful understanding. Still, these books likely accord Roosevelt and his presidency more attention than that given to most other American presidents. The current "standards movement" remains problematic. Still, even if it achieves only modest success in the coming years, subsequent attention to and portrayals of Franklin D. Roosevelt in high school American history courses, not just in school textbooks, may increase.

ENDNOTES

1. See, for example, O. L. Davis Jr., Gerald Ponder, Lynn M. Burlbaw, Maria Garza-Lubeck, and Alfred Moss, *Looking at History: A Review of Major U.S. History Textbooks* (Washington, DC, 1986); O. L. Davis Jr., and Sherry L. Field,

"Portrayal of the United Kingdom in Elementary School Social Studies Textbooks of the United States," *Education Today*, in press; O. L. Davis Jr., and Sherry L. Field, "Forgotten for 146 Years: How Do We Remember Poland Treatment of Poland in U.S. Elementary Social Studies Textbooks," *Neodidagmata*, in press; Sherry L. Field, "The Legacy of Lincoln in the Elementary Classroom," in *Abraham Lincoln: Contemporary*. ed. Frank J. Williams and William D. Pederson (Campbell, CA: Savas Woodbury, 1995): 205-15.

2. The six books are: Carol Berkin, Alan Brinkley, Clayborne Carson, Robert W. Cherny, Robert A. Divine, Eric Foner, Jeffrey B. Morris, Arthur Wheeler, and Leonard Wood, *American Voices: A History of the United States - 1865 to the Present* (Glenview, IL: Scott Foresman, 1992); James West Davidson, Mark H. Lytle, and Michael B. Stoff, *American Journey: The Quest for Liberty Since 1865* (Texas edition) (Englewood Cliffs, NJ: Prentice Hall, 1992); Thomas V. DiBacco, Lorna C. Mason, and Christian G. Appy, *History of the United States: Civil War to the Present*, vol. 2 (Boston: Houghton Mifflin, Co., 1992); Robert A. Divine, T. H. Breen, George M. Frederickson, and R. Hal Williams, *America: The People and the Dream: The Later Years*, vol. 2 (Glenview, IL: Scott Foresman, 1992); John Garraty, *The Story of America: 1865 to the Present*, vol. 2 (Austin: Holt, Rinehart and Winston, Inc., 1992); and Gary Nash, *American Odyssey: The United States in the Twentieth Century* (Lake Forest, IL: McMillan-McGraw Hill, 1992).

3. Robert A. Divine et al., *America*.

4. James W. Davidson, Mark H. Lytle, and Michael B. Stoff, *American Journey*, 635.

5. Thomas V. DiBacco, Lorva C. Mason, and Christian G. Appy, *History of the United States*, 428.

6. Gary Nash, *American Odyssey*, 362.

7. Davidson, 781.

8. Nash, 361.

9. Nash, 361.

10. Nash, 358.

11. Nash, 366.

12. Nash, 367.

13. Davidson, 383.

14. Carol Berkin et al., *American Voices*, 451.

15. Divine, 294.

16. Nash, 333.

17. John Garraty, *The Story of America*, 363.

18. Divine, 295

19. Nash, 360.

20. Davidson, 386; DiBacco, 356.

21. DiBacco, 723.

22. Nash, 362.
23. Ibid., 370-76.
24. Berkin, 470; Garraty, 377.
25. Nash, 373.
26. Garraty, 375.
27. Berkin, 476.
28. Garraty, 378.
29. Divine, 304.
30. Garraty, 409.
31. Ibid., 405.
32. DiBacco, 725.
33. Davidson, 472; DiBacco, 409; Divine, 326; Nash, 444-46.
34. Divine, 325.
35. Nash, 462-63.
36. Garraty, 425.
37. Davidson, 485.
38. DiBacco, 509.
39. Nash, 631.
40. See, for example, Richard Jensen, "The Culture Wars, 1965-1995: A Historian's Map," *Journal of Social History* 29 (October, 1995): 17-37.
41. *National Standards for United States History: Exploring the American Experience. Grades 5-12.* (Los Angeles, CA: National Center for History in the Schools, University of California, 1994). Subsequent references to this source indicate appropriate page numbers only.
42. Ibid., 193.
43. Ibid., 195.
44. Ibid., 197.
45. Ibid., 199.
46. Ibid., 201.
47. Ibid., 203.
48. This possibility seems especially prominent in the consideration of standards related to the historical thinking. For example, one recent research report concludes that current high school world history textbooks provide woefully inadequate attention to "historical analysis and interpretation." To overcome these deficits, revisions of the textbooks likely would need to include both more substantive content (e.g., historical sources) and assistance (e.g., directions, advice) for their appropriate use. See Stuart J. Foster, James W. Morris III, and O. L. Davis Jr., "Prospects for Teaching Historical Analysis and Interpretation: National Curriculum Standards for History Meet High School History Textbooks," *Journal of Curriculum and Supervision*, in press.

11

Teaching FDR to the Next Generation

Matthew Ware Coulter

We who teach the history of the 1930s and 1940s are fortunate. Not only does the period feature a wide variety of fascinating topics, it also offers one of history's most compelling figures in Franklin D. Roosevelt. FDR provided a wealth of materials to use in exploring the period of his presidency. This chapter describes a pair of assignments that use primary source materials, both written and filmed, to facilitate student writing and group discussion. The assignments are designed to use writing more, as opposed to simply using more writing, and to engage beginning college students in learning about FDR and his times. Evaluative research suggests that assignments using these methods can improve student writing. They can also making teaching more enjoyable while providing alternatives to the lecture and textbook format.[1]

Over twenty years ago, FDR historian George Wolfskill noted that "even getting students to read the textbook is a miracle only slightly less difficult than turning water into wine." He might have added that getting students to listen critically to lectures is equally hard. For today's traditional students, the Great Depression and World War II are ancient history. Born in the 1970s and 1980s, they represent the visual and image-oriented "Generation X" and can be considered postmodern students. While lecturing and reading are time-honored ways of teaching history, postmodern students are accustomed to more than two learning channels. They "came of age" enjoying random access to information, effortlessly and endlessly searching for something more interesting. For many, the words "boring" and "lecture" form a single word, boring lecture. They are used to changing channels when they become bored. Using a variety of teaching techniques, therefore, can help meet the needs of today's students.[2]

The following assignments are used in a one-semester United States history course covering the period from 1877 to the present. The assignments are the third and fourth among a total of eight. "The Age of Roosevelt, 1933-1945" forms the second unit of the course and accounts for 450 minutes of classroom time. The two assignments together require about seventy-five minutes, which includes thirty minutes viewing time for a documentary film. Remaining time in the unit is divided between lecturing, video viewing, and testing. Each assignment generates up to five points of credit and accounts for about one and 1.5 percent of the points possible in the course. Class sizes range from thirty to forty students.

When the students receive the Roosevelt assignments, they are building on efforts at collaborative learning gained earlier in small discussion groups. Students were grouped by the instructor, with an emphasis on providing balance for such characteristics as gender, age, and place of origin. When students initially assemble in groups, their only task is to introduce themselves. This helps overcome the tendency of some students to ignore other students and focus only on what the teacher says and does. In their second meeting, which takes place during the first unit, the groups consider a question about the industrialization of the late nineteenth century.

The first Roosevelt assignment opens the second unit. In the previous class meeting, students received a copy of Roosevelt's 1933 inaugural speech. For their writing assignment, they were to first read the speech, looking in particular for what FDR saw as the primary cause or causes of the Great Depression. Roosevelt clearly expressed himself on the question. After describing the impact of the depression on America, FDR noted the essential cause in the eighth paragraph of his speech. "Primarily, this is because the rulers of the exchange of mankind's good have failed through their own stubbornness and their own incompetence, have admitted their failure and abdicated," Roosevelt said. "Practices of the unscrupulous money changers stand indicted in the court of public opinion, rejected by the hearts and minds of men."

Roosevelt's inaugural speech stirred a nation in 1933 and can still excite FDR historians seventy years later. Conveying this excitement to today's students requires more than simply telling them that FDR delivered an important address. Postmodern students, the grandchildren of the generation who heard FDR's address, may approach the speech with their "been there and done that" attitudes. In my experience, however, most students enjoy working with primary sources when they receive clear directions. Getting them to read the speech is substantially easier than turning water into wine, and they are usually able to identify what FDR saw as causing the depression. When the students assemble in class, they join their groups and discuss their findings. After five to ten minutes of group discussion, students receive the writing part of the assignment. They are asked to write for five minutes on the following question: "In his First Inaugural Address in 1933, what did Franklin D. Roosevelt identify as the primary cause(s) of the Great Depression?"

The short assignments serve as a springboard to discussion, allowing the student writing to be used for more than just teacher reading and scoring. After the students complete their writing, they do a "read around" in the groups with each student reading his or her answer. Once students realize that they are going to share their writing with their peers, they often become more motivated to write something that sounds literate. Students learn from each other through discussion of their writing, instead of from listening to the professor and taking notes. As an added benefit, the small-group work promotes student interaction and builds trust in the classroom. After the read around and group discussion, students return to their regular seats. Having had focused time to process and consider the speech, they will usually offer their reactions for a discussion if asked to do so.

To finish the classroom work, students watch a two-minute excerpt of the speech taken from the *20th Century Video Library*. I then offer my remarks. Knowing that today's traditional students grew up in the age of the "credibility gap," I tell them that there was a time when Americans believed the words of a president. I encourage them to listen to future inaugural addresses as one way to be aware of public issues. By the end of the assignment, students have read the speech, talked about it, written about it, watched part of it, and heard the teacher's thoughts about it.

For me, the final part of the assignment remains: grading the papers. Grading time must be carefully controlled when many assignments are used. With eight writing assignments in the course, forty students per section, and a community college teaching load of five classes, over 1,500 writing assignments can be generated in a semester. I take less than a minute to read and score a typical five-minute writing assignment, with the majority of students receiving the maximum possible five points. Responding to student writing does not have to be unmitigated toil, especially if interesting questions are posed and if students have been given a fair chance to think about their answers. The following are five unedited responses from a summer, 1995, class at Collin County Community College in Plano, Texas.[3]

Student Responses to the First Assignment on FDR

> In FDR's Inaugural Address he identified many primary causes of the Great Depression. One serious cause was the morals and values of the people had diminished. Taxes had risen greatly and their ability to pay has fallen. People in the 30s bought and borrowed with no remorse. "Primarily, this is because the rulers of the exchange of mankind's goods have failed through their own stubbornness and incompetency." Everything seemed to freeze dealing with exchange. Banks and citizens seemed to be blamed—who else is there?
>
> One of the primary causes that Roosevelt blamed the depression on was mere stubbornness and incompetence. He goes on to tell

about the "horrible practices of the unscrupulous moneychangers." These people who so thoughtlessly kept buying on the margin, are now subject to public opinion. It is the mistakes of a chosen few that now ruined millions of people. He goes on to say they should be, "Rejected by the hearts of men."

After recapping some of the major effects of the Great Depression on Americans, Franklin D. Roosevelt puts the blame on "the rulers of exchange of mankind's good." These "rulers" being the big business owners of the trusts. "Unscrupulous money changers" have valued monetary profit as being more important than social values. FDR strongly believes that this nation, if given the power, can restore this economy once again. Employment is the key to accomplish "needed projects to stimulate and reorganize the use of natural resources."

Franklin D. Roosevelt identified the fact that the laissez-faire ideas in our capitalist system had been abused by the greed of those seeking monetary gain. He subtly blamed the Republican's idea of encouraging private citizens to volunteer efforts to stop the depression instead of intervening and regulating the actions that were taking place in banks and large corporations.

FDR placed most of the blame for the Great Depression on the "money changers" of the time, and their errors in judgement concerning economics and the stock market. At the time, everyone was getting rich off of playing the stock market. This caused a lot of excitement and people extended a lot of credit to stock buyers, and many "junk bonds were created just to be sold and make money off of." The money changers incompetence came in to play as too much money began to flood the market. Because of this, FDR condemned them and urged the US to take charge and better the community.

Second Assignment on FDR

The students' work with FDR's inaugural speech allows me to refer to it while lecturing on the New Deal. Student misperceptions can be addressed at appropriate times. For example, I can point out the inaccuracy of the last student's statement that in pre-Depression times "everyone was getting rich off playing the stock market." When discussing Roosevelt's early foreign policy efforts, I can point to the lack of emphasis on international affairs demonstrated in his speech. The movement into global affairs and World War II sets up the second Roosevelt writing assignment. In an event familiar to FDR historians, but absent from most survey textbooks, Roosevelt met with King Ibn Saud of oil-rich Saudi Arabia while enroute to the United

States after the Yalta Conference. The context and substance of this meeting forms the topic for the second assignment.

The importance of petroleum to modern U.S. and world history forms one theme of the course, an approach that allows students to connect larger events to state and local history. Oil played an important role in Texas history during the twentieth century. In the 1930s, as FDR called for a "moral embargo" on exports to Italy, East Texas oil producers struggled with problems of excessive supply and low prices. Italy provided a much needed market for East Texas oil. Fifty years later, suburban Dallas voters approved a bond referendum to create Collin County Community College during a time when high oil prices fueled a booming Texas economy. In the 1990s, American soldiers found themselves in Saudi Arabia and Kuwait, fighting to protect U.S. access to the massive oil reserves of those countries. In a Texas community college history class, FDR's meeting with King Saud can easily be made relevant to students. In a different setting with another instructor, some other event might better serve to engage the students. In this case, the assignment also reflects my own research interest in Roosevelt's policies toward the Middle East.

With students having earlier in the course considered the importance of oil in U.S. history, it becomes important to develop other vital aspects of American policy toward the Middle East. In the first unit of the course, the rise of nationalism, including Zionism, was considered. The clash of Arab and Jewish nationalism at the 1919 Paris Peace Conference was mentioned. Within the context of World War II, the disaster of the Holocaust complicated greatly the tensions between Arabs and Jews. Increasing numbers of Jews, including many Jewish Americans, demanded creation of a Jewish nation-state in Palestine. Arab leaders, including King Saud, opposed the Jewish state. Roosevelt struggled to find a balance between those who insisted that American access to Arab oil was a vital national interest and those who passionately voiced their conviction that a Jewish state was a vital humanitarian interest. For today's traditional-age students, the Holocaust is perceived as more ancient history. I want them to comprehend both sides of Roosevelt's dilemma before they consider what happened when he met with King Saud.

Perhaps the best way to get image-oriented Generation X students to think about the Holocaust is to show it to them. Many good video works are available on the subject. I use *Night and Fog*, a 1955 film directed by Alain Resnais. The French narration begins a soft multicultural touch to the classroom, while English subtitles allow students to follow along. Most of the scenes come from the World War II era and are shocking enough to stir even those students jaded by violence-saturated motion pictures and television programs. After watching the film, students can more easily understand why the world's Jews were so deeply committed to the goal of a nation-state.

With an understanding of the importance of oil to America and the importance of a Jewish state to Holocaust survivors and others, students are prepared to consider FDR's meeting with Ibn Saud. They receive a copy of the official State Department memorandum of the meeting, taken from the *Foreign Relations of the United States* series. The record shows that when FDR pressed Ibn Saud to accept a Jewish state in Palestine, the king rejected the proposal and recommended giving Holocaust survivors "living space in the Axis countries which oppressed them." He said the "Arabs would choose to die rather than yield their lands to the Jews." Roosevelt promised that he "would do nothing to assist the Jews against the Arabs and would make no move hostile to the Arab people."[4]

I ask students to ponder three questions as they read the memorandum. First, I ask how they would describe Roosevelt's position toward Zionism and Arab nationalism. Second, I ask what factors FDR had to consider in shaping a policy on the Palestine issue. Finally, I ask them to characterize King Saud's position toward Zionism and Arab nationalism in Palestine. As with the first Roosevelt assignment, students take the handout home with them and have until the next class meeting to read and think about the primary source. When they come to the next class, they assemble in their groups and discuss their findings as preparation for the writing. After five to ten minutes of discussion, I distribute the writing part of the assignment. Students get an opportunity to take on the role of president of the United States because they are asked to imagine themselves as FDR. They have five minutes to answer the following questions: "What would you have said in response to the King's statements regarding Zionism and Palestine? For what reasons would you have responded in this way?"

The procedure used in the previous assignment is repeated, with students "reading around" after the five minutes of writing time has lapsed. Small-group discussion follows, and, after students return to their regular seats, a full class discussion can take place. By this time, students have considered the importance of oil, have viewed the inhumanity of the Holocaust, have read the official record of FDR's meeting with King Saud, have talked about the meeting and its context, and have written about the meeting. With such preparation, many students are ready and willing to participate in a class discussion that can easily be made relevant to contemporary issues. I point out that making foreign policy decisions is rarely as simple and clear-cut as some political commentators would like people to believe. I ask my students to be circumspect before criticizing any president's foreign policy.

The age of Roosevelt came to a close when FDR died two months after meeting King Saud. For the students, the assignment closes off the second unit of the course. For me, again, the grading remains. As before, I work quickly and devote less than one minute to reading and scoring the typical student response. Most students receive the full five points credit. The following are five unedited responses from the summer, 1995, course.

Student Responses to Second Assignment on FDR

> I would assure the King Saud that the U.S. will not interfere with the affairs of Arabs disliking the Jews in their homeland. It is important to keep a friendly term between the U.S. and the Arabs for simply the fact the Arabs have the largest oil field in the world. Assisting the Jews against the Arabs would mean the cut off of the supply of oil from the Arabs. However, as the President, I would not assist the Arabs driving out the Jews either. After all, the war was fought somewhat on the bases of saving the Jews from Nazi's destruction. I would stand neutral and let it take [care] of itself.
>
> If I was Roosevelt I would concentrate mainly on keeping good relations with Kind Saud while not saying anything completely against the Zionist Movement. First of all, I would have agreed to King Saud's idea of returning the Jewish people back to their homeland if that is where they wanted to go. Unfortunately, since they all would not want to return, I would respond to his idea about returning them in a place in conquered lands diplomatically stating that it is a good idea but not giving any positive or negative responses. I would agree that the Arabs presently have a legal right to their lands but would look down, but not openly, on his statements that the Jews are bad people who they cannot get along with. This diplomatic approach would be in order to keep good relations with Saudi Arabia who has much oil which gives them great amount of power. Also, I would have to keep in mind Jewish pressure from home.
>
> Even though I personally see no problem with Jews and Arabs both living in Palestine together, I know they will not reconcile with each other for a very long time. As it stands now, King Saud has made it clear that the Arabs feel that zionism is a great threat and they would rather die than give their lands to the Jews. Since there is a pretty large and powerful Jewish Population in the U.S. and since Saudi Arabia supplies the U.S. with a very large amount of oil at a good price, I would choose to remain neutral. It is in the U.S.'s best interest.

I would have answered King Saud in a similar manner that President Roosevelt did. In staying neutral in this fight, Roosevelt showed his compassion for both sides of this issue and therefore was not able to take sides with either one. Also, his neutrality was very diplomatic in that, although he agreed with both the Arabs and Jews that each should have their own land, since America relied heavily on Saudi Arabia & the Middle East for petroleum, he himself insured that no animosity was stirred up between the U.S. President & the Arabian King. In staying neutral, FDR did not condone violence or fighting for the land, only that the office of the U.S. president would not interfere.

Clearly, as president of the U.S., I would need to keep in mind the economic importance of good relations with Arab nations–that is, the importance of oil for the good of the U.S. However, I *hope* I would point out that Jews had as much claim to Palestine as Arabs. I do realize that diplomatically speaking, this could be disastrous, but I hope I would have the character to acknowledge the Jews claim to Palestine–hopefully maintaining peaceful relations w/Arab nations as well.

Conclusion

Aspects of modern U.S. history developed in the class and sharpened through the Roosevelt assignments receive further attention later in the course. Knowledge gained from the assignments and skills exercised in working with the primary source documents are used again and again. In the third unit, covering the period from 1945 through 1963, students read and view excerpts from John F. Kennedy's inaugural address. They write for five minutes about his speech, contrasting JFK's emphasis on international affairs against FDR's focus on domestic problems. In subsequent units, students consider U.S. policy in the Middle East during the 1967 Six Day War, 1973 Yom Kippur War, and 1991 Persian Gulf War. The 1973 oil embargo and its impact on the world, the United States, and Texas are considered. Throughout the course, the small groups continue to work. The student writing continues to serve as a starting point for class discussion. Over the semester, with numerous opportunities to write and discuss, student writing and class discussion improve. The results support research on student writing which suggests that effective teaching of writing requires frequent short assignments with immediate feedback.[5]

The age of Franklin Roosevelt provides a fertile field from which history teachers can draw primary source materials to integrate into their classes.

Other eras offer similar opportunities. In American history to 1877, I use small groups and ten short writing assignments in much the same manner as described above. In one assignment, students consider Abraham Lincoln's view on the Fugitive Slave Act as expressed in the 1858 Lincoln-Douglas debates. Of course, not only presidents are entitled to receive attention in today's history classes. One way to move toward a more multicultural and inclusive course is to use primary sources generated by previously excluded groups.

Integrating primary source materials and short in-class writing assignments into a course may initially take more time than preparing another lecture, but ultimately requires less of the instructor's energy and more of the students' energy. Using well designed assignments allows students to write and think more, while the instructor can lecture less and make responding to student writing more enjoyable. Once designed, the assignments can be used over and over again in subsequent semesters. Refinements can be added or made as necessary. Watching, writing, and discussing become methods of teaching and learning, rather than something done simply to break the monotony of lecturing, reading and quizzing.[6]

The assignments described above show ways to promote teaching and learning that have worked well for this history instructor in his current teaching situation. Students are freed from a steady diet of "boring lectures" and reading assignments they often do not do anyway. The teacher is also freed—from delivering yet another lecture, from dealing with classes where few students have read the textbook and discussion is impossible, and from grading essays for which students have had too little focused time to prepare. Probably all college teachers will have to, in some way or another, react to the influx of postmodern students into their classrooms. For those lucky enough to teach the history of the FDR period, making the adjustments can be challenging and rewarding.

ENDNOTES

1. Gail Hughes-Wiener, "Teaching and Testing Writing Across the Curriculum." Paper read at the Eighth Annual National Testing Network in Writing Conference, November 11, 1990, New York, NY.

2. George Wolfskill, *Happy Days Are Here Again! A Short Interpretative History of the New Deal* (Hinsdale, IL: The Dryden Press, 1974), 213; Matthew Ware Coulter, "Modern Teachers and Postmodern Students," *Community College Journal* 17 (January 1983): 51-58.

3. The Plano campus of Collin Community College enrolls approximately 8,000 students. Drawing from a largely suburban population in a relative affluent area, the

majority of students are "traditional age" (18 to 22 years old), and have plans to transfer and complete a four-year degree.

4. *Foreign Relations of the United States, 1945,* 8 (Washington, DC: Government Printing Office, 1969), 2.

5. Elizabeth F. Haynes, "Using Research in Preparing to Teach Writing," *English Journal* 67 (January 1978): 82-88.

6. Matthew Ware Coulter, "Designing Writing Assignments So Students Can Succeed," *Social Science Perspectives Journal: Proceedings of the 1987 St. Louis Conference* 1 (1987): 292-302.

CHRONOLOGY

Abraham Lincoln

Feb	12	1809	Lincoln born near Hodgeville, Kentudky (now Larue County)
		1816	Lincoln family moves to southwestern Indiana
Oct	5	1818	Lincoln's mother dies at age thirty-four
Dec	2	1819	Lincoln's father, Thomas, marries Sarah Bush Johnston
Apr		1828	Lincoln makes his first flatboat trip down the Mississippi River to New Orleans
Mar	1	1830	Lincoln's family moves again to about ten miles west of Decatur, Illinois
Apr-July		1831	Lincoln family moves again to nearby Coles County, Illinois
Mar		1831	Lincoln makes his second flatboat trip to New Orleans
			Lincoln moves to New Salem, Illinois, where he resides for six years
Apr	7	1832	Lincoln selected captain of his militia company
Aug	6		Lincoln defeated as Whig candidate for Illinois House
			Lincoln serves briefly in Black Hawk War

May	7	1833	Lincoln appointed postmaster of New Salem
Jun	15	1833	Lincoln becomes a county surveyor
Aug	4	1833	Lincoln enters a partnership in a New Salem tavern
		1833	Lincoln wins an Illinois House seat
Sept	9	1836	Lincoln licensed to practice law
Aug	1	1836	Lincoln reelected to Illinois House
Apr	15	1837	Lincoln moves to Springfield, Illinois, the new capital
		1837	Lincoln becomes law partner of John Todd
Mar	1	1837	Lincoln admitted to Illinois bar
Aug	6	1838	Lincoln elected to third term in Illinois House
		1839	Meets Mary Todd
		1840	Lincoln becomes engaged to Mary Todd and elected to fourth term in Illinois House
Aug	14	1841	Lincoln becomes law partner of Stephen Logan
Nov	4	1842	Lincoln marries Mary Todd
Aug	1	1843	Robert Todd Lincoln is born, first son

Dec	9	1844		Lincoln starts his own law practice and takes William H. Herndon for a partner
		1844		Lincoln buys their Springfield home
Mar	10	1846		Edward Baker Lincoln is born, second son
Aug	3	1846		Lincoln wins congressional seat as a Whig
May	22	1849		Lincoln granted U.S. Patent No. 6,469
Aug	21	1849		Lincoln offered secretaryship of Oregon Territory but he declines
Feb	1	1850		Lincoln's second son Eddie dies
Dec	21	1850		William Wallace Lincoln is born, third son
Apr	4	1853		Thomas "Tad" Lincoln is born, fourth son
Nov	7	1854		Lincoln reelected to Illinois House but declines seat to be eligible for U.S. Senate
Feb	8	1855		Lincoln loses election as U.S. Senator
Feb		1856		Lincoln helps to launch Republican Party in Illinois
Jun	16	1858		Lincoln wins Republican nomination for U.S. Senator

Aug	21	1858	Lincoln-Douglas series of seven debates (Aug-Oct)
Nov	2	1858	Unsuccessful senate candidate
Feb	27	1860	Lincoln's Cooper Institute speech
May	9	1860	Constitutional Union Party selects John Bell
May	16	1860	Lincoln is nominated as Republican Party presidential candidate after the third roll call.
Jun	18	1860	Northern Democrats select Stephen A. Douglas
Jun	28	1860	Southern Democrats select John C. Breckinridge
Nov	7	1860	Lincoln wins plurality of the votes and 180 electoral votes in contrast to 123 for his three rivals combined
Mar	4	1861	Chief Justice Roger B. Taney administers oath of office
Apr	12	1861	Civil War begins
Apr	19	1861	Lincoln calls for 75,000 volunteers Lincoln proclaims blockade of Confederate states Lincoln suspends habeas corpus
Jul	4	1861	Construction begun on the Trans-Continental Telegraph line

Jul	27	1861	Lincoln appoints General George B. McClellan commander of the Potomac
Nov	1	1861	Lincoln names McClellan commander of the Union Army
Jan	13	1862	Lincoln names Edwin Stanton as new secretary of war
Feb	20	1862	Son Willie dies at age eleven
Mar	11	1862	Lincoln dismisses McClellan as general in chief
May	20	1862	Lincoln signs Homestead Act
Jul	1	1862	Pacific Railroad Act
Jul	2	1862	Lincoln signs Land Grant College Act
Sep	22	1862	Lincoln issues the preliminary Emancipation Proclamation
Nov	5	1862	Lincoln relieves McClellan as commander of the Potomac
Dec	1	1862	Lincoln proposes a constitutional amendment for gradual, compensated emancipation in loyal slave states
Jan	1	1863	Lincoln signs the final Emancipation Proclamation
Feb	25	1863	Lincoln signs the Currency Act, creating a national banking system

Chronology

Sep		1863	Lincoln gives U.S. Grant command in the West
Oct	14	1863	Lincoln signs charter for National Academy of Sciences
Nov	19	1863	Lincoln delivers Gettysburg Address
Dec	8	1863	Lincoln issues Proclamation of Amnesty
Jun	7	1864	Lincoln renominated on first ballot by the National Union Party
Mar	9	1864	Lincoln promotes U.S. Grant to commander-in-chief
Aug	29	1864	Democrats nominated McClellan and Pendleton for president and vice president
Oct	12	1864	Chief Justice Roger B. Taney dies
Nov	8	1864	Lincoln receives 55 percent of the vote
Feb	3	1865	Hampton Roads (Virginia) Conference
Mar	4	1865	Lincoln's second inaugural address
Apr	4	1865	Lincoln enters defeated Richmond
Apr	14	1865	Lincoln assassinated by John Wilkes Booth

Franklin D. Roosevelt

Jan	30	1882	FDR born, Hyde Park, New York
Jan	24	1903	FDR received a B.A. from Harvard University
Mar	17	1905	FDR and Anna Eleanor Roosevelt marry
May	3	1906	Daughter Anna born
Dec	23	1907	Son James born
Mar	18	1909	Son Franklin Jr. born; died November 8
Sep	23	1910	Son Elliott born
Nov	7	1912	FDR reelected to New York Senate
		1913	President Wilson's assistant secretary of the Navy until 1920
Mar	17	1916	Son John born
Jul		1920	FDR nominated as vice president candidate of Democratic Party
Nov	7	1920	FDR defeated with Democratic presidential candidate James N. Cox
Aug		1921	FDR stricken with polio

Nov	7	1928		FDR elected governor of New York
Nov	7	1930		FDR reelected governor of NY
Nov	7	1932		FDR elected president
Mar		1933		FDR inaugurated as thirty-second president
Mar	4	1933		Good Neighbor Policy to Latin America
Mar	9	1933		"Hundred Days" congressional session
Mar	31	1933		Civilian Conservation Corps created
May	12	1933		Agricultural Adjustment Act
				Federal Emergency Relief Act
May	18	1933		Tennessee Valley Authority (TVA)
Jun	13	1933		Home Owners Loan Corporation
Jun	16	1933		Federal Deposit Insurance Corporation (FDIC) Farm Credit Administration National Recovery Administration and Public Works Administration created by National Industrial Recovery Act (NIRA)
Nov	16	1933		United States recognizes USSR
Mar	24	1934		Philippine Independence Act

May	31	1934	Platt Amendment repealed with Cuban Treaty
Jun	6	1934	Securities and Exchange Commission (SEC)
Jun	12	1934	Reciprocal Tariff Act
Jun	19	1934	Federal Communications Commission (FCC)
Jun	27	1934	Railway Pension Act
Jun	28	1934	Federal Housing Administration (FHA)
Apr	8	1935	Works Progress Administration (WPA)
May	27	1935	NIRA declared unconstitutional
Jul	5	1935	Wagner Labor Relations Act
Aug		1935	First Neutrality Act
Aug	14	1935	Social Security Act
Aug	26	1935	Federal Power Commission
Jun	6	1936	Agricultural Adjustment Act declared unconstitutional
Feb		1936	Second Neutrality Act
Feb	29	1936	Soil Conservation and Domestic Allotment Act
Jun	26	1936	Merchant Marine Act
Nov	7	1936	FDR reelected president, second term

Dec		1936	Buenos Aires Inter-American Conference
Feb	5	1937	FDR's Supreme Court packing plan
Apr	12	1937	"Switch in time that saved the nine" case (*NLRB v. Jones and Laughlin Steel Corporation*)
May		1937	Third Neutrality Act
Jun	22	1937	Senate rejects FDR's Supreme Court packing plan
Jun	25	1938	Fair Labor Standards Act
Dec		1938	Pan-American Conference, Lima, Peru
Apr	3	1939	Administration Reorganization Act
Jun		1939	England's George VI visits
Sep	5	1939	United States proclaims its neutrality in European war
Sep	16	1940	Selective Training and Service Act
Nov	7	1940	FDR reelected president, third term; Wendell Willkie loses
Jan	6	1941	FDR's "Four Freedoms"
Mar	11	1941	Lend-Lease Act
Aug	14	1941	Atlantic Charter
Dec	7	1941	Pearl Harbor attack

Dec	8	1941	United States declares war against Japan
Dec	11	1941	Germany and Italy declare war against United States; United States declares war against them
Jan	14	1943	Casablanca Conference
Nov	28	1943	Teheran Conference
Jan	6	1944	D-Day invasion by Allies
Jun	22	1944	G-I Bill of Rights (Servicemen's Readjustment Act)
Aug	7	1944	Dumbarton Oaks Conference, basis for United Nations Charter
Nov	7	1944	FDR reelected president, fourth term
Feb	4	1945	Yalta Conference
Apr	12	1945	FDR dies at Warm Springs, Georgia

BIOGRAPHICAL DIGEST
Abraham Lincoln

Adams, Charles Francis (1807-86). Son of John Quincy Adams and the U.S. minister to Great Britain who played a major role in assuring Britain's neutrality during the American Civil War.

Alexander II, Czar (1818-81). Succeeded his father (Nicholas I) in 1855. After Russia's defeat in the Crimean War (1853-56) and peasant unrest, he was forced to emancipate the serfs in 1861 but was assassinated twenty years later. A moderate in foreign policy.

Bates, Edward (1793-1869). Lincoln's conservative but loyal attorney general from St. Louis, Missouri.

Beveridge, Albert (1862-1927). Progressive Republican U.S. senator from Indiana (1900-22), who wrote biographies of John Marshall and Abraham Lincoln.

Bismarck, Otto von (1815-98). German "Iron Chancellor" who defeated Austria in the Austro-Prussian War. He was made imperial chancellor and prince (1871-90), after the defeat of Napoleon III in the Franco-Prussian War when the German Empire was created.

Blair, Montgomery (1813-83). From a prominent American family he became the lawyer who defended Dred Scott and served as Lincoln's postmaster general (1861-64).

Booth, John Wilkes (1838-65). Actor son of Junius Brutus Booth's second family in Maryland who assassinated Abraham Lincoln in Ford's Theater to avenge the South's defeat during the Civil War.

Brady, Matthew B. (1823-96). The photographer of Abraham Lincol and the large battles of the Civil War.

Bright, John (1811-89). British politician of Quaker descent who entered parliament in 1843, and held office under Gladstone.

Buchanan, James (1791-1868). Though personally opposed to slavery and secession, his passive personality and rigid constitutional views were ineffective as the U.S. fifteenth president (1857-61).

Calhoun, John C. (1782-1850). A successful South Carolinian politician, as well as one of the two brightest mid-nineteenth century American minds, who nonetheless came up with the irrational concept of the "concurrent majority" as a solution to the sectional crisis. Richard Hofstadter aptly captured his essence as "the Marx of the Master Class."

Carpenter, Francis B. (1830-1900). The portrait painter who painted Lincoln reading a draft of the Emancipation Proclamation to his cabinet and author of *Six Months at the White House with Abraham Lincoln*. (New York: Hurd and Houghton, 1866).

Charnwood, Lord (1864-1945). British author of the first great one-volume biography of Abraham Lincoln.

Chase, Salmon P. (1808-73). Ohio politician and one of the nation's leading antislavery politicians, who served as secretary of the treasury until 1864 and then was appointed chief justice of the U.S. Supreme Court.

Clay, Henry (1777-1852). Known as "the great compromiser" and for his "American system" for national development, he was a friend of Mary Todd's father and the political hero of Abraham Lincoln.

Davis, Jefferson (1808-89). President of the Confederate States of America during the Civil War, he had served in the U.S. Senate (1847-51, 1857-61).

Douglas, Stephen A. (1813-61). Known as the "Little Giant," a senator from Illinois (1847-61), who debated Abraham Lincoln in 1858.

Douglass, Frederick (1817-95). The most literate ex-slave in history who became a leading abolitionist.

Fillmore, Millard (1800-74). The thirteenth U.S. president who assumed the office after Zachary Taylor's death in 1850. In 1856 he sought the presidency again as the Know Nothing Party candidate.

Franz, Josef (1830-1916). The conservative autocratic emperor of Austria from 1848 and king of Hungary from 1867.

Fremont, John C. (1813-90). The Republican party's first presidential candidate in 1856 who was defeated by James Buchanan.

Garibaldi, Giuseppe (1807-82). One of the creator's of a unified Italy who led guerilla campaigns against Austria and allowed King Victor Emmanuel II to rule (1861-78).

Grant, Ulysses S. (1822-85). Abraham Lincoln's effective Civil War general, a persistent and innovative fighter, who won military campaigns and later became the eighteenth president of the United States (1869-77).

Greeley, Horace (1811-72). Influential editor of the New York *Tribune* during the Civil War who was defeated for the U.S. presidency in 1872.

Hamlin, Hannibal (1809-91). Abraham Lincoln's first term vice president who was a senator from Maine (1848-56, 1869-81).

Hay, John (1838-1905). Abraham Lincoln's secretary (1860-65), who later became a secretary of state (1898-1905) and authored with J. G. Nicolay a 10-volume biography of Lincoln (1890).

Herndon, William H. (1818-91). Abraham Lincoln's third and final law partner from 1843 who wrote one of his most important biographies (1889).

Johnson, Andrew (1808-75). The only southern senator who did not join the Confederacy, he was made military governor of Tennessee, was elected vice president in 1864, and became president after Lincoln's assassination.

Juarez, Benito P. (1806-72). First Mexican president of Indian descent (1861-67), sometimes called the "Abraham Lincoln of Mexico."

Keckley, Elizabeth (1818-1907). Mary Todd Lincoln's African American dressmaker in Washington, D.C., who wrote an account of her life with the First Lady.

Lee, Robert E. (1807-70). Declined Abraham Lincoln's offer of command of the Union armies in 1861 and instead became the commander of the Confederate armies, placing loyalty to Virginia above the Union. He was the son of Henry "Light Horse Harry" Lee (1756-1818), who had served with George Washington.

Leopold I (1790-1865). The uncle of England's Queen Victoria, he was elected Belgian king in 1831. Helped to create national unity and implemented some reforms.

Lieber, Francis (1800-72). German-born U.S. political scientist who assisted Alexis de Tocqueville. Lieber wrote the first codified rules of war for the Union army which influenced the nineteenth century Geneva and Hague conventions.

Lincoln, Abraham (1809-65). Sixteenth president of the United States (1861-65) who preserved the Union, ended slavery, thereby becoming America's greatest president and democracy's premier political leader and its most eloquent writer.

Lincoln, Edward B. (1846-50). The second son of Mary and Abraham Lincoln who died before they moved to Washington, D.C.

Lincoln, Mary Todd (1818-82). The daughter of a prominent Kentucky family, she married Abraham in 1842. A woman ahead of her times, she reared their four children while promoting Lincoln's political career. After the death of her second son in 1862, she grew eccentric, especially after the assassination.

Lincoln, Nancy Hanks (1748-1818). Abraham Lincoln's mother from Virginia who married his father, Thomas, in 1806. She died when Abraham was nine years old. They had two other children, a daughter, Sarah, and a son, Thomas, who died in infancy.

Lincoln, Robert Todd (1843-1926). Eldest son of the Lincolns' who briefly institutionalized his mother and became a corporate lawyer.

Lincoln, Sarah Bush Johnston (1788-1869). Abraham Lincoln's stepmother who married Thomas Lincoln in 1819.

Lincoln, Thomas (1778-1851). Abraham Lincoln's father who moved to Kentucky in the 1780s.

Lincoln, Thomas "Tad" (1853-71). Lincoln's fourth and youngest son.

Lincoln, William Wallace "Willie" (1850-62). The Lincolns' third son and their favorite.

McClellan, George B. (1826-85). Controversial Union general whom Abraham Lincoln made supreme commander and was popular with his troops but passive on the battlefield. Ran against Lincoln as the presidential candidate of the Democratic Party in 1864.

Marti, José (1853-95). Cuban poet and hero of its independence movement who lived in the United States and admired Lincoln.

Marx, Karl H. (1818-83). Wrote the *Communist Manifesto* (1848) on the eve of the failed European revolts of 1848 and covered the American Civil War as a foreign correspondent from London for the *New York Daily Tribune* (1852-52).

Masters, Edgar Lee (1869-1950). American poet who wrote a critical biography of Abraham Lincoln.

Maximilian (1832-67). Austrian archduke made emperor of Mexico in 1864 by Napoleon III. He was defeated by Benito Juarez's forces and executed.

Napoleon III (Louis Napoleon Bonaparte, 1808-73). The son of Louis Bonaparte, king of Holland, nephew of Napoleon I, who was elected president of France but then made himself emperor of France (1852-70).

Nicolay, John G. (1832-1901). Abraham Lincoln's private secretary from 1860-65.

Palmerston, Viscount (1784-1865). British prime minister 1855-58 and 1859-65, who led Britain to victory in the Crimean War and kept out of the American Civil War.

Pierce, Franklin (1804-69). Fourteenth American president (1853-57) and the youngest to that time who led the Democratic party to defeat Winfield Scott, the last national candidate of the Whig party. A passive president, he backed the Kansas-Nebraska Act repealing the Missouri Compromise leading the northern part of the Democratic party to split.

Pope Pius IX (1792-1878). His reign began in 1846 with liberal reforms but became reactionary after the Revolutions of 1848 with the notion of the Immaculate Conception in 1854 and papal infallibility in 1870. Served the longest papal reign.

Sandburg, Carl (1878-1967). American poet and biographer who won the Pulitzer Prize for *Abraham Lincoln: The War Years* in 1940.

Sarmiento, Domingo F. (1811-88). Argentine ambassador to the United States who wrote first Lincoln biography in Spanish. Served as Argentine president 1868-74—perhaps its best.

Schurz, Carl (1829-1906). Exiled after the German Revolution of 1848, he supported Lincoln, who named him minister to Spain in 1861. Served as a brigadier-general during the Civil War.

Seward, William H. (1801-72). Leading contender for the 1860 Republican presidential nomination, Lincoln appointed him secretary of state. Scholars rate him as one of the greatest secretaries of state.

Speed, Joshua F. (1814-82). Lincoln's closest friend from 1837 to 1841 in Springfield, Illinois.

Stanton, Edwin M. (1814-69). Lincoln's secretary of war (1862-65).

Stuart, John Todd (1807-85). Lincoln's first law partner, political mentor, and Mary Todd's cousin.

Sumner, Charles (1811-74). U.S. abolitionist and radical Republican, assachusetts (1851-74) who served as chairman of the senate foreign relations committee (1861-71).

Taney, Roger B. (1877-64). Became the first Catholic to serve on the U.S. Supreme Court when Andrew Jackson named him chief justice to replace John Marshall. Served from 1836 to 1864. Wrote the *Dred Scott* decision in 1857 which contributed to the Civil War.

Vallandigham, Clement L. (1820-71). An Ohio congressman (1858-63) and leader of the Copperheads (peace Democrats) who was court martialed for treason in 1863 and "exiled" to the Confederacy until 1864 when he returned to Ohio.

Vance, Mariah (1819-1904). African American housekeeper of the Lincolns during their last ten years in Springfield, Illinois.

Victor, Emmanuel II (1820-78). Served as king of Sardinia 1849-61 and became the first king of a united Italy from 1861-78.

Victoria (1819-1901). British queen from 1837 who married Prince Albert in 1840. They had nine children. She disliked both prime ministers Palmerston (1784-1865) and Lord William Gladstone (1809-98).

Welles, Gideon (1802-78). Lincoln's secretary of the Navy (1861-65), who blockaded the Confederate coast and built the Union fleet of ironclads.

Whitman, Walt (1819-92). The poet of Lincoln who in 1866 wrote "O Captain! My Captain!" and "When Lilacs Last in the Dooryard Bloom'd" dealing with the president's death.

Franklin D. Roosevelt

Anderson, Marian (1897-1993). African American opera singer who performed at the Lincoln Memorial after her DAR concert at Constitution Hall was cancelled in segregated Washington, D.C. The alternate site was arranged with the help of Eleanor Roosevelt.

Beard, Charles A. (1874-1948). American historian, best known for *An Economic Interpretation of the Constitution of the United States*, who became an isolationist opponent of FDR.

Black, Hugo L. (1886-1971). Democratic U.S. senator from Alabama (1927-37) who became FDR's first appointee to the U.S. Supreme Court (1937-71) and one of its greatest justices.

Brownlow, Louis (1879-1965). Journalist and public administrator appointed by FDR to chair the committee on administrative management in 1936. The following year "the Brownlow Report" was issued and called for additional administrative assistance for the chief executive. It eventually led to the creation of the White House Office.

Burns, James MacGregor (1918-). A major political biographer whose authoritative *Roosevelt: The Lion and the Fox* (1956), the first of a two-volume biography, established his national reputation.

Byrnes, James F. (1879-1972). U.S. senator from South Carolina from 1931 to 1941, associate justice, U.S. Supreme Court from 1941-42 and U.S. secretary of state, 1945-47.

Capra, Frank (1897-1991). Legendary Hollywood movie director who won three Academy Awards for best director in the 1930s. His Hollywood films celebrated the common man as a hero during the Great Depression.

Churchill, Winston (1874-1965). British prime minister from 1940 to 1945 and 1951 to 1955.

Civilian Conservation Corps (CCC). The only New Deal program which originated with FDR himself.

Corcoran, Thomas G. (1900-81). An adviser to FDR who took a leading role in FDR's third term decision. "Tommy the Cork" became so controversial by 1941 that he resigned to enter private law practice.

Davis, John W. (1873-1955). Democratic candidate for president in 1924.

DeGaulle, Charles (1890-1970). French officer who started the Free French movement in England and asserted himself as one of the Allies during World War II.

Dewey, Thomas E. (1902-71). Republican governor of New York from 1943 to 1955 and unsuccessful presidential candidate in 1944 and 1948.

Douglas, William O. (1898-1980). FDR's former chairman of the Securities and Exchange Commission appointed to the U.S. Supreme Court (1939-1975), serving longer than any other justice. He also ranks as one of the greatest justices in Supreme Court history.

Early, Stephen T. (1889-1951). FDR's press secretary from 1937 to 1945.

Farley, James A. (1888-1976). A principal New York strategist in FDR's 1932 and 1936 presidential campaigns who broke with him over third and fourth term issues. He served as the chair of the Democratic National Committee (1932-40) and U.S. postmaster general (1933-40).

Frankfurter, Felix (1882-1965). Long-term professor at Harvard University whom FDR appointed an associate justice of the U.S. Supreme Court (1939-62). The political liberal and judicial restraintist is considered one of the great Supreme Court justices in American history.

Garner, John Nance (1868-1967). Democratic congressman from Texas (1903-33) who became FDR's first vice president (1933-41).

Goodwin, Doris Kearns (1942-). Political scientist and biographer whose *No Ordinary Time, Franklin and Eleanor: The Home Front in World War II* (1994) provides insight into the Roosevelts.

Great Depression. The stock market crash of October 24, 1929 triggered the largest economic crisis in American history. More than 5,000 banks closed and more than a quarter of the labor force was unemployed in 1933. The New Deal restored hope, but it took World War II to restore prosperity.

Hirohito (1901-89). Japanese emperor from 1926 who occupied a god-like status until after World War II.

Hitler, Adolf (1889-1945). Austrian-born dictator of Nazi Germany from 1933 to 1945.

Hopkins, Harry L. (1890-1946). One of FDR's closest advisers from New York. Headed the FERA, the CWA and the WPA, and served as secretary of commerce from 1939 to 1940.

Hughes, Charles Evans (1862-1948). Former progressive Republican Governor of New York (1906-10), secretary of state (1921-25), and chief justice of the U.S. Supreme Court (1930-41).

Hull, Cordell, (1862-1948). Democratic congressman from Tennessee (1907-21, 1923-33), who served as FDR's secretary of state (1933-44).

Ickes, Harold L. (1874-1952). FDR's secretary of the interior (1933-46) and close associate of Eleanor Roosevelt in promoting civil rights, including Marian Anderson's concert at the Lincoln Memorial.

Jones, Jesse H. (1874-1956). FDR's first administrator of the Federal Loan Agency and secretary of commerce in 1940.

LaGuardia, Fiorello H. (1882-1947). Dynamic mayor of New York City (1933-45), known as "the Little Flower."

Landon, Alfred M. (1887-1987). Republican governor of Kansas (1935-36) who became the 1936 Republican presidential candidate.

LeHand, Marguerite "Missy" (1898-1944). FDR's secretary and confidant who served as the hostess of the Little White House in Warm Springs, Georgia.

Leuchtenburg, William (1922-). American political historian and author of the classic, *Franklin D. Roosevelt and the New Deal* (1963) and the study of how subsequent presidents used FDR's legacy, *In the Shadow of FDR* (1983).

Long, Huey P. (1893-1935). Populist demagogue from Louisiana, "The Kingfish" was a potential electoral threat to FDR.

MacArthur, Douglas (1880-1964). Army general who in 1941 was recalled from retirement to serve as commander of the U.S. Army in the Far East and in 1942 Allied supreme commander of the Southwest Pacific.

Marshall, George C. (1880-1959). Served as the chief of staff from 1939 to 1945, who influenced Allied strategy during World War II.

Moley, Raymond (1886-1975). A political scientist from Ohio (Ph.D., Columbia University, 1918), who taught at Columbia University from 1923 to 1954, and organized the "Brain Trust" for which he served as the unofficial leader in the early 1930s. He broke with FDR in the late 1930s.

Mussolini, Benito (1883-1945). Fascist dictator of Italy from 1924 to 1943.

New Deal (1932-45). The term that FDR began using in 1932 to describe his domestic policies during the Great Depression.

Norris, George W. (1861-1944). Progressive Republican congressman from Nebraska (1903-43) and "father" of the Tennessee Valley Authority.

Perkins, Frances (1882-1965). First female cabinet member in U.S. history whom FDR appointed as secretary of labor (1933-45).

Peron, Juan D. (1895-1974). The head of an army clique which took over the Argentinian government in 1943. Served as secretary of labor and gained union loyalty, and then became president (1946-55).

Randolph, A. Philip (1889-1979). Founding president of the Brotherhood of Sleeping Car Porters (1925-69). Persuaded FDR and Harry Truman to end segregation in the defense industry in 1941 and the armed services in 1948.

Rayburn, Sam (1882-1961). Democratic congressman from Texas (1913-61), who served as majority leader (1937-41), minority leader (1947-49, 1953-55), and House Speaker (1940-61).

Robinson, Joseph (1872-1937). Democratic senator from Arkansas (1913-37), who served as minority leader (1923-33) and majority leader (1933-37).

Roosevelt, Anna Eleanor (1884-1962). Eleanor Roosevelt married her distant cousin FDR in 1905. After rearing five children, she became the greatest American First Lady, serving as FDR's political partner, his social conscience, and then after his death as an informed First Lady of the world.

Roosevelt, Franklin D. (1882-1945). America's greatest president of the twentieth century and the only president who served more than two terms (1932-45). An active and flexible personality, he successfully adapted the presidency to meet the challenges of the Great Depression with ad hoc New Deal measures, and the military threat of the Axis powers during World War II.

Schlesinger, Arthur, Jr. (1917-). Award-winning American historian who authored the three-volume biography of *FDR, The Age of Roosevelt* (1957, 1959, 1960).

Smith, Alfred E. (1873-1944). Democratic governor of New York (1923-28), who became the first Catholic nominated for president by a major party. He lost the 1928 election to Republican Herbert Hoover.

Stalin, Joseph (1879-1953). Soviet dictator who was in office from 1929 until his death.

Stone, Harlan Fiske (1872-1946). Associate justice of the U.S. Supreme Court (1925-41), whom FDR elevated to chief justice (1941-46). He ranks as one of the greatest justices in Supreme Court history.

Truman, Harry S (1884-1972). Democratic senator from Missouri (1935-45), who served as FDR's third vice president (January 1945-April 1945).

Vanderberg, Arthur H. (1884-1951). Republican senator from Michigan (1928-51), who was a leading isolationist until Pearl Harbor. He became a supporter of a bipartisan foreign policy, including the UN, NATO, and the Marshall Plan.

Wallace, Henry A. (1880-1965). FDR's second vice president (1941-45) who had served as his first secretary of agriculture (1933-40).

Warren, Robert Penn (1905-89). Author of *All the King's Men* (1946), the greatest American political novel of the twentieth century which captures the essence of a charismatic autocrat, paralleling the life of Louisiana's Huey Long.

Willkie, Wendell L. (1892-1944). A former Democrat (1914-33) who led business opposition to FDR's New Deal and became the Republican presidential candidate in 1940. His running mate was Charles L. McNary from Oregon. Both died in 1944.

SELECTED BIBLIOGRAPHY

Abraham Lincoln

Baker, Jean H. *Mary Todd Lincoln. A Biography.* New York: W. W. Norton, 1987.
Boritt, Gabor S. *Lincoln and the Economics of the American Dream.* Memphis: Memphis University Press, 1978.
Boritt, Gabor S. and N. O. Forness, eds. *The Historians' Lincoln:Pseudohistory, Psychohistory, and History.* Urbana: University of Illinois Press, 1988.
Boritt, Gabor S. ed., *The Lincoln Enigma: The Changing Face of an American Icon.* New York: Oxford University Press, 2001.
Braden, Waldo W. *Abraham Lincoln, Public Speaker.* Baton Rouge: Louisiana State University Press, 1991.
Charnwood, Lord. *Abraham Lincoln.* New York: Henry Holt, 1917.
Current, Richard N. *The Lincoln Nobody Knows.* New York: Hill and Wang, 1958.
Davis, William C. *Lincoln's Men: How President Lincoln Became Father to an Army and a Nation.* New York: The Free Press, 1999.
Davies, James C. *Human Nature in Politics.* New York: John Wiley, 1963.
Dirck, Brain R. *Lincoln and Davis.* Lawrence: University Press of Kansas.
Donald, David H. *Lincoln.* New York: Simon and Schuster, 1995.
_____. *Lincoln Reconsidered: Essays on the Civil War.* New York: Vintage, 1961.
Fehrenbacher, Don E. *Prelude to Greatness: Lincoln in the 1850s.* Stanford: Stanford University Press, 1962.
Fehrenbacher, Don E. and Virginia Fehrenbacher, eds. *Recollected Words of Abraham Lincoln.* Stanford: Stanford University Press, 1996.
Fishman, Ethan, William D. Pederson, and Mark J. Rozell, eds. *George Washington: Foundations of Presidential Leadership and Character.* Westport, CT: Praeger, 2001.
Fletcher, George P. *Our Secret Constitution: How Lincoln Redefined American Democracy.* New York: Oxford University Press, 2001.
Franklin, John Hope. *The Emancipation Proclamation.* Garden City, NJ: Doubleday, 1963.
Gary, Ralph. *Following in Lincoln's Footsteps: A Complete Annotated Reference to Hundreds of Historical Sites Visited by Abraham Lincoln.* New York: Carroll and Graf, 2001.
Gienapp, William E. *Abraham Lincoln and Civil War America: A Biography.* New York: Oxford University Press, 2002.

Guelzo, Allen C. *Abraham Lincoln: Redeemer President.* Grand Rapids, MI: William B. Erdmans, 1999.

Hatchett, William. *The Life of Abraham Lincoln: Out of the Wilderness.* Urbana: University of Illinois Press, 1994.

Hofstadter, Richard. *The American Political Tradition and the Men Who Made It.* New York: Knopf, 1948.

Holzer, Harold. *The Lincoln-Douglas Debates: The First Complete, Unexpurgated Text.* New York: HarperCollins, 1993.

Hubbard, Charles M., Thomas R. Turner, and Steven K. Rogstad, eds. *The Many Faces of Lincoln. Selected Articles from the "Lincoln Herald."* Mahomet, IL: Mayhaven Publishing, 1997.

Jaffa, Harry V. *Equality and Liberty.* New York: Oxford University Press, 1965.

_____. *Crisis of the House Divided.* Chicago: University of Chicago Press, 1982.

_____. *A New Birth of Freedom: Abraham Lincoln and the Coming of the Civil War.* Lanham, MD: Rowman and Littlefield, 2000.

Lew, Yu-Tang Daniel, ed. *The Universal Lincoln.* Taiwan: Chinese Culture University Press, 1995.

Leech, Margaret. *Reveille in Washington.* New York: Harper and Row, 1941.

Lincoln, Abraham. *Lincoln on Democracy.* Edited and introduced by Mario M. Cuomo and Harold Holzer. New York: HarperCollins, 1990.

Long, David E. *The Jewel of Liberty. Abraham Lincoln's Re-Election and the End of Slavery.* Mechanicsburg, PA: Stackpole, 1994.

McPherson, James M. *Abraham Lincoln and the Second American Revolution.* New York: Oxford University Press, 1990.

_____. *Battle Cry of Freedom: The Civil War Era.* New York: Ballentine Books, 1988.

_____, ed. *"We Cannot Escape History." Lincoln and the Last Best Hope of Earth.* Urbana: University of Illinois Press, 1995.

Morris, Jan. *Lincoln: A Foreigner's Quest.* New York: Simon and Schuster, 2000.

Mahin, Dean B. *One War at a Time: The International Dimensions of the American Civil War.* Washington, DC: Brassey's, 1999.

Miller, *William L. Lincoln's Virtues: An Ethical Biography.* New York: Knopf, 2002.

Neely, Mark E., Jr. *The Abraham Lincoln Encyclopedia.* New York: McGraw-Hill, 1982.

_____. *The Last Best Hope of Earth. Abraham Lincoln and the Promise of America.* Cambridge, MA: Harvard University Press, 1993.

_____. *The Fate of Liberty: Abraham Lincoln and Civil Liberties.* New York: Oxford University Press, 1991.

_____. *Southern Rights: Political Prisoners and the Myth of Confederate Constitutionalism.* Charlottesville: University of Virginia, 1999.

Oates, Stephen B. *With Malice Toward None: The Life of Abraham Lincoln.* New York: Harper and Row, 1977.

Ostendorf, Lloyd and Walter Olesky, eds. *Lincoln's Unknown Private Life. An Oral History by His Black Housekeeper Mariah Vance, 1850-1860.* Mamaroneck, NY: Hastings House, 1995.

Padover, Saul K., ed. *Karl Marx on America and the Civil War.* New York: McGraw-Hill, 1972.

Paludan, Phillip S. *The Presidency of Abraham Lincoln.* Lawrence: University Press of Kansas, 1994.

Pederson, William D. *The "Barberian" Presidency.* New York: Peter Lang, 1989.

William D. Pederson and Ann M. McLaurin, eds. *The Rating Game in American Politics.* New York: Irvington, 1987.

Pederson, William D. and Norman W. Provizer, eds., *Great Justices of the U.S. Supreme Court.* New York: Peter Lang, 1993.

Pederson, William D. and Frank J. Williams, eds., *International Abraham Lincoln Journal.* Shreveport, LA: International Lincoln Center, 2000.

Provizer, Norman W. and William D. Pederson, eds., *Grassroots Constitutionalism.* Lanham, MD: University Press of America, 1988.

Peterson, Merrill D. *Lincoln in Memory.* New York: Oxford University Press, 1994.

Pitt, H. G. *Abraham Lincoln.* Phoenix Mill, UK: Sutton Publishing, 1998.

Rawley, James A. *Abraham Lincoln and A Nation Worth Fighting For.* Wheeling, IL: Harlan Davidson, 1996.

Rietveld, Ronald D. *Lincoln's Views of the Founding Fathers.* Redlands, CA: Lincoln Memorial Shrine, 1992.

Riddle, Donald W. *Congressman Abraham Lincoln.* Westport, CT: Greenwood Press, 1979.

Safire, William. *Freedom.* Garden City, NJ: Doubleday, 1987.

Simon, John Y., Harold Holzer, and William D. Pederson, eds. *The Lincoln Forum: Abraham Lincoln, Gettysburg and the Civil War.* Mason City, IA: Savas Publishing, 1999.

Simon, Paul. *Lincoln's Preparation for Greatness: The Illinois Legislative Years.* Urbana: University of Illinois Press, 1971.

Strozier, Charles B. *Lincoln's Quest for Union: Public and Private Meanings*. New York: Basic Books, 1982.

Temple, Wayne C. *Abraham Lincoln from Skeptic to Prophet*. Mahomet, IL: Mayhaven Publishing, 1995.

Tidwell, William A. *April '65: Confederate Covert Action in the American Civil War*. Kent, OH: Kent State University Press, 1995.

Thomas, Benjamin P. *Abraham Lincoln: A Biography*. New York: Knopf, 1952.

Vidal, Gore. *Lincoln*. New York: Modern Library, 1993.

Waugh, John C. *Re-electing Lincoln: The Battle for the 1864 Presidency*. New York: Crown Publishing, 1997.

White, Ronald C., Jr. *Lincoln's Greatest Speech: The Second Inaugural*. New York: Oxford University Press, 2002.

Williams, Frank J., William D. Pederson, and Vincent J. Marsala, eds. *Abraham Lincoln: Sources and Style of Leadership*. Westport, CT: Greenwood Press, 1994.

Williams, Frank J. and William D. Pederson, eds., *Abraham Lincoln: Contemporary. An American Legacy*. Campbell, CA: Savas Woodbury Publishers, 1995.

Williams, Frank J. *Judging Lincoln*. Carbondale: Southern Illinois University, 2002.

Williams, T. Harry. *Lincoln and the Radicals*. Madison: University of Wisconsin Press, 1941.

Wills, Garry. *Lincoln at Gettysburg: The Words that Remade America*. New York: Simon and Schuster, 1992.

Wilson, Douglas L. *Honor's Voice: The Transformation of Abraham Lincoln*. New York: Knopf, 1998.

Wilson, Douglas L. and Rodney O. Davis, eds. *Herndon's Informants: Letters, Interviews and Statements About Abraham Lincoln*. Urbana: University of Illinois Press, 1998.

Franklin D. Roosevelt

Berthon, Simon. *Allies at War: The Bitter Rivalry among Churchill, Roosevelt and DeGaulle*. New York: Carroll and Graf, 2001.
Beasley, Maurine, Holly C. Shulman, and Henry R. Beasley, eds. *The Eleanor Roosevelt Encyclopedia*. Westport, CT: Greenwood Press, 2001.
Berger, Jason. *A New Deal for the World: Eleanor Roosevelt and American Foreign Policy, 1920-1962*. New York: Columbia University Press, 1981.
Black, Alida M. *Casting Her Own Shadow: Eleanor Roosevelt and the Shaping of Postwar Liberalism*. New York: Columbia University Press, 1996.
Buhite, Russell D. and David W. Levy, eds. *FDR's Fireside Chats*. Norman: University of Oklahoma Press, 1992.
Burns, James M. *Roosevelt: Lion and the Fox*. New York: Harcourt, Brace, 1956.
_____. *Roosevelt: Soldier of Freedom*. New York: Harcourt Brace Jovanovich, 1970.
Burns, James M. and Susan Dunn. *The Three Roosevelts: Patrician Leaders Who Transformed America*. New York: Atlantic Monthly Press, 2001.
Caroli, Betty. *The Roosevelt Women*. New York: Basic Books, 1998.
Casey, Steven. *Cautious Crusade: Franklin D. Roosevelt, American Public Opinion and the War Against Nazi Germany*. New York: Oxford University Press, 2001.
Cashman, Sean. *America, Roosevelt and World War II*. New York: New York University Press, 1989.
Cole, Wayne. *Determination and American Foreign Policy*. Lanham, MD: University Press of America, 1995.
Collier, Peter and David Horowitz. *The Roosevelts: An American Saga*. New York: Simon and Schuster, 1994.
Cook, Blanche W. *Eleanor Roosevelt: 1884-1933*, vol. 1; *Eleanor Roosevelt, 1933-1938*, vol. 2. New York: Viking Penguin, 1993; 1999.
Curtis, Sandra R. *Alice and Eleanor: A Contrast in Style and Purpose*. Bowling Green, OH: Bowling Green University, Popular Press, 1994.
Dallek, Robert. *Franklin D. Roosevelt and American Foreign Policy, 1932-1945*. New York: Oxford University Press, 1979.
_____. *Franklin D. Roosevelt as a World Leader*. New York: Oxford University Press, 1995.

Davis, Kenneth S. *FDR: The New Deal Years, 1933-1937: Into the Storm, 1937-1940; The War President, 1940-1943.* New York: Random House, 1986, 1993, 2000.

Daynes, Byron, William Pederson, and Michael Riccards, eds. *The New Deal and Public Policy.* New York: St. Martin's Press, 1998.

Dickinson, Matthew J. *Bitter Harvest: FDR, Presidential Power and Growth of the Presidential Branch.* New York: Cambridge University Press, 1996.

Divine, Robert A. *Roosevelt and World War II.* Baltimore: Johns Hopkins Press, 1969.

Doenecke, Justus D. *Storm on the Horizon: The Challenge to American Intervention, 1939-1941.* Lanham, MD: Rowman and Littlefield, 2000.

Donn, Linda. *The Roosevelt Cousins.* New York: Random House, 2001.

Dunn, Dennis J. *Caught Between Roosevelt and Stalin: America's Ambassadors to Moscow.* Lexington: University Press of Kentucky, 1998.

Edens, John A. *Eleanor Roosevelt: A Comprehensive Bibliography.* Westport, CT: Greenwood Press, 1994.

Farnham, Barbara R. *Roosevelt and the Munich Crisis: A Study of Political Decision Making.* Princeton, NJ: Princeton University Press, 1997.

Feis, Herbert. *Roosevelt, Churchill, Stalin: The War They Fought and the Peace They Sought.* Princeton, NJ: Princeton University Press, 1957.

Ferrell, Robert H. *The Dying President: Franklin D. Roosevelt, 1944-1945.* Columbia: University of Missouri Press, 1998.

Fleming, Thomas. *The New Dealers' War: FDR and the War Within World War II.* New York: Basic Books, 2001.

Flynn, George Q. *Roosevelt and Romanism: Catholics and American Diplomacy, 1937-1945.* Westport, CT: 1976.

Freidel, Frank. *Franklin D. Roosevelt: A Rendezvous with Destiny.* Boston: Little, Brown, 1990.

Fried, Albert. *FDR and His Enemies.* New York: St. Martin's Press, 1999.

Gallagher, Hugh. *FDR's Splendid Deception.* Arlington, VA: Vandamere Press, 1994.

Glendon, Mary Ann. *A World Made New: Eleanor Roosevelt and Universal Declaration of Human Rights.* New York: Random House, 2001.

Goodwin, Doris K. *No Ordinary Time: Franklin and Eleanor Roosevelt: The Home Front in World War II.* New York: Simon and Schuster, 1994.

Graham., Otis L., Jr. and Megan R. Wander, eds. *Franklin D. Roosevelt, His Life and Times: An Encyclopedia View.* New York: Macmillan, 1985.

Gurewitsch, Edna P. *Kindred Souls: The Friendship of Eleanor Roosevelt and David Gurewitsch.* New York: St. Martin's Press, 2002.

Harper, John L. *American Visions of Europe: Franklin D. Roosevelt, George F. Kennan and Dean G. Acheson*. New York: Cambridge University Press, 1994.

Hearden, Patrick. *Roosevelt Confronts Hitler: America's Entry into World War II*. Dekalb: North Illinois University Press, 1987.

Herzstein, Robert E. *Roosevelt and Hitler: Prelude to War*. New York: Wiley, 1994.

Hoopes, Townsend and Douglas Brinkley. *FDR and the Creation of the United Nations*. New Haven, CT: Yale University Press, 1997.

Kennedy, David. *Freedom from Fear. The American People in Depression and War, 1929-1945*. New York: Oxford University Press, 1999.

Kimball, Warren F. *Forged in War: Roosevelt, Churchill, and the Second World War*. New York: William Morrow, 1997.

Kinsella, William E., Jr. *Leadership in Isolation: FDR and the Origins of the Second World War*. Rochester, VT: Schenkman Books, 1970.

Klein, Jonas. *Beloved Island: Franklin and Eleanor and the Legacy of Campobello*. Forest Dale, VT: Ericksson, 2002.

Langer, William A. *The Undeclared War, 1940-41*. New York: Harper, 1953.

Larrabee, Eric. *Commander in Chief—Franklin D. Roosevelt: His Lieutenants and Their War*. New York: Harper and Row, 1987.

Leuchtenburg, William E. *Franklin D. Roosevelt and the New Deal, 1952-1990*. New York: Harper and Row, 1963.

_____. *In the Shadow of FDR: From Harry Truman to Bill Clinton*. Ithaca, NY: Cornell University Press, 1993.

_____. *The FDR Years: On Roosevelt and His Legacy*. New York: Columbia University Press, 1995.

Maney, Patrick J. *The Roosevelt Presence: A Biography of Franklin Delano Roosevelt*. New York: Twayne, 1992.

Marks, Frederick W. *Wind Over Sand: The Diplomacy of Franklin Roosevelt*. Athens: University of Georgia Press, 1988.

Marolda, Edward J. *FDR and the U.S. Navy*. New York: St. Martin's, 1998.

McJimsey, George. *The Presidency of Franklin Delano Roosevelt*. Lawrence: University Press of Kansas, 2000.

Miller, Dwight and Timothy M. Walch, eds. *Herbert Hoover and Franklin D. Roosevelt: A Documentary History*. Westport, CT: Greenwood Press, 1998.

Morgan, Ted. *FDR: A Biography*. New York: Simon and Schuster, 1985.

Newton, Verne W., ed. *FDR and the Holocaust*. New York: St. Martin's Press.

Olson, James S., *Historical Dictionary of the New Deal: From Inauguration to Preparation for War*. Westport: CT: Greenwood Press, 1985.

O'Neill, William L. *A Democracy at War: America's Fight at Home and Abroad in World War II*. New York: Free Press, 1993.

Perlmutter, Amos. *FDR and Stalin: A Not So Grand Alliance, 1943-1945*. Columbia: University of Missouri Press, 1993.

Perras, Galen R. *Franklin D. Roosevelt and the Origins of the Canadian-American Security Alliance, 1933-1945: Necessary, but Not Necessary Enough*. Westport, CT: Praeger, 1998.

Persico, Joseph E. *Roosevelt's Secret War: FDR and World War II Espionage*. New York: Random House, 2001.

Pike, Frederick B. *FDR's Good Neighbor Policy: Sixty Years of Generally Gentle Chaos*. Austin: University of Texas Press, 1995.

Polenberg, Richard. *The Era of Franklin D. Roosevelt, 1933-1945: A Brief History with Documents*. New York: St. Martin's, 2000.

Robinson, Greg. *By Order of the President: FDR and the Internment of Japanese Americans*. Cambridge, MA: Harvard University Press, 2001.

Rosenbaum, Herbert D. and Elizabeth Bartelme, eds. *Franklin D. Roosevelt: The Man, the Myth and the Era, 1882-1945*. Westport, CT: Greenwood Press, 1987.

Rossi, Mario. *Roosevelt and the French*. Westport, CT: Praeger, 1993.

Rubinstein, William D. *The Myth of Rescue: Why the Democracies Could Not Have Saved More Jews from the Nazis*. New York: Routledge, 1997.

Ryan, Halford R. *Franklin Roosevelt's Rhetorical Presidency*. Westport, CT: Greenwood Press, 1988.

Sainsburg, Keith. *Churchill and Roosevelt at War: The War They Fought and the Peace They Hoped to Make*. New York: New York University Press, 1994.

Savage, Sean J. *Roosevelt: The Party Leader, 1932-1945*. Lexington: University Press of Kentucky, 1991.

Schlesinger, Arthur M., Jr. *The Age of Roosevelt: The Politics of Upheaval*. Boston: Houghton Mifflin, 1960.

Sears, John F., ed. *Franklin D. Roosevelt and the Future of Liberalism*. Westport, CT: Greenwood Press, 1990.

Stinnett, Robert B. *Day of Deceit: The Truth About FDR and Pearl Harbor*. New York: Free Press, 1999.

Szalay, Michael. *New Deal Modernism: American Literature and the Invention of the Welfare State*. Durham, NC: Duke University Press, 2000.

Underhill, Robert. *FDR and Harry. Unparalleled Lives.* Westport, CT: Praeger, 1996.

Van Minnen, Cornelis A. *FDR and His Contemporaries: Foreign Perceptions of an American President.* New York: St. Martin's, 1992.

Ward, Geoffrey C. *A First-Class Temperament: The Emergence of Franklin Roosevelt.* New York: Harper and Row, 1989.

Weiss, Stuart L. *The President's Man: Leo Crowley and Franklin Roosevelt in Peace and War.* Carbondale: Southern Illinois University Press, 1996.

Winfield, Betty H. *FDR and the News Media.* Champaign: University of Illinois Press, 1991.

Wolf, Thomas, William Pederson, and Byron Daynes, eds. *Franklin D. Roosevelt and Congress: The New Deal and Its Aftermath.* Armonk, NY: M.E. Sharpe, 2001.

Young, Nancy, William Pederson, and Byron Daynes., eds., *Franklin D. Roosevelt and the Shaping of American Political Culture.* Armonk, NY: M.E. Sharpe, 2001.

LIST OF CONTRIBUTORS

Matthew Ware Coulter is professor of history at Colin County Community College in Plano, Texas.

James Chowning Davies is professor emeritus at the University of Oregon.

Matthew D. Davis is assistant professor of secondary education/educational foundations at Rowan University.

O. L. Davis, Jr. is the Catherine Mae Parker Centennial professor of curriculum and instruction, the University of Texas at Austin.

Sherry L. Field is professor of education, University of Texas at Austin.

Glen Jeansonne is professor of history at the University of Wisconsin, Milwaukee.

David E. Long is associate professor of history at East Carolina University.

William D. Pederson is the Endowed American Studies Chair and Director of the International Lincoln Center at Louisiana State University in Shreveport.

Ronald D. Rietveld is professor of history at California State University, Fullerton.

C. Todd Stephenson is an instructor at St. Andrew's Episcopal School in Austin, Texas.

Frank J. Williams is the Chief Justice of the Supreme Court of Rhode Island and founding chair of the Lincoln Forum.

INDEX

abolitionists, 80, 191
Adams, Charles F., 258
Adams, John, 20, 26, 34
Admiral Yamamoto, 178
Agricultural Adjustment
   Administration, 177, 256
Alexander II, Czar, 258
American Youth Congress, 35
Anderson, Marian, 129, 265
Anglemyer, Mary, 137
Animal Farm, 190-91
Arab, 242, 244, 245
Aristotle, 76, 188
Atlantic Charter, 44, 232

Bach, Johann Sebastian, 185, 199
Bacon, Henry, 131
Baltimore, Maryland, 66
Bankhead, William, 69
Barnard, George Grey, 140
Bates, Edward, 258
Beard, Charles A., 32, 265
Beethoven, 6, 185-188, 193, 194-199, 201-212
Belgium, 34
Bennett, Charles, 136
Bethune, Mary McLeod, 222
Beveridge, Albert J., 258
Bevin, Ernest, 160
Bismarck, Otto von, 258
Black Hawk Indian War, 81, 155,
Black, Hugo L., 265
Boers, 116
Bonn, 185, 196, 199, 202, 205
Borglum, Gutzon, 131
Booth, John Wilkes, 252, 258

Bowers, Claude, 13
Brady, Matthew B., 258
Bretano, Antonie, 202-205, 207
Bretano, Bettina, 202
Breuer, Marcel, 136
Bright, John, 258
Brownlow, Louis, 265
Buchanan, James, 30, 191, 258
Buck, H., 51-52
Buddha, 76, 187-188
Burnham, Scott, 207
Burns, James MacGregor, 113, 163-164, 177, 265
Burns, Robert, 99
Butler, Benhamin F., 67-68
Byrnes, James, 71, 265

Calhoun, John C., 259
Cameron, Simon, 67
Capra, Frank, 265
Carpenter, Francis B., 259
Carter, Jimmy, 175, 177
Casablanca, 47, 233,
Charnwood, Lord, 259
Chamberlain, Neville, 34, 161
Charmley, John, 159
Chase, Salmon P., 160, 259
Chicago, 43, 63, 70, 72
Christianity, 113, 189-190, 193
Churchill, Winston, 5, 34, 44, 47, 94, 116, 154, 158, 159-165, 166, 167, 194, 232, 265
Civilian Conservation Corps, 170, 265
Clay, Henry, 81, 84, 259
Cleveland, Grover, 12, 39, 171
Clinton, Bill, 171
Cohen, Ben, 95

281

Colville, John, 161
Comacho, Manuel, 222
Confucius, 188
Conkin, Paul, 139
Cooper Institute Address, 38, 252
Copperheads, 43, 44
Corcoran, Tommy, 95, 266
Coughlin, Charles, 181
Coulter, Matthew W., 7, 238,

Dante, 118
Danton, Maryland, 25
Davies, James C., 4, 6, 7, 75, 164
Davis, Jefferson, 259
Davis, John W., 266
Davis, Matthew D., 228, 281
Davis, O. L., 228, 282
Davis, Speed, 108, 142
Declaration of Independence, 6, 20, 43, 163, 166, 185,
DeGaulle, Charles, 266
Denmark, 34
Dewey, Thomas E., 50, 61, 266
Douglas, Stephen A., 50, 84, 101, 252, 259
Douglas, William O., 71, 266
Douglass, Frederick, 259
Dunkirk, 34, 165

Early, Stephen T., 266
Eben, Mary, 35
Edwards, Ninian, 81
Eisenhower, Dwight, 158, 221
Emancipation Proclamation, 253
Enlightenment, 198, 206
Eroica Symphony, 207
Fascism, 115

FDR Memorial Commission, 128, 141
Farley, James A., 266
Fehrenbacher, Don E., 67
Ferrell, Robert H., 70
Fillmore, Millard, 26, 259
Fireside Chat, 16, 123, 127
First Hundred Days, 256
Ford, Henry, 108
Four Freedoms, 165, 258
Fowler, Delbert, 137
Fowler, Henry, 40
France, 36
Franco, 113-114
Frankfurter, Felix, 95, 143, 266
Franklin, Benjamin, 14
Franz, Joseph, 259
Frederick the Great, 206
Fremont, John C., 156, 259
Freidel, Frank, 54
Freud, 94
Fugitive Slave Act, 245

Garibaldi, Giuseppe, 260
Garner, John Nance, 266
Generation X, 238, 242
George, Lloyd, 161
Gettysburg Address, 12, 17, 25, 43, 113, 166, 254
Gettysburg Eternal Light Peace Memorial, 23
Gingrich, Newt, 137
Goddess of Liberty, 42
Goethe, 98, 200
Good Neighbor Policy, 222, 256
Goodwin, Doris Kearns, 266
Grant, Ulysses S., 20, 26, 253, 260
Great Depression, 3, 7, 13, 63, 163, 171, 172, 181, 183, 216,

225, 234, 238, 239, 241, 266
Greeley, Horace, 108, 260
Griffith, D.W., 41
Guerin, Jules, 135
Gunderson, Dorann H., 141
Gunther, John, 165

Halleck, Henry W., 157
Halprin, Lawrence, 131
Halstead, Anna Roosevelt, 143
Hamlin, Hannibal, 62, 260
Hart, Gary, 176
Harvard University, 12, 44, 90, 91, 102, 103, 116, 185, 255
Hassett, William, 51
Hay, John, 10, 11, 66, 156, 260
Haydn, 185, 199
Heiligenstad Testament, 209
Herndon, Billy (William) H., 78, 100-101, 252, 260
Herod, 189
Hickok, Lorna, 96
Hirohito, Emperor, 267
Hitler, Adolf, 116, 117, 174, 177, 206, 267
Holland, 34
Holmes, Oliver Wendell, 103, 181
Holocaust, 129, 242, 243
Holt, Joseph, 66
Homestead Act, 253
Hoover, Herbert, 13, 27, 30, 33, 34, 54, 175-176, 219, 221, 231
Hopkins, Harry, 35, 73, 267
Howe, Louis, 89-90, 94, 173
Hughes, Charles Evans, 267
Hull, Cordell, 267

Hyde Park, NY, 12, 27, 51, 95, 96, 138, 144, 172, 255

Ickes, Harold, 69, 267
International Labor Organization, 45

Jackson, Andrew, 12, 13, 20, 21, 22, 28, 39, 191
Jackson Day Dinner, 29, 32, 42
Japan, 42, 115
Jeansonne, Glen, 5, 171, 181, 280
Jefferson, Thomas, 12, 14, 20, 21, 26, 28, 34, 39, 41, 43, 128, 145, 191
Jefferson Memorial, 31, 130, 134, 146
Jesus, 6, 76, 185, 186-190, 193, 210
Johnson, Andrew, 62, 64, 67, 68, 72, 260
Johnson, Lyndon, 171 175, 224
Jones, Jesse, 26, 267
Juarez, Benito R., 260

Kansas-Nebraska Act of 1854, 79, 101
Keckley, Elizabeth, 84-85, 103, 260
Keegan, John, 162
Keller, George, 132
Kelly, Edward J., 71
Kennedy, John, 174, 175, 176, 183, 224, 245
Keogh, Eugene, 137
King, Ernest, 158
King, Martin Luther, 129, 174

LaGuardia, Fiorello, 267
Lamon, Ward Hill, 66
Land Grant College Act, 160
Landon, Alf, 267
Langer, Susanne K., 6, 210
Lao-tzu, 188
Larrabee, Eric, 157, 158
Lash, Joe, 96
Laski, Harold, 52
League of Nations, 175
Lee, Robert E., 260
LeHand, Marguerite (Missy), 88, 89, 94, 173, 267
Lend-Lease Act, 49, 157, 258
Lenin, 206
Leopold I, 260
Lerner, Max, 30, 36
Leuchtenburg, William, 267
Leviticus, 187
Liberty League, 38
Lieber, Francis, 261
Life, 52-53
Lincoln, Edward (Eddy), 83, 251, 261
Lincoln, Mary Todd, 4, 6, 7, 11, 26, 27, 75-80, 81-82, 91, 97, 102-103, 104, 107, 114, 193, 261
Lincoln, Nancy Hanks, 77, 261
Lincoln, Robert Todd, 47, 102, 140-141, 143, 261
Lincoln, Sarah Bush Johnson, 249, 261
Lincoln, Thomas, 77, 249, 261
Lincoln, Thomas ("Tad"), 102
Lincoln-Douglas debates, 191, 245, 251
Lincoln Memorial, 5, 131, 133, 135, 139, 144, 146
Lincoln Memorial Commission, 130

Lippmann, Walter, 15, 17
Long, David E., 4, 61, 281
Long, Huey P., 6, 110, 181-184, 267
Luce, Henry, 108
Ludwig, Emil, 23
Luxembourg, 34

MacArthur, Douglas, 6, 49, 230, 268
Mahomet, 76
Maitland, F. W., 167
Malcolm X, 174
Maney, Patrick J., 54
Mantle, Mickey, 174
Marling, Karal Ann, 135
Marshall, George, 158, 268
Marti, José, 262
Marx, Karl, 262
Masters, Edward Lee, 262
Maximilian, 262
Mayan, 154-155, 162, 164
Merrill, Louis Taylor, 67
Miller, Earl, 96
Mills, Clark, 130
Missouri Compromise, 79
Moley, Raymond, 16, 31, 268
Morgan, Ted, 12
Morgenthau, Henry, 95
Morison, Samuel Eliot, 27
Mozart, 197, 199, 201, 209
Mumford, Louis, 136
Murphy, Frank, 25
Mussolini, Benito, 268

Napoleon, 116, 117, 206-207
Napoleon III, 264
National Gallery, 41

National Recovery Act (NRA), 16
National Recovery Administration, 177, 256
National Republican Club, New York, 14, 29
Nazism, 34, 42, 93, 114, 164
Neef, Christian Gottlob, 198, 211
New Deal, 16, 21, 23, 28, 30, 32, 34, 38, 41, 53, 54, 69, 93, 101, 114, 138, 163, 176, 216, 217, 218, 221, 225, 230, 231, 232, 241, 268
New Salem, Illinois, 14, 80, 249, 250
New York Times, 133
Nicolay, John G., 65-66, 68, 156, 262
Night and Fog, 242
Ninth Symphony, 194, 208, 210
Nixon, Richard, 224
Nora, Pierre, 129
Norris, George W., 268
Northwest Ordinance, 79
Norway, 34, 47, 96

Orwell, George, 190
Owens, Mary, 81

Palestine, 185, 18, 242, 243, 244, 245
Palmerston, Viscount, 262
Patterson, Judith, 142
Peabody, Endicott, 87
Pearl Harbor, 11, 46, 49, 96, 104, 172, 220, 221, 232, 258
Pederson, William D., 5, 280

Pentateuch, 187
Perkins, Frances, 89, 268
Peron, Juan, 268
Peterson, Merrill, 10
Phelps, J.W., 26
Phi Beta Kappa, 105
Philadelphia, 36
Pierce, Franklin, 262
Pierce, George, 12
Pogo, 179
Poland, 31
Pope Pius IX, 262
Presley, Elvis, 174

Randall, James G., 66, 102
Randolph, A. Philip, 268
Rayburn, Sam, 268
Reagan, Ronald, 139, 171
Reich, Alan, 142
Republican party, 10, 62, 182, 191, 193, 251
Resnais, Alain, 242
Revenue Act of 1862, 64
Revenue Act of 1942, 64
Rietveld, Ronald D., 3, 281
Robinson, Joseph, 268
Rogers, Will, 14
Roosevelt, David, 141
Roosevelt, Eleanor, 6, 7, 34, 37, 51, 69, 75-80, 89, 91, 93, 95, 104, 107, 109, 112, 114, 143, 165, 167, 172-173, 216, 220-221, 222, 223, 255, 268-269
Roosevelt, James, 11, 143
Roosevelt, Sara Delano, 85-86, 91, 97
Roosevelt, Theodore, 10, 11, 13, 15, 21, 29, 39, 54, 88, 89, 109, 128, 145, 146, 156, 222, 224
Root, Elihu, 132

Rosenman, Samuel, 69
Ruckstuhl, Frederick, 141
Rutherfurd, Lucy Mercer, 88, 92-93, 94, 96, 109, 112, 173
Rutledge, Ann, 80-81

Saint-Gaudens, Augustus, 44, 140, 141
Sandburg, Carl, 16-17, 22, 26, 31, 35, 40, 43, 44, 45, 48-49, 52, 53, 263
Sarmiento, Domingo F., 26, 263
Saud, King Ibn, 242, 242, 243-244
Saudi Arabia, 109, 241, 242, 244
Schlesinger, Arthur, Jr., 269
Seagraves, Eleanor Roosevelt, 137
Seward, William H., 106, 160, 263
Shakespeare, 99, 102, 103, 211
Shaw, Stanley, 138
Sherwood, Robert, 37-38
Shields, James, 82, 84, 91
Sisyphus, 112, 210
Smith, Alfred E., 270
Social Security Act, 163
Socrates, 205, 210
Sohier, Alice, 9
Soloman, Maynard, 202, 207
Speed, Joshua F., 82, 263
Springfield, Illinois, 39, 101, 250
Stalin, Joseph, 116, 205, 229, 269
Stanton, Edwin M., 100, 106, 157, 253, 263
Stephenson, C. Todd, 5, 128, 281
Stimson, Henry L., 115

Stone, Harlan Fiske, 269
Stuart, John Todd, 82, 263
Sumner, Charles, 26, 80, 103, 263
Surratt, Mary, 47
Sutton, Stewart, 141

Taft, William Howard, 141
Taney, Roger B., 16, 252, 254, 263
Tapke, Peter, 135
Taylor, A.J.P., 159
Teichman, Ray, 142
Thanksgiving Day Proclamation, 26
Thatcher, Margaret, 164
Thirteenth Amendment, 160
Thomas Jefferson Memorial Foundation, 135
Thoreau, Henry David, 135
Tilton, Clint Clay, 66
Time, 32, 46, 53, 108
Trent Affair, 156
Truman, Harry, 49, 54, 62, 64, 71, 72, 220, 222, 269
Tsongas, Paul, 177
Tully, Grace, 18, 54

United Nations, 48, 222
U.S.S. *Potomac*, 42

Vallandigham, Clement L., 43, 44, 45, 107, 263
Vance, Mariah, 4, 83, 102, 263
Vandenberg, Arthur H., 269
Victor Emmanuel II, 264
Victoria, 264

Vienna, 185, 196, 198, 199, 200, 203, 204, 208, 211, 22

Wagner, Richard, 20
Wallace, George, 176
Wallace, Henry, 37, 62, 69-70, 71, 269
Warm Springs, Georgia, 51, 89, 96, 130, 137, 259
Warren, Robert Penn, 269
Washington, George, 5, 6, 12, 25, 31, 39, 41, 54, 55, 128, 165, 166, 172, 191, 219, 223
Washington Post, 134, 136, 141
Washington Temperance League, 102, 111
Watrous, George D., 137
Watson, General "Pa," 95
Welles, Gideon, 264

West Potomac Park, 131
Whig Party, 162, 166, 249
Whitman, Walt, 51, 52-53, 264
Williams, Frank J., 5, 281
Williams, Norma C., 138
Willkie, Wendell, 36, 39, 40, 232, 258, 270
Wilmington, Delaware, 38, 50
Wilson, Woodrow, 12, 39, 46, 54, 115, 136, 221
Wolfskill, George, 238
World War II, 3, 37, 53, 129, 155, 163, 171, 194, 211, 215, 216, 218, 220, 222, 223, 225, 234, 238, 241, 242

Yalta Conference, 94, 95, 233, 242, 259

Zionism, 243, 244

For Product Safety Concerns and Information please contact our EU
representative GPSR@taylorandfrancis.com
Taylor & Francis Verlag GmbH, Kaufingerstraße 24, 80331 München, Germany

www.ingramcontent.com/pod-product-compliance
Lightning Source LLC
Chambersburg PA
CBHW070235230426
43664CB00014B/2316